Leonid Latynin was born in 1 the Volga. In the private libra priest he discovered the pre-re culture such as the poetry of Akhmatova, Tsvetayeva, Bely and Blok, the art of Bakst, Dobuzhinsky and Vrubel, which was in total contrast with the castrated literature taught at school. 'The Silver Age' art became for him a symbol of opposition to the impoverished and colorless provincial life of the Stalin period.

After a series of manual jobs and the army service he graduated from Moscow University upon which he worked in various publishing houses while writing poetry and studying pre-Christian Russian culture. He published six collections of his verse, but he only managed to publish his novels after perestroika: *The Face-Maker and the Muse* in 1988; *Sleeper at Harvest Time* in 1993, and *Stavr and Sara* in 1994. *Sleeper at Harvest Time* was published in French translation by Flammarion in 1992, and in English translation by Zephyr Press in 1994.

'Latynin's apocalyptic novel has been published just at a time when his grim predictions are coming true...' — *Le Monde*

'Latynin is a convincing and disquieting ethnographer but he is also a born storyteller, perfectly at home in this fragmented age. ...His incantations possess a magic power...' — *Magazine litteraire* (Paris)

Glas New Russian Writing

a series of contemporary Russian writing
in English translation
edited by Natasha Perova & Arch Tait

VOLUME 21

Back issues of Glas:

Leonid Latynin

The Face-Maker and the Muse

Translated by Andrew Bromfield

glas

GLAS Publishers (Russia)
Moscow 119517, P.O.Box 47, Russia
Tel./Fax: +7(095)441 9157;
E-mail: perova@glas.msk.su

GLAS Publishers (UK)
Dept. of Russian Literature,
University of Birmingham,
Birmingham, B15 2TT, UK
Tel/Fax: +44(0)121-414 6047;
E-mail: a.l.tait@bham.ac.uk

WORLD WIDE WEB:
http://www.bham.ac.uk/glas

USA and Canada:
Ivan R. Dee, Publisher
1332 North Halsted St.,
Chicago, Illinois 60622-2694, USA
Tel: 1-312-787 6262
Fax: 1-312-787 6269
Toll-free: +1-800-462-6420
E-mail: elephant@ivanrdee.co

Contributing editor: Joanne Turnbull
Camera-ready copy: Tatiana Shaposhnikova

Front cover picture and illustrations
by Andrei Nefyodov (courtesy of the author)

ISBN 5-7172-0047-1
US ISBN 1-56663-275-7

Printed at the "Novosti" printing press, Moscow

CONTENTS

FROM THE AUTHOR

This novel was written in the 1970s, and although it made the rounds of many journals and publishing houses, and filled a fat file in my desk with reviews expressing indignation, fright, puzzlement, embarrassment and gratitude, I never had occasion seriously to anticipate its publication. It was well worthwhile, nonetheless, to see one's text through the eyes of that time.

Readers of *samizdat* were engrossed in the anti-utopia — Orwell, Zamyatin, Huxley, Kafka — and my novel was inevitably perceived in terms of that familiar code. As a matter of fact I did not mean to write an anti-utopia or a social satire, let alone a political pamphlet replete with veiled allusions: the diagnosis delivered by my readers was a clear case of anti-utopianism. In fact I had not had the slightest interest of laying out another *Foundation Pit*, renaming the Castle 'the City', or transforming Big Brother into the Official (this latter character in my novel is not situated at the summit of the pyramid, he is an individual who stands on the boundary between God and Man). The experience of the anti-utopia is the experience of prophetic insight into the logic of the future. The Trojan Laocoon — the first anti-utopian — implored his fellow-citizens not to fall into the role of 'uniformists' dragging their own doom into the city. The people would not listen to him, and the Gods punished him, in order to teach others not to stick their noses into the spokes of the wheel of history.

Prophets who foretell the past are mere artisans, and they really have no chance of making good on their predictions (unless, that is, history comes full circle). Retrospective prophecy is senseless, furthermore, because reality has now clearly exceeded the bounds of human imagination.

The anti-utopia is today a genre of the past. Even a decade ago some already felt that we were living in a post-utopian period, although in our country a farcical version of utopia was still being energetically played out — a self-parody of utopia, retreating ever further from its original idea. I was therefore interested less in society's denial of the individual than in a free individual's denial of society. Is the creative calling opposed to the world of the anti-utopia from within, or does it facilitate it from without? If, as Berdyaev claims, creative work is 'the opposite of egocentrism', if it is a striving towards something higher, the attempt to create a 'new heaven and a new earth', then who bears responsibility for the failure of the creative act? My hero, the Face-Maker, is an artist tormented by a prosperous existence in a sickeningly self-satisfied world devoid of freedom. Initially he is a man of ambition rather than a creative artist. As he makes the moral ascent towards the ideal, the claims of ambition are dissolved in the noble and altruistic goal of transforming the world and creating a new individual. But the artist's greatest victory proves to be a crushing defeat: his creation is not a new reality, merely a standard cultural artefact; not a new person, but a new face, a new canon, a new image. The moment when the artist realizes his defeat is the very moment when the crowd makes its appearance, ready to accept his creative failure as a true revelation — and then the 'false heaven' created by the artist collapses on his head and kills him.

Where does the boundary lie between supreme success and total defeat of an artist who imagines himself to be a god at the very moment when he is transformed into a devil? How does the meaning of life justify his creative act, if his daring does not lead to atonement?

The *Face-Maker and the Muse* is basically a novel about the fate of an artist and a prophet, about his rise and his downfall, about his responsibility for the metamorphoses undergone by his own ideas. The novel is, if you wish, a metaphor for the fate of the artist in the world. But this metaphor is still not the essence of the matter.

The idea of a novel and its plot are like the protective sheath of a telephone cable. The cable does not exist in order to protect the wires from the elements and physical damage (time and the state), or to contain as many fine fibres of wire as possible (sub-plots and messages), but in order to provide a route and a direction for the movement of a certain force, which for some is the opportunity to hear a person who lives behind the stone wall of alienation, or beyond the fantastic distances of geography and political system, while for others it is the opportunity to be heard by them. For yet others this is a channel of communication through which they can conduct a dialogue.

1989

Prologue

When you look down on the Volga from the high bank of the Chuvil hills, the river doesn't seem very wide at all: in their simple-minded fashion the hills rob the eyes of what meagre space there is. In those parts we call the hills 'mountains' — Cathedral Mountain, Peter and Paul Mountain, Cold Mountain, Resurrection Mountain and finally, Hospital Mountain, bearing on its summit the red-brick building of the old hospital, built at the turn of the century in the drab provincial style. And standing beside it, a house from the same period, occupied from times immemorial by our family and our neighbours.

I saw them build the new wing on to that house and I watched my first teacher move into it after his arrival from foreign parts.

An accent that wasn't from the Volga, a glance filled with unworldly compassion, a light that burned all night in the window — these were all unusual things in our town, which no longer ranked as a regional centre. But the local authorities tolerated this strange man, for in that period immediately after the war a teacher was a great rarity anywhere in our region — and the mongrel yard-dogs tolerated his white poodle with the same feeling of irritation.

A few years ago the wing of the house had caught fire, and although the flames were extinguished quite quickly (they hardly touched the main house at all), the teacher was choked to death by the smoke.

In the very farthest corner of the attic, under a thick layer of gray dust, I discovered a bundle of papers, neatly wrapped in newspaper and bound round with fine copper wire.

Later, at home in Moscow, when I had read everything that my

Teacher had written, I recalled, like some blurred and faded spectral vision, a walk we had taken together long before.

It was an oppressive, cotton-wadded, dense, viscous night in autumn. We went down to the river, almost feeling our way along by touch, and walked to the water's edge. The moon and stars were hidden behind the clouds. It was pitch-black, just as it should be on an overcast autumn night on the Volga.

Suddenly, somewhere far, far away from us on the opposite bank, a wavering flame flared into life, and by the light of the campfire we could just make out the dim shape of a solitary figure.

'A campfire, now there's a good idea,' said the Teacher. 'Just think, now: the moon and the stars are hidden by the clouds, and the power of darkness seems complete, but it only makes a fire lit by anyone even brighter and easier to see.'

It cost us quite some time and effort before we could get our own campfire burning. The earth was damp, the branches were heavy and wet. But eventually the campfire became a blaze, and I found myself in quite unfamiliar surroundings — a glimmering, bloated landscape, with something that might be a bush or might be some strange rustling creature waving its paws at me, the strange rocky trunk of an unfamiliar tree and eyes that had appeared out of the darkness, bearing reflections of our distorted faces and the tight-bundled flames of the campfire.

The man on the far bank waved to us. The Teacher returned his wave and laughed.

It seems that was all I could remember. Except, that is, for the words 'night realism' and a thought which I can now only paraphrase approximately: 'one more thing that used to unite people is coming to an end.'

The Teacher's papers contained a novel and a mass of plans and drafts. The novel begins with the following words: 'THE SOOT TOOK TO THE AIR RELUCTANTLY...'

The Face-Maker
and the Muse

The soot took to the air reluctantly and drifted away behind his back, so that through the flames — brighter now and scarcely visible in the grey light of day — the Face-Maker could see the City, separated from his eyes under the awning by a dry distance that lent it an unusual appearance.

From the street, from out of the rain, the City looked grayer and more blurred, and you could only ever see a small part of it. But from here, from high up, through the flame, the dry air and then the rain, the City trembled slightly, detached itself from the earth and hung in the air, as though it had finally ceased pretending and become what it really was.

At first a warmth appeared around the rain, and in the wind that felt pleasant, but then the tongues of flame ceased caressing the soles of his feet with their warmth and began caressing him with their heat. They burnt his feet and suddenly, without any warning at all, one of them licked him in the groin. The Face-Maker jerked convulsively and then remembered that he was bound fast and his convulsion was merely internal. He sensed as well that his body was prepared to accustom itself to the fire. It had exuded sweat, it was defending itself against the heat. At this point the wind pressed against the tongues of flame, and they leaned reluctantly away from the Face-Maker's body. It was suddenly strangely cold, but that wasn't true, it was a normal cold, the cold he was used to, only before the fire. The Face-Maker shuddered. Having detached itself from the earth, the City appeared to be trying to fulfill the fundamental purpose of its existence by clambering up the hill on the top of which the Face-

Maker now lived. But high as he might live, the House behind his back was higher still. From the roof of that House the Face-Maker could probably have seen most of the City, while all he could see now were the neat, even rows of the houses that bent around the hill in a semicircle, surrounding it on all sides — as though an ancient amphitheatre that had been pulled inside out but otherwise left untouched by the hand of time had raised itself up from the surface of the earth on its steps and was scrambling up the hill — without the slightest fuss, without any of the rows attempting to overtake the others: in their coordinated ascent they maintained a strict and regular order, sequence and balance. From here he could see quite clearly how regular the distance between the rows was. Only at one spot did a wide band of separation split the ranks of houses into two equally great detachments, in the way an army divides when it moves, pushing its commanders ahead of itself, with the soldiers marching just far enough behind for the gap to be sensed and seen even at a distance, just far enough behind for the leaders and the masses not to be confused.

Yet another gust of wind bent the fire back towards the Face-Maker's body. The flames had grown taller in the meantime and they licked at the Face-Maker's face. His eyebrows flared up, then drooped, turned pale and vanished, leaving behind nothing but white wisps of ash. The tongues lifted their tender caress still higher, and his hair disappeared as though it had ducked back inside his skull: the way a ground squirrel glances out for a minute and then ducks back into its burrow when it hears an enemy approaching. The smell of burning hair is disgusting, probably even more disgusting than the pain.

The Face-Maker closed his eyes, but the City was still there in them, still just the same as when the Face-Maker saw it from here for the first time: those even semi-circles embracing the hill. His eyelids grew hot. One, no longer able to withstand the heat, suddenly burst, and the eye, unable to withstand the light and the fire, shriveled away and saw the world no longer. The last thing the Face-Maker glimpsed through it was the front row of houses flattened, stretched and bent sharply backwards, as though in attempting to resist the other rows advancing upon it, it had suddenly given way and snapped under the pressure. And after that, nothing but a red mist. The Face-Maker tried to throw his head back and tip his living eye further inside himself, and he felt the force of the fire slacken. Perhaps it was the wind, or perhaps the junk piled up under his feet had burned through and collapsed and the flames had retreated, slipping down to pursue the burnt-out junk. The Face-Maker opened his remaining eye. Of course, he had only imagined it — the first row was still there, choking the hill in the grip of its even, regular semi-circle. His shriveled eye had made him overlook the fact that his legs had already begun to burn. The charred and twisted sole must be cramping his leg, but he couldn't feel the pain of the twisted muscles through the pain of his smouldering foot. His brain could only theorize about it, and meanwhile his body, independent of his brain, went on resisting the heat through its strongest centre of pain, even though future causes were already at work, reconciling the Face-Maker with it.

Now the fire must have clambered on to a heap of papers, for it leapt up and thrust a lance into the Face-Maker's heart. He had been prepared for trial by fire, but not to this extent, it was time to take the Face-Maker down now, he had already lost one eye and it would be harder for him to work from now on. The flames spurted up again, brighter now and wider, and the City disappeared behind them.

The awning above him caught fire and the flame broke through to the outside. The Face-Maker spat salty saliva in his delight: now the rain would come pouring in. But no, it was too late. Before they could reach the flames, the streams of rain turned to steam and evaporated. Fire was stronger than water. Sooner or later, of course, the flames would weaken and the rain would have its way, because fire is temporary, it is only there for as long as there is something to burn, no matter how strong it might be, while the rain in this City was permanent. But that would not do the Face-Maker any good: by the time the rain had conquered and the flames were exhausted, what would be left of his body? Certainly not anything that could go down the hill and open the door behind which the Muse was waiting.

It became a little cooler though it might not be able to defeat the fire, the water had made it more bearable. It was too risky to open his eye. The skin on his belly began to burst open and the cracks crept around his hips. The Face-Maker could no longer feel any pain below his knees.

And even so he had been lucky. He had managed to acquire a Name. He was the Face-Maker, and not just Seventy-Seven, as he had been two years earlier. And the Muse, his Muse — today she had a Name as well.

Calm down, remember. What has no fear of fire? Stone? Stone. His body still seemed to obey his thought, for everything that was still alive in the Face-Maker now became stone. And that was only right — if there is no way out, then you have to invent one. Once again his thoughts, like a runner who has stumbled, struggled to their feet and trudged on, limping slightly. Yes, thought the Face-Maker, yes that's right, if he opened his remaining eye now it would burn up, and if he opened his mouth, his speech and his breathing would burn up, and if he felt the pain, his brain would not survive it.

The Face-Maker laughed. He didn't have to think up ways out any more. Everything was simple now, he was stone and stone is not afraid of fire, it simply turns red and brittle, exuding sweat in order to even out the temperature, in fulfillment of the law of future causes.

And then the doubt appeared as suddenly as an abyss yawning just around the corner in a place where only yesterday there was a road. If he'd become stone, would he be able to work? Would they be able to manage without him? Not everyone was capable of correcting people who were made different to match a single face like the one on the wall in the hall in the House behind him. He had learnt every detail of that face in years of work. Even here, high above the City, even now having hidden his only living eye deep inside himself, the Face-Maker could see that face as clearly as if he was looking at himself in a mirror only a foot in front of him.

Toss a match into a haystack and you'll see what will happen to the Face-Maker's doubts: nothing but red ash drifting on the wind. Nothing else. Nothing but a blackened patch on the ground, and probably even less of a trace left by future memory. Although it really did exist, that haystack made out of grass which has not yet sprouted, the red bees did fly on the wind, the ground-squirrels did hide away from the fire in their burrows and there was a smell of scorched hair and the smoke of flesh that had become stone.

Chapter One

The Choice

I

It is raining everywhere except here inside. No matter how strong, how constant, how persistent, how cold or all-powerful the rain might be — the blue rain of the river in its slanting lines, the red rain of the sun in its large check patterns, the green rain falling down through the leaves on to the point of the hood of your cloak, across your shoulders, down on to the ground and then into the stream of the gutter, into the canal and on out of the City — no matter how strong it might be, this rain, here inside a human being it is thought that flows, that swells with the blood, that emerges from the mouth as steam or congeals in the brain as memory that might be needed some day. Everything outside a human being is subject to the laws of nature, but nothing here inside a human being is subject to any laws at all. He can live his entire life underground, that is, within himself, and no one will ever know, because he will walk home through the streets of the City just as the Face-Maker is walking home from work at this very moment, because at home his Muse is waiting for him, the Muse who was granted to him by chance, his own faithful Muse, just as our Muse is waiting for our Face-Maker at this very moment. The rain simply keeps on falling downwards, but the blood inside the body moves in its own unswerving, anomalous direction, quite independent of the direction of the rain. This, or something like this, is the way the Face-Maker reasons in his joy at the fact that sooner or later, if you remain exclusively faithful, the thing you are waiting for will happen. But even so, the hour of a person's encounter with his own fundamental identity is unexpected and fortuitous, possibly even disastrous, it might even be better if it never arrives at all, for the longer you live in anticipation of this hour, the more meaningful your life will become. This, or something like this, perhaps even in words something like these, is the way the Face-Maker reasons on the deserted street of the City, not even aware that thought is protecting him from what is happening outside him; he walks on, unaware of the rain squeezing his body with its cold, heavy hands and bowing his head down towards the stone that serves the inhabitants of the City so forcefully by lying beneath their feet.

II

How everything has changed! Only yesterday the Face-Maker had walked along these same streets with almost exactly these thoughts, feeling the rain on the folds of his cloak, and then on the folds of his skin, accepting the weight of this torrent pouring down from above. Today the rain is still pouring down, perhaps even more heavily, but the Face-Maker is totally insensible to it.

The thing he has been waiting for for years has happened.

On one occasion already, in his impatience at waiting so long, the Face-Maker had forfeited the final remnants of his gaiety, then after the Commission he had simply become indifferent to fear, and begun over again working secretly to prepare himself for today — without knowing, of course, that it would be today. The Official had appeared in the laboratory during the final quarter of an hour before the lunch-break and the patient lying on the table had pulled the sheet up over her breasts as she gaped wide-eyed at him, and attempted to get up. That was when the Face-Maker had seen the Official in her eyes.

The Official gestured for the patient to get up from the table. She wrapped herself more tightly in the sheet against the cold and stood up. Then she realized she was being banished from the surgery, and she hurried out.

The Face-Maker stood there with his arms dangling awkwardly, the fingers of one hand still clutching a scalpel. He tried to assume a more independent pose: he bent his arm and tossed the scalpel with an easy movement into the white nickel-plated instrument box, but the ease was evidently more pretense than reality, and in his agitation the throw proved awkward. The scalpel clattered on to the bottom of the box and bounced, skidding over the edge and flying point-first towards the floor, glinting momentarily like a fisherman's spinner in the water before it was extinguished.

The Face-Maker was astonished to discover within himself the traits he had possessed before the Commission. Firstly, he was nervous, and secondly, he had lost control of himself to such an extent that his agitation was visible to others. The Face-Maker was overjoyed, the way a person who has fallen over a cliff is overjoyed, on re-emerging from unconsciousness into life and feeling himself all over, to discover that he is not only alive, but unharmed, his arms and legs obey him, his eyes see and his ears hear. Unable to believe the evidence of his senses, he is overjoyed even at his own disbelief.

This meant that beyond the bounds of his daily routine the Face-Maker still possessed all the same old feelings. The Official's arrival was something that went beyond his daily routine, something from a higher plane, from a life in which the Face-Maker had had no place until today. From the life which last year the Face-Maker had been in such haste to enter that he had almost broken his neck in the attempt. But perhaps his experience in indifference and self-control could serve him well enough even in this other life, if only he could impress upon himself the idea that the Official's visit might be something new, but it was still a part of daily reality, it was almost like the return of his old freedom, just with a certain extra tension.

But even this fancied freedom lasted scarcely more than a moment before it was gone like a spike driven into a railway sleeper — the first blow secures it, and after the second there is nothing left but the head showing on the surface. Not only had the Official himself come — and his appearance in itself was a sure sign that you were somehow involved in the principal affairs of the City — but there had been a second blow, the one which took away the Face-Maker's fancied freedom: the Official had come to see the Face-Maker on business. He began to speak.

His speech stacked itself away on the shelves of the Face-Maker's memory like bolts of cloth in a haberdashery shop. The Face-Maker saw the meaning, but not the words, for the external sense of words never expresses what the speaker really wants to say to you, his desire to astonish or conquer you, to crush or compel you to love him or to stop loving him, and all the rest... You have to filter all this out from the spoken word like salt from water, and not everyone is capable of this. The Face-Maker, though, was a master of the technique of translating words into meaning.

The Official was suggesting that the couple the Face-Maker was working on should be altered to become the Principal Couple — but although his couple and another were both involved in the Choice, the distance between them was as insurmountable as a precipice for a tortoise or a pane of glass for a butterfly, and the distance was even greater that separated our Face-Maker from his teacher, the Great Face-Maker, who was preparing the Principal Couple.

The Face-Maker did not know what to do with his hands, he stood up... picked up the scalpel... he sniffed (which was tantamount to disrespect), became even more embarrassed, carefully placed the scalpel in the box. The scalpel clinked once and was silent. Apparently heartened by this steely signal from fate, he shuddered once and — to external appearances at least — regained control of himself.

The proposal was as unexpected and impossible as a proposal that a girl from the *corps de ballet* should dance the leading role in a major competition. Of course, the Face-Maker was precisely that, a Face-Maker, but the gap between him and the Great Face-Maker was wider than that between the prima ballerina and a chorus girl.

The Great One was unique.

Of course, he could have regarded the proposal as a test of the extent of his own secret vanity, but testing that was obviously not a job for the Official. To regard the visit as a test would have been the extreme limit of fear and mistrust, and even after the Commission, the Face-Maker, like all who had acquired a name, knew only moderate fear.

Today the Official was neither joking nor testing him. For all his experience in mistrust, the Face-Maker gave precedence to the simple sense of the proposal in the Official's words. In any case, it appeared that he could wait until the following day before deciding whether or not to accept. Yes, taking everything together, the interpretation of a combined test and deception could effectively be ruled out. But the Face-Maker did not entirely dismiss this meaning, he simply assigned it a subordinate position in the system of possible variants, and regarded the simple sense of the proposal as the fundamental one. The effort cost him all the energy that he had accumulated and conserved. This was the first step towards the life-goal for which he had been preparing — with the Muse's help, of course. But had he really been preparing? And was he ready now?

The rain grew stronger and finally forced a breach in the Face-Maker's concentration — a small, narrow breach just large enough for a single drop — and it seeped through into the Face-Maker's consciousness, like a mouse that twists and stretches itself in order to wriggle into a room through a crack in the floor. The Face-Maker's shoulders twitched, and once again he saw himself alone on the street in the rain, hunched and wretched, hiding away from people within himself, the way he had seen himself almost all his life, apart from those moments when he thought of the Muse, who waited for him in the dry apartment, pretending to read something, when she was really listening to hear the bang of the front door, which meant that in a moment the door would open. In contrast with the Face-Maker, who was waiting for his hour to come, she had long since been prepared to live in any way that life allowed, whether that meant success or living out the rest of their years as they had been living, always waiting for each other and glad to see each other, and... Perhaps the Muse would have preferred the second option, because success was something unknown and even frightening, it would open up another way of life which might distort and perhaps mutilate everything that had been built up in the course of their long and faithful relationship, perhaps making them more tender and loving, but perhaps finally pulling them apart. She did not want these potential blessings or misfortunes, she was happy to exchange them for what they had already, which she treasured, and which made her happier than many of the people she encountered at work or afterwards. Sadly this choice did not depend on her, however, she was dependent on the Face-Maker, and he was dependent on many different things, including the Official, as had been confirmed by that day's meeting.

III

If that day's meeting had not taken place, there would have been no novel. Their previous life is not the subject of this novel, it is a life like everyone else's; and the things that are known to everyone, that everyone can see, are not, even in their most pronounced form, the subject-matter of the novelist, but of the chronicler of social mores. The subject-matter of a novel is something concentrated in one or several individuals, which entirely changes the lives of all people living, changes them and the shape of their days, so that the chroniclers of the future may continue to perfect their art and describe the subtle forms of realities which came into being without their assistance. Therefore our novel begins with that day's meeting, which affects the destiny of everyone living, not only the Face-Maker and the Muse. Of course I need not have written that, I could have left it for the critic to guess: when they finish building a house they take away the scaffolding, and only an architect would know where to position the support if the building had to be renovated. But I want to leave the critic with no work to do, because his fate is to serve the chronicler, he is the second half of this pair, which feeds itself by gathering the corn planted earlier by a sower who scattered his own substance on the soil in place of grain.

How strange it was: until today nothing had depended on the Face-Maker, everything — his work, his pay, his routine — had been decided without him being involved, and he had been entirely dependent on people above him, but today his own voluntary decision would determine whether or not he would carry out the work proposed by the Official, because this was something you could not be ordered to do.

IV

The Face-Maker slipped. He just barely managed to keep his balance, like a tight-rope-walker, and his hand touched the building's cold, windowless wall. The next house was his. He moved on cautiously, spreading his legs wider to make doubly sure. If not from the sky, then from the ground, the rain had still succeeded in distracting his attention. Even when you were absorbed in thought you still had to take it into account. End up smashing the back of your head against the stone, and all your great decisions and desires would flow out and down through a crack in the earth's crust, mingle with the rain and disappear, flowing out beyond the city along the canal that ran down the hill. Special caution was needed: today he needed that crust more than ever, he should carry it with care.

Replying to the Official's proposal was not so simple. On the one hand, there was the prospect of what he longed for: the Face-Maker would occupy the first rung on the ladder and become the Great Face-Maker, and that would be followed by everything the Face-Maker had been striving for, or at least, what he had thought he was striving for initially. On the other hand, this was the same adventurism that had nearly cost him Departure. Of course, the Official was involved in this piece of adventurism, but everybody knew what became of verbally delivered official proposals if something went awry in the course of their implementation. The proposers simply forgot their proposals, and the responsibility was borne by those who were implementing them. In this case the person who was supposed to implement the proposal was the Face-Maker, and he had already been through one Commission, and only recently... And then again, who wants to take over from someone who is alive and working, especially when he is your teacher and his work is excellent, far better, in fact, than your own? Of course, the Face-Maker could have disputed this, but only in his imagination. He had never carried out any Real Operations of Likeness of the same class as the Great Face-Maker. Last year's operation had been an amateur affair, and in the present circumstances working by eye was simply pointless. Yes, the proposal was sufficiently complicated for an unconsidered answer to mean... These are the thoughts that circle around the two hemispheres of the Face-Maker's brain, in the way that pigeons loosed into the sky by an experienced fancier will swirl around and around and are quite incapable of stopping, and it requires an effort of will-power to drive them back into the dovecote so that you can calmly inspect each of them at close quarters and let them rest. The true dovecote of the Face-Maker's thoughts was the Muse — which brings us back to the person without whom our Face-Maker would not exist. The Face-Maker owed everything that he was and everything he could do to the Muse, and she was with him everywhere — when he was relaxing, absorbed in his thoughts, and when he worked with the scalpel at home, to improve his fingers' control over the instrument. Only once had the Face-Maker ever decided to act on his own, when he had launched into last year's undertaking.

If the Face-Maker had asked the Muse, simply and clearly, whether he ought to do it, she would have managed to persuade him to refuse, for the chance always comes to do the same thing with less risk. But last year the Face-Maker had almost stopped talking to the Muse and decided for the first time to do without her help. Ignoring the Muse's persistent requests to tell her what was happening, he set out to realize his plan, remarking nonchalantly that nothing was happening that hadn't happened before to someone or other.

The Muse calmed the Face-Maker; the means were various, but always as a result the Face-Maker's thoughts would become quiescent, and fold away their wings, just a little nervously at first, and then settle down and allow themselves to be handled.

Show me the person who can identify the species of a bird flying in darkness — and the state of anxiety is a darkness, filled with the rustling of wings and clamorous cries.

Museum Attendant Two Hundred and Ninety Two — such were the post and the number of our Muse when she met the Face-Maker at one of the Likeness Operations. She was younger then, and so was he. The Face-Maker had leaned his chest across her uncovered body in his usual manner, but scarcely had he raised his scalpel to the first upper quadrant of her face, as he had done a thousand times before, when he felt the entire surgery reel and roll, turning entirely upside down. Then it had begun to expand and shrink alternately, as though it had been transformed into some kind of pendulum. When the Face-Maker recovered his composure half an hour later, he was quite simply delighted that the Muse was still alive, although less in need of the Likeness Operation, than of basic resuscitation, but that wasn't really a problem. If the Face-Maker was to take her as his wife, then there would in any case have to be another operation, as a result of which she would be given a name. Perhaps, in fact, she was first given a name and then the Likeness Operation was carried out, but regardless of the order of events, a week or two later the Muse, like the other lucky ones (and cases like this were as rare in the history of the City as wells in the desert) was transformed from a Museum Attendant into a Muse, with a face which was a corresponding likeness of the Image.

In general it would be just as impossible to say which had priority in the City — the number or the corresponding face — as to decide whether the chicken or the egg came first in human history. Therefore, in the City, which was full to overflowing of order and justice, blind chance still remained the main factor in determining a citizen's fate. Something happened, and as a result people's numbers changed, and then so did their faces — or the reverse. And the Face-Maker, on whom the citizen's fate might appear to depend, had only to perform the operation corresponding to the citizen's class, nothing more and nothing less. There was no making head or tail of the whole mysterious business.

In any case, it does not matter whether the name or the face came first, but a certain Two Hundred and Ninety Two became a Muse. Any ordinary person would quite simply say she had been lucky. 'Fate' was the Face-Maker's only comment on the matter. Not by any means that they were both in the habit of keeping silent; all of their time together they spent talking — and how they missed each other!

V

But this day, as we know, is a special one. The Muse is as sensitive to joy as a dog is to scent — and to grief, too — the Muse is sensitive to any departure at all from the humdrum routine of life. She won't show it straight away, she may not ask any direct questions, and she won't try to talk about what the Face-Maker is feeling, but in their idle chatter and nonsense she will weave a spell of confusion around him with her very intonation, and somehow or other an hour later the Muse will know everything. The Face-Maker has still not been able to understand how this happens. But he has noticed one thing: when some special occasion entirely transcends the limits of a routine occasion, the Muse, alas, is once again powerless. Of course, she guesses at what has happened, and picks up half of it from conversation, but as far as complete understanding is concerned... On these occasions there is no way to break the Face-Maker down.

Today is one of those very special occasions, a difficult day for the Muse. But since the Face-Maker barely survived on the one occasion when he relied on himself to deal with a doubly-important occasion, he is no longer quite so reserved. Almost on the threshold, almost before the Muse had time to take off his cloak and thrust it into the drier, to lead him into the dining-room, pressing her face to his back and embracing him from behind, the Face-Maker had informed her of the Official's visit, and the proposal, and the decision which has to be communicated the next day. But the first question the Muse asked took the Face-Maker by surprise: in view of all the possibilities — on the one hand the moral question, and on the other the fulfillment of the Face-Maker's own personal destiny (in general people's lives are governed by a social destiny, in the present case, for instance, the destiny of the City) — it turned out the Face-Maker had forgotten something quite fundamental:

'But have the deadlines been extended?' the Muse asked him. 'It's twice the amount of work.'

'Three times,' said the Face-Maker, sinking down into an armchair as he pondered the problem. He recalled that not a word had been spoken about it, and therefore there could be no question of any extensions.

'Well, if that's the case, there's really not much point in thinking about it,' said the Muse, 'I think one lesson should be enough for you. Show a wise man a feather, and he'll show you the fox that ate the chicken.'

'What's a fox got to do with it?' asked the Face-Maker, his mind on something else entirely.

The Face-Maker paid no attention to the Muse's explanation, with its Official and its fox and its chicken, and he suddenly came to his own decision, the way a man who has set out to fetch water but finds gold on the way will run home, not to the well. He took a firm grasp of his own idea and changed the conversation to a different subject, a subject that our couple had developed to such a high degree that all he had to do, for instance, was to roll his tongue up into a tube and stick it out slightly and move it about a bit. Or else simply form the shape of the sounds 'oo-wah' with his lips.

'Wait,' said the Muse, 'you've come to a decision, and so have I, and I think there can only be one opinion here.'

She told him how unbearable it was for her to wait for him every day since the Commission, and how the agony of his possible Departure tormented her, and how she saw today's visit as a sign of destiny's desire to test him and remind him of last year's lesson, from which it followed that he shouldn't have any desires or regrets.

It should be said that if the Face-Maker had thought as she did that evening, or if he had not been preoccupied with a decision he had already taken, or let us say — for the sake of accuracy — with another desire, and if he had listened to the Muse's arguments, then perhaps what was to happen in the City would not have happened. But how could the Face-Maker take the Muse's arguments seriously when he had been struck so hard by his own inspiration? We must, of course, give the Muses their due — they are always absolutely right. I can see that doubts have begun to appear as to whether the event might not possibly have occurred without my Face-Maker. Yes, it could have and it would have. But not necessarily now, in fact, definitely not now. An event can only take place when two equally necessary conditions are fulfilled — its readiness to occur and the presence of the person who sets the event in motion. If it were not for my Face-Maker, this novel would not exist, there would be a different novel, perhaps with the same epilogue, but not today, and other people would set the time in motion in a different manner. I am as sure of this as a man who is neither drunk nor blind is sure there is a birch tree in front of him when he is standing there looking at it.

Ah, birch tree, what a soft, white trunk you have, how tender and pleasant it is to my fingers. My fingers feel warm and sensitive as if they were stroking birch-bark, I hear the leaves rustling, and the wind whispering gently in the torn fibers of the birch's skin.

VI

Once again the Muse gave way to him. She put her arms on the Face-Maker's shoulders and around his neck, slid them down over his smooth, cool skin, bent her head and pressed herself to him, softly and tenderly.

If everything the Face-Maker had planned had indeed come to pass, and if he were to have turned the world upside down and transformed it into the very shape and substance of his own secret desires, then these same hands would still have been placed on his shoulders in the same way, these same lips and fingers would still have felt his body swelling and his thought broken off when it was only half-spoken, half a phrase, half a thought... Light began moving backwards through time, confusing the sequence of numerals and the ordinal numbers of the time zones. The Muse knew this, but the Face-Maker did not know it, his boat swung high into the air and a wind sprang up and swelled the sail. The red oars were lowered into the water, and a pillar of fire sprang up and raised the boat high on its crest, with its white sail and its red oars. The lightning struck, and its branches spread out across the sky, shielding the boat from the slow fire, and then its roots grew down through the boat and it flared up. Burning slowly, slowly, the boat dropped back into the sea and lay on its calm waves, and the red oars were extinguished, and the scrap of scorched sail slowly dragged it to the shore, only half-alive, scorched pink by the fire.

VII

They lay for a long time without moving. The Muse got up first. It was as pointless talking to the Face-Maker after this as trying to persuade a telegraph post to sink roots into the earth and shed its wires. First she had to revive him, to teach him to talk, and only then could she start asking him for things. So the Muse simply stood up without speaking. But in order to completely rid her conscience of the guilt to come, which she might well feel if there had been the slightest chance at all of bringing the Face-Maker back to the conversation that had been taking place, and changing his mind, the Muse took his hand and tried to make him sit up. The Face-Maker was not capable of speaking, or arguing, or agreeing, he simply continued being absent. There was no way anyone could rouse him from this state within the next half hour, but the Muse did not give up straight away, she felt so sorry for the Face-Maker now. Why this feeling, as though she was losing him today? And it hurt her so, as though it had all happened yesterday and today it was all beyond repair. But the sensation of pain is one thing, and our actions are another, and the Muse quietly dressed, pulled on her cloak and went out into the street. She had decided to attempt to change something; since she couldn't change him, she would change the circumstances.

The Hundreds, whom the Face-Maker was preparing for the Choice, were her friends. In fact, it was the Muse who had found them for the Face-Maker. Every Face-Maker preferred to work with faces that they not only knew, but with which had some kind of personal connection, and the couple's personal connection with the Face-Maker lay in the fact that the Muse was their friend. This friendship had endured from a time long before, when they and the Muse had lived in rooms next door to each other — the Hundreds had been living together even then. It had all begun with the male Hundred's courtship of the Muse — he was then Two Hundred and Ninety Five — which came to absolutely nothing, but developed into a friendly relationship with his partner. That was all quite a long time ago now. In some way alike in the past, now they were very different from each other. But without faithfulness to our memories, how could we carry on living? This friendship had somehow dragged on, without, in fact, bringing the Muse much pleasure. But she had not made any other friends, when you have a Face-Maker for a partner, you hardly need other people. His energy, his desires and problems are quite enough: from thinking of something new to do in bed, to his delirious desire to make a new face for you, because he is fed up with this one. And then there was her own work; although she now had the right to give it up, the Muse had carried on in her job, and to some extent this had weakened the thoughts which sometimes seemed about to drive her mad. Sometimes, indeed, these thoughts could even produce some deft and simple result by transforming themselves into something both useful and calm. Today she really felt less than ever like going to see the Hundreds, but she had to — for the Face-Maker. Once again everything was settling back into place.

On the street the rain grabbed hold of her and squeezed her, as though it was trying to make her small and light, so that its streams could knock her off the pavement and carry her away out of the city. Her heart began to ache from the pressure. What if it did knock her, then who would help her? There was nothing around her but Stone, and Stone is not afraid of the rain. Numbers. Bridges. Not a single tree. Not a single branch. Not a single bird. Not a single living soul. It was rare for anyone to venture out on the street, and then they went alone, glancing over their shoulders, and only if they were driven by some exceptional need: there were almost no needs at all, everyone socialized within the limits of their ten-units, that it, within the limits of their house. So the streets steamed in quiet solitude, and mist rose from the canal, the only sound was the monotonous noise of the rain, there was no other sound at all. The silence of the noise. The silence of the rain. The silence of the stone walls. The silence of the mist. The silence was deafening.

VIII

How tired-looking female One Hundred's face was. A working day spent on the table under the knife — no wonder she was exhausted! The Muse's glance accidentally fell on One Hundred's breasts and she remembered what the Face-Maker had said about not wanting to touch those white, pointed, fleshy mounds, so that when he was operating he put on an apron that made him look like a housewife. Maybe so, well, doesn't he always say he puts on an apron.

But then, he puts one on when he makes corrections to the Muse too. In that case, so he says, it's only because he's afraid of disfiguring her face again. She would have to try asking him to work without an apron, perhaps that feeling had gone a long time ago. Or perhaps, when he was working with One Hundred, he put on an apron because that excited him too.

The first five minutes of a conversation between two people who have known everything about each other for a long time is enough to find out all the Muse needs to know. For all the honour due to old friendships and other such nonsense, the Hundreds' chances of making the leap to becoming the Principal Couple are so minute, they couldn't even dream of it, so if the chance did somehow come up... At this point female One Hundred's face becomes soft, silent, dreamy, feminine just as it should be up on the stage during the Choice. And she wouldn't even have to think. What she would do without even having to think about it the Muse didn't even try to discover. She simply noted there was no point in expecting any help from One Hundred and dropped the matter. What was there to talk about anyway? Everything had been clear from the very start. She might as well ask a woodpecker not to drill holes in trees.

But though she understood that, just as she had with the Face-Maker, she went back over things for herself to see if there might be a chance. There was no chance. There was nothing she could count on here either. The avidity with which female One Hundred seized on the possibility of such unimaginable good fortune finally convinced the Muse she had miscalculated. Winding up the business part of the conversation without revealing the serious intent behind this five minutes of idle chatter, the Muse agreed to go out into the garden with her and watch male One Hundred working with his birds, so that she wouldn't have to go straight away and leave the sharp-witted female One Hundred with anything for her mind to work on (after all, she was tired enough from dealing with her own problems, so what did she want with the Muse's as well?)

They walked through the hall and opened the light lattice-work door into the garden, an almost aerial door that didn't creak or squeak but swept back like a flapping wing. The male One Hundred was standing with his back to them in his linen shirt. He was just getting a bird out of its cage and he answered the quiet question — could they watch? — with a nod, without turning round. As he carefully lifted the bird out it tried to flutter its wings, but it couldn't. It tensed up tightly as though it was trying to make itself smaller and escape from his fingers. The hand tightened still further and now it feels squashed. It is really frightened now. Its heart has already been squashed within its body, its heart is no longer beating at all. The bird is living without any heart. The palm of the hand presses tighter, harder against the soft, yielding, subtle flesh of the tiny bird. Crack — the body split open like a nut, there was a sudden spurt and then a stream of blood, and it fell in quiet drops, pink and thin. The hand was stone, pressing harder and stronger, and the brownish, pinkish flesh oozed out between the fingers.

She could see female One Hundred becoming excited. The Muse shuddered, but she could appreciate the skill. She hadn't seen much of this craft, but as far as she could tell he was a real Master. Male One Hundred was already reaching for the next one, while all around him the birds were singing in the yellow trees.

Maybe tomorrow they would find themselves struggling in the strong hand of the master, but they didn't know that, or perhaps they'd simply got used to the idea and they carried on flying about lightheartedly while they still could, with the thin dry branches of the indoor garden trembling under their own fluffy and fragile little bodies.

'Let's go,' female One Hundred tugged at the Muse's arm, 'I'll make you some tea.'

While they enjoyed their tea, another ten minutes went by in idle chatter. He came in and washed his hands, but there was a brown spot on his sleeve, just by the hemmed edge — he'd squeezed a bit too hard and the blood had splashed. He sat down by the Muse. His eyes were still focused on his work, red, severe.

'It's the same every day now,' female One Hundred announced with a casual air.

'Every day?' male One Hundred queried. 'No it's not, there are breaks. It's like they say in the City: "you can't do everything all the time". Sometimes you have to do just some of it, and only some of the time.'

Female One Hundred's smile spread so far that the edge of her right lip almost touched her ear and then halted there in a crooked curve. Her man was obviously in good form today. And if he was in good form, then she knew his standard two-hour program off by heart, so female One Hundred was happy to join in the conversation that followed this great aphorism and make her own lively contribution. After all, it meant that she got two hours of freedom as well.

Viewed from the outside the content of the conversation was approximately as follows: male One Hundred says he likes the rain when he gets worked up, for then it is pleasant to go out and walk under the dense lashing downpour and cool one's body and come back after the walk with the feeling that the body is stronger than the rain.

The warmth of the City, he says, and a human being are not subject to the rain's power, and then follow other similar cliches that male One Hundred has always forced down his partner's ears with indifferent inspiration. And with the same indifferent inspiration she always agrees with him and assures him that she understands exactly what he means. She has always waited for him to come back and heated some water and prepared a towel, and... at this point she became even more pink and tender... if we shift from the language of pulling wool over eyes and magic spells for toothache to the language of real meaning, then male One Hundred's lyrical passage conveyed the information that he was going to see a woman and the reminder that for female One Hundred this was nothing new or surprising.

In turn she had conveyed the fact that she'd understood male One Hundred and wouldn't mind having a couple of hours' fun herself. All three of them understood this language very well. It's nice to deal with intelligent people, you never have to tell them what you think, because they'll understand, and while they talk about the usefulness of hot water for cooling the body, they'll let you slip your hand into their pocket and assure you that they won't notice a thing. Experience shows that in court cases between people who employ such a system there are only half as many guilty parties as there are among people who are more direct.

'Goodbye then, my love,' male One Hundred already had his cloak on.

'Goodbye, my darling,' replied the delicately pink female One Hundred, shedding a few tears as she wound her warm arms around his neck. 'Just be very careful with your face — it's our future after all.'

She watched him on his way for a whole minute to make sure he wouldn't come back, as he sometimes did. Once she'd waited for the prescribed period, she threw off her house-coat and pulled on her linen shirt with its sleeves covered in small pink splashes. The cloak went on top. She apologized to the Muse. Since the time of the Choice was approaching and she would have to move out of this house, she'd like to visit another couple of neighbours that she hadn't got to know yet. And of course, go to see the Museum Director, who she felt absolutely nothing for, in fact, he actually disgusted her with his white narrow chest that was bald as a knee-cap, but he was the only man in her life who had a name — and what woman with a number wouldn't be flattered to be allowed into the bed of the Director himself. Of course, the Director wasn't a Face-Maker, but for the One Hundreds even a Director was like a pair of wings for a homeless cat.

The Muse was astonished that she would have to do so much in such a short time.

'Never mind, I used to get even more done, when I still didn't know much. But now! Ohoh!' She winked at the Muse and tied the ribbons of her hood in a bow.

'Bye...' she kissed the Muse on the cheek.

The Muse went back to the table, and then walked through into the garden. She had to think of something, or at least do everything she possibly could do, so that she wouldn't have to feel guilty about the past, so she would be able to stay calm. She sat down in the chair where male One Hundred crushed his birds. The birds were singing, leaves were falling. It was quiet.

IX

Female One Hundred went up to the next doorway and tugged impatiently on the handle. The doors opened. There was nobody in the hallway. She took off her cloak and hung it up. She gently pushed the second door and it swung back. The room was empty too. And the next one after that. The third room was half-dark, damp and warm. She started suddenly — a pair of eyes was watching her. They were astonished, full of fear. Only they came in like this. The fear was like a bird in a cage, when the door is already open and the hand is reaching in for the bird.

'Are you One Hundred and One?'

'No, I'm Ninety-Nine.'

'I'm One Hundred. I live next door.' She held out her hand.

The fear flapped its wings, flitted past the hand and disappeared from view.

'I only have a few minutes to spare.'

'Come on, I'll make you some tea.' Ninety-Nine stood up.

'I only have a few minutes.' One Hundred went across to him. 'I only have a few minutes, and then I'll go. Come here,' she pulled Ninety-Nine towards herself. She felt him go tense and start breathing heavily, she felt his heart beating fast. A thin shaving began lifting from the surface of the wood — transparent, long, unvarying — but the plank was still not ready and One Hundred began to think the material wasn't properly seasoned and it wasn't worth wasting any more time.

Even though she could feel her partner slowly going insane, and she knew he'd never known anything like it in his life, and it would be a little unkind to leave now. But there was no time!

She was like a man carrying water who won't let a dying old man drink his fill because up ahead the water is needed by people who are digging a well in order to provide water for the whole world. Sometimes the water-carrier comes too late to find anyone alive, and then he goes back and finds the person he left behind is dead too.

'There's no time, I told you, I only have a few minutes.'

His heart was heaving and pounding like a car stuck in the mud, his legs were trembling. He let go of her. She went out into the hall and threw on her cloak. He came up to her, pressed himself against her.

'Wait a minute.'

'Tomorrow, do you hear? I'll come tomorrow.'

She slipped out of the door and out on to the street. The rain greeted her with its coolness, but it didn't cool her, it embraced her body tightly with its flowing streams. Still carrying with her the touch of his hands by her lips, beside her ear, she began to hurry, and the power of this uncooling excitement bore her through the wet, black, gleaming, slippery streets to the doorway she longed to enter. The door was standing open.

'Hello, you're ten minutes late.'

'He left ten minutes later than usual.'

'Is that the truth?'

But he wasn't listening to her any longer. He'd been waiting for her and he didn't even give her time to take off her cloak.

X

The Muse tidied up the garden. She washed away the traces of blood and flesh. She swept up the fallen leaves. She hadn't thought of anything that was any use. She wanted to go back home, to her own garden, to the Face-Maker, away from these secrets, away from this filth. She put on her cloak. The door swung open.

'I can't wait till tomorrow.' Standing in the doorway was Ninety-Nine, his hair tousled, his eyes narrowed to slits, absolutely drunk.

The Muse feels sorry for him, she even delays a little before she utters her all-powerful magic phrase, for now it is up to her whether Ninety-Nine remains alive or attends the Commission that evening. And now he'll understand that too. The fox was chasing a rabbit, but it had fallen into a trap — click.

'I have a name.' The Muse even shook her head, as though she was asking for forgiveness.

It was all gone, scattered, disappeared. Ninety-Nine was suddenly as soft as rice pudding, sweat sprang out on his forehead, he lost control of his tongue.

'Alright, off you go, don't just stand there. I won't tell anyone.'

Holding on to the wall, Ninety-Nine staggered out through the door. The Muse followed him.

It was useful to have a name. If he'd come bursting in like that in the days before she knew the Face-Maker, she'd have had to scratch and struggle and defend herself. Lord, how hard it was for women without a name. It was hard enough for men without one. It meant you were defenseless and dependent. The Muse and the Face-Maker were both dependent on bigger names, but then that wasn't as crude, it was on a different level, although if the names were equal, then it was all just the same... But anyway she felt sorry for the young man.

'What energy that woman has,' she thought about female One Hundred, 'she must have left too soon.'

The Muse had barely taken a few steps away from the entrance when she was almost knocked off her feet by female One Hundred.

With her head thrust out in front of her like a duck about to land on the water, she was flying home. When she heard that he hadn't come back yet she sighed in relief and whisked in through the doorway. A few more steps, round the corner, and there was male One Hundred coming towards her. This was very different. He was lumbering along in a leisurely, thoughtful fashion. He stopped and looked at her in a way that made her want to wash her eyes out, which she did, by tipping her face up towards the sky.

'Wonderful weather, I don't even feel like going home, if it wasn't for the time...' One Hundred winked. 'Maybe I could walk you home?'

The Muse shuddered.

'No, thank you,' she said, thinking: 'What a pig he really is.' But she smiled, said goodbye and walked on, afraid he might try to change her mind.

He didn't turn away immediately. His mouth twisted into a rueful grin. It was a pity he didn't have a name, or else he'd have taken her ages ago. True, a name wasn't all there was to it, what he could manage, bringing her round here, probably wouldn't have suited. But anyway, why go to all that bother, when there was plenty of it lying around just waiting behind every door. It wasn't as if the ones with names had bodies that were any different.

Or perhaps they did. His thoughts became glued to the word 'name' and began wrapping themselves around it like tow on a spindle. Not straight away, not right now... but in theory at least anyone in the City could acquire a name. One Hundred wiped his face and bent his head forward so that the rain couldn't fall on to his skin. There were three days left until the Choice of the Principal Couple, and his operation was being performed by the Muse's Face-Maker, which meant he'd get second place. Which meant he'd no more chance of getting a name than of seeing his own ears. But what if a miracle happened? A miracle could always happen.

That stopped him dead, and from that moment on, forgetting all about the Muse and female One Hundred and female One

Hundred and Six, he began waiting for a miracle. This is how a chance thought that flits through the mind suddenly becomes obvious, anticipation is engaged and expectations start working, but exactly why no man could possibly explain to save his life. What takes place somehow takes place outside of us, we only feel it taking place! And don't even imagine for a second that there were any immediate changes in his external life. He walked home. The rain fell on him. Tomorrow once again he would spend his working day on the operating table. In the evening he would watch video recordings with female One Hundred and crush birds, and then go out about his own business. That was a good idea of mine, he thought, about my own business. Then he would come back home like today. All of it was so much the same you might have thought he was already coming home tomorrow or in ten years' time from now — each of his days was exactly like any other. But now this feeling of expecting a miracle had appeared in him. He tried to understand why it had happened. He could view the day in its entirety: nothing special had happened. The Muse had come visiting before. Yes. But the last time she had come was two weeks ago, she wasn't supposed to come again for another two weeks, but she had come today. How on earth could the Muse's visit have changed anything in his life? Of course, if she'd needed to find anything out or let them know anything, she'd have done it through the Face-Maker. Oh, how wonderful it was to live in a city where there were never any surprises. It meant that straight off, from one tiny single little fact, you could guess that something unusual was about to happen. But that wasn't all there was to it, not just these thoughts. He had been visited by the anticipation of a miracle. It was a sensation as clear and as simple as the resistance of his face to the rain, as the hands and lips of female One Hundred and Six that he was still carrying with him. He had a warm, happy feeling. Even the life of a simple man with a three-figure number has its joys. As they say in the City, joy can come to a sparrow if only it has faith. One Hundred was smiling at something as he entered the house.

She was there to meet him in her housecoat as always, as though she hadn't seen him for an eternity. He bared his teeth even more at the sight of her outstretched arms, which removed his cloak and then tenderly embraced his neck. He surprised himself by moving closer to her, which surprised her even more. After these walks they both usually went straight to bed and slept, but this time, perhaps because of this new sensation of his, perhaps because today's walk hadn't been such a great success — he was bored with female One Hundred and Six and he'd wasted his time crushing his own birds, because his partner had made him crush some of hers: in the first place he was a real master at it, and in the second place he was already excited and she wasn't... today was probably the first time he'd wondered whether it was really worth so much time and effort. It was almost the same as it was with female One Hundred anyway. Perhaps even one Hundred held him a little more tenderly, but then...

She put her hand on his shoulder and the shoulder was warm, even hot, the way the mud in which two pigs are jostling on a summer's day can be warm and even hot; the mud is deep and greasy, it flows over their legs and gets stuck in their bristles, it sticks to their snouts, and one pig pushes the other over and they begin wallowing in the sloppy mess — warm, hot and stinking. They enjoy the smell and the warmth and the chance to roll over in it from one side on to the other, round and round in circles, slopping the mess around. Good, is it? Very.

XI

It felt good to them. But in this particular case it has no real significance for the action. While their bodies are engaged for the second time in displacing a mass of mud equal to their own mass, there will be plenty of time for us to take a look at the person who wound the spring that has set the Face-Maker in motion. One tooth of its cog has already engaged his thoughts through the proposal to perform an operation according to new data. The Muse has now set herself in motion with the Face-Maker's thought and transmitted the motion to the Hundreds, and without really understanding how it all came about, they have not stopped moving since. Even when they do stop, they will still continue spinning around the major axis.

And so, already four people in this city are living differently, they are already sick, infected with the idea of movement — without any understanding of the real nature of their ailment. For their actions coincide with their desires, and externally they continue to lead the same life as they think they were leading before today, and subtle distinctions are of no importance. But anyone who knows the future will easily understand the changes that are really taking place, although no one in the City knows that except perhaps the person who wound the main spring of the action, but even he would never have done that, if he had realized the true scope and the consequences.

We are speaking, of course, of the Official who proposed that the Face-Maker should prepare the Principal Couple, when according to the writ of the law only the Great Face-Maker can work on them. Why, then, has the Official condemned to change such a well-arranged and reliable mechanism as the City, the management of which is not easy, but which runs nonetheless in a well-oiled groove?

Habit and tradition are the essence of life, and when they are disrupted, no one knows where it may lead.

Perhaps it is for the noble goal of equality for the population of the City?

Perhaps it is an attempt to liberate them from the eternal fear of Departure?

Perhaps... and then another and yet another great reason in the name of which cities and people are broken.

Alas... It is shameful even to speak out loud, but the entire affair — unfortunately, unhappily, God alone knows why it had to happen — turns out to be no more than a question of purely personal enmity between the Official and the Great Face-Maker, an enmity which began the day before our Face-Maker was rescued and freed from the Commission by the Official. When an enmity like this flares up, adventurers have to be saved from Commissions. And in this case, sad though it may be to admit it, in the eyes of the Law the Face-Maker was precisely that. But naturally nothing like that would happen again, at least not for the present. At least, that was what he and the Muse had thought, but... the Official had needed the Face-Maker again in precisely the same capacity.

As for the causes which led to the quarrel between the Official and the Great One, I think that if God himself had happened to witness the quarrel he would have been unable to define them precisely, except, perhaps, for the external sequence leading from the first clash a year ago to the most recent one, following which the Official had made his approach to the Face-Maker. Even we can do that much; they were fed up with each other, they had not shared their power out between them. But then, what need was there to share, when one was in charge of faces, the other of persons? Or perhaps a person and his face are actually the same thing? Anyway, there's no way of telling which is more important. But one way or another, there's no doubt that there was a quarrel, and nothing more need be said.

If the reason were ever to be mentioned, then both of them would be ashamed to remember it.

In general terms, one of them is first, and the other is second, but that's just for the uninitiated, in actual fact they are both first.

That's the catch, of course — there can never really be two people on top. There is only one outcome, in the end. The only possible one.

They quarreled that first time, and then again yesterday, over — aagh... no, I can't say it... my tongue won't... let us leave that to their consciences and take a look at where events are leading as a result. Of course, there is no result as yet, but there can be no doubt that things are moving towards it. The Official is also worried; after all, to consent to a second dubious venture, and after the Commission — no sane person would be likely to do that. As for the Face-Maker, it is actually possible to hope that he is really insane. Speaking from a rational point of view, of course. Even at the Commission the Face-Maker had stubbornly insisted that the cause of his admitted offense was not adventurism, but experimentation, and he hadn't seemed to be lying. Very possibly that was the only kind of people who suited the Official — although they are few and far between — they stubbornly carry through their own portion of the work, supposing that they are doing it for themselves. But of course, you have to keep a sharp eye on them. It was a good thing that the Official (a fastidious manager — he saw a long way ahead) had earlier palmed off the Muse on the Face-Maker so that she could act as a kind of brake on him, or he would have broken out even earlier, and then today's undertaking would have simply fallen apart, and he had, alas, no one else like the Face-Maker in view. Then it would have been a matter of just carrying on, hating the Great One all the while, overflowing with hatred for the monster and yet carrying on smiling. Alright, calm down, the Official told himself, it doesn't matter what names you call him, what matters is that you must play by the rules. What will happen tomorrow? Who will come out on top, the Muse or the Face-Maker?

The hour is late, time even for the Official to go to sleep. The body is a steed that has to be well maintained, or it won't carry you, and there is a good sleeping draught to help him get to sleep more quickly. Alas, in order to survive in the City and not risk losing his name — a wise move even for the Official — he had gradually been forced to give up women altogether, for at such moments even the Official was a human being who might let something slip, and unnecessary witnesses meant a significant statistical possibility of failure.

Ugh! the Official actually spat in disgust; what kind of language was that. He'd heard far too many of all those coefficients and indicators. It was a good thing he had this. A few minutes later he was calm, he took a shower, and immediately a mood of complacency set in. Maybe he shouldn't do anything, damn the Great Face-Maker, after all, he'd put up with him for so many years. No... perhaps he shouldn't... but before he had reached any decision he fell asleep, and he slept no worse than any ordinary One Hundred and Forty, unburdened by any lofty concerns. This was another of the Official's peculiar features; in any situation he slept well and took his decisions easily. He never tormented himself when his duties required him to act in one particular way and not another. The same applied to his personal problems, insofar as his personal problems and the problems of the City were all the one to him, since he was the City itself. But sssssssh! Let us not disturb the man's sleep. After all, he has a hard day tomorrow, for all his cool composure. After all, he has also transgressed the bounds of custom — that is, of his own self — and as an individual he is also part of the dynamic system which he has set in motion, which he cannot halt or modify, for even as the City sleeps it is gathering speed.

XII

But sleep, like insomnia, does not last for ever. Morning is here already.

Street lamps.

Rain.

Wet, black walls gleaming like agate, like statues in a graveyard, solemnly modest and monumental on a small scale.

Who is the first person to be met by anyone walking along the low black banks of the canal? Why, the person with the most work to do, of course. That means the Official. He made his way through the streets, slipping through them almost like a shadow without thinking, without looking around him, without noticing anybody or anything. He only stopped once in order to lower his hand into the water of the canal and rub it through his fingers. All normal. He couldn't feel a thing, or rather, he could feel exactly what he ought to feel. Further along he took a run and then slid across a slippery stone slab like a little boy, stopping where the Muse had visited the Hundreds, beside the entrance. He stood still for a moment and thought. Was it worth thinking it over? No. It had already been decided for certain yesterday. Would he manage it before they came out? Yes!

Why has the Official come all the way down to the house where the Hundreds live so early in the morning, when he has never before been seen beyond the houses of the names? Because before he hears the Face-Maker's answer, the Official must see for himself the material with which he is working. Why didn't he do that sooner, before he went to see the Face-Maker? Before the Face-Maker is brought into motion by the spring, any sequence of actions is acceptable, it's not until afterwards that only one specific series is possible, but right now... Right now the Hundreds have got up. They were already dressed and ready to continue their work with the Face-Maker, they had even walked to the doorway when the Official appeared in it. They both took a step backwards. They knew who it was there in front of them, he was in their thoughts all the time — they grinned at him. And once again that lucky mosquito bit into male One Hundred's heart, he could feel it. The Official didn't have much time. He smirked and went up to female One Hundred, ran his fingers over the skin of her face, turned back the skin of her eyelids, opened her mouth with his finger. He unbuttoned her shirt and dropped it so that it slid down and settled in a heap around her feet.

'Take a step forward.' She took a step forward. The Official went down on his knees, lifted up her right leg, lifted up her left leg, examined her ankles carefully, ran his hand over her feet. Smooth, pink, regular, like the light from a red lamp in the mist. He sat her in the armchair. He asked male One Hundred to bring the lamp closer and then ran his fingers over her skin like a pianist fingering the keys. On one side his fingers felt the skin fail to respond to his touch, like a sticking key; he dug his finger harder into the skin — aha, the reaction was there inside, deeper. Female One Hundred's body was tuned well and it played very promisingly. He touched her neck one last time with his right hand, ran the back of one crooked finger over her lips and waited for the complete response, then gently withdrew from contact. The body went on resounding for several minutes: it would do. After an inspection of male One Hundred, equally thorough, methodical and professional, he asked him to lift his head slightly. One Hundred lifted his head.

'That'll do.' The Official was already on his way to the door.

The Hundreds looked at each other. They were happy. They rushed into each other's arms.

'Oh Lord, I'm so happy,' she said. 'That was the Official.'

He stroked her hair and cried with her. He felt almost insane with joy. Red-eyed and happy, they began getting dressed.

XIII

Now the Official and the Face-Maker are both moving in the direction of the House, and both their heads glow in the mist. When a person's thoughts are vivid they can be observed from above. You can see the Face-Maker's light crawling along, much slower than the Official's: the Face-Maker is still thinking things through, but the Official is already acting. A person who is acting always moves faster than a person who is thinking about how he should do something, or whether he should even do it at all. I've already mentioned the City's resemblance to an inverted amphitheatre. Now the two of them are moving up from the aisles, shining in the rain and the mist, in order to meet at a single point, where the *deus ex machina* should put in its appearance, and very soon now the Official, having overtaken the Face-Maker, will be snuffed out by the doors of the House. The Official will be snuffed out, without having noticed or paid the slightest attention to the rain or the black marble walls, and in general without having felt anything at all. But that's only right — what time has a person who is involved in action for sensations? His only concern is the next action to be performed. And there is the Face-Maker, still toiling along, afraid of his decision, ensnaring himself in the thought that everything will happen at the last moment, will be exactly what must happen. And that's right, for when he has acted without thinking, things have always turned out as they had to, as fate determined. It was actually rather convenient not to have to take responsibility for anything. And so it unexpectedly turns out that the decision and the sensation are the truth, and all the calculations in advance are just lies to yourself. (But then what if it's really all the other way round). And perhaps the Muse is right, and he'll give it all up — these are the thoughts of the Face-Maker, as if he's trying to understand himself. And he feels everything, feels it today especially keenly and more deeply than usual, because doubt means paying attention to everything around you. The rain today is eternal and more tangible than ever, its heavy, masterful hands fumble across the Face-Maker's body, seeking to discover what he has concealed from external view, and if there is nothing, then they look within. His skin submitted to these hands, and through it the Face-Maker could feel the rain rummaging inside him, it became more difficult to breathe; a fist seemed to squeeze his heart, and it attempted to make various movements like a bird, to fly, to pull itself free, but it could only twitch within itself. The sweat stood out even more strongly on his face in the rain, and the Face-Maker stopped. Halt. Nothing was decided as yet. The fist unclenched, his heart shot forward convulsively at first, and then its wings began once again to work easily and smoothly. His heart was beating regularly, the rain washed away the sweat and no more appeared. Lord, thought the Face-Maker, I'm not like everyone else, dependent on everything that happens, I've chosen my own road, myself. Now they all depend on me.

XIV

As he strides around the Face-Maker's office the Official, of course, does not know what the Face-Maker is thinking, but he's in a good mood nonetheless. The candidates are perfectly suitable. The strange thought even flashes through his head that he ought to visit her afterwards. But this thought is no more than an attempt to calm the agitation that he always carries around with him nowadays. He would have killed off this agitation if it was necessary, but all he needed to do was just stabilize it a little. The Official knows that when a man is agitated he is more sensitive to things, and he needed to be more sensitive, because there was a great deal that depended on the Face-Maker's decision at this very moment; it was not just the bare fact that was important here, but just how reliable the decision was. That was something no amount of brain could figure out, but feelings could decode the answer and the degree of agreement or disagreement with absolute reliability. There were some kinds of disagreement which offered a greater guarantee of satisfactory execution than... The Face-Maker came in. He hadn't expected to see the Official here, he had deliberately come ten minutes early in order finally to make up his mind here, within these familiar walls, and to rehearse all the possible versions of his answer, even to use the walls for testing how convincing the answers were. Not that it hadn't worked out, he would have to do it right there in front of the Official. What was this, an opportunity, or... The Official had come early, which meant he was agitated himself, which meant it was an opportunity. Let's try another version. The Official had come early, which meant he wanted to create the illusion of agitation, which meant... But you can never work anything out if you carry on thinking that way. That's right. You wanted to rely on your own feelings. Okay, then feelings it is. But the Muse, who probably knows my feelings better than I do, came to an absolute and simple decision — refuse, not directly, not out loud, but using any genuinely objective reason as an excuse. A reason like that makes it convenient for everyone.

For the Face-Maker to refuse, for the Official to accept his refusal. A reason? The Face-Maker decides to follow all of the Muse's advice, so that at least he won't be reduced to making petty excuses to her.

'I'm not sure my couple will suit.'

'I've had a look at them, they'll suit alright. Good material.' He even raised his palm to his nose once again — the smell was still there, a very suitable smell. 'Yes, they'll suit.'

'But do I have enough skill?' — The question is not asked directly, the Face-Maker seems to be asking as though he himself is certain, but he doesn't know whether the Official is sure about it.

'You'll have all the data you need,' the Official explains to the Face-Maker.

Meaning: be grateful this proposal was made to you and not to someone else, because there are a dozen Face-Makers with enough skill to do what's needed using this material. But the Face-Maker wasn't born yesterday either. Maybe a dozen might have done it, but they'd come to him, then the Official seems to let slip by accident that he's not the first, but things didn't work out with the others. Maybe it's the truth. It could very well be the truth. The co-authors of power. Fear and so-called justice are in some senses more important than the Official. But the Face-Maker knows perfectly well what truth and untruth mean for the Official — he has to get the job done, and it doesn't matter how. All the rest can be called by any names that are convenient or acceptable to the partner in trade. In any case, the essence of the matter as not in the words, but in the job. Of course, it's more pleasant for any man to torture his victim in the belief that he's doing it exclusively for the salvation of the victim's soul, rather than simply doing it for the money. But on the other hand, what does the victim care about the executioner's motives, when the fire is scorching his body, when the current...

So the result of this conversation (even though it isn't actually spelt out in so many words), is that the Face-Maker will not be given any guarantees at all and if things go wrong he alone will answer for everything. Clarity has at least been achieved, and the Face-Maker is relieved. This version of the situation suits him. If he alone is answerable, then this really is an opportunity. Because then the Official will not come round even once to stick his nose into the work, which means that while he's trying to meet the deadlines for the operation (which are already too tight) he will be free of one inconvenience, perhaps the major one. As a consequence, success might be possible. But what if it isn't possible? Is it possible anyway for him to go on trying for as long as he has already lived, or even longer, or has he already reached his limit? It makes no sense to go on spinning his wheels inside himself, like a tank stuck in a quagmire, sinking deeper and deeper into the bog for another twenty years.

Brrr... Is that the only meaning to his life, is that his only prospect for the future? But the Face-Maker is no fool, he expresses his agreement in a vague and indefinite form. The Official is even less of a fool, and he reminds him that this conversation of theirs has never taken place. That's all there is to it. It's very simple — the spring has turned the drum, and the drum has a cogwheel on its axle, the teeth engage with the teeth on a smaller wheel, so tightly that there's no way they can be separated, and now it seems there's no way of telling who's moving whom. No time to try working it all out, either. Cog will engage with cog and any moment the Hundreds will be caught up in the movement. In order not to bump into them, the Official leaves by the opposite door of the House. The movement hasn't reached the pendulum yet, the hands are still not moving, not even the very keenest sight can yet discern the face of the new time, but deep inside a wheel set on the same axis as the fate of the City has already shuddered into motion, the steed of history has become restive and we're on our way.

And, damnation, the Face-Maker is excited. This is not just a conversation, it's the start of a new life. His hands are even shaking. His fingers are trembling, and this trembling is a pleasant thing. He has known for a long time how to make use of his excitement and coordinate it and the movement of his fingers with the sketch-plan of an operation. There's a great pleasure in selecting the part of the sketch, the facial correction and the rhythm that match your own excitement. It's exactly like holding a chisel to a piece of wood spinning on a secure axis and removing a beautifully regular shaving: the wood become smooth and perfect, more smooth and perfect than when you cut wood lying still, clamped in a vice, or if there is no vice, then in your hand — no matter how keen your eye or how steady your hand, the surface won't turn out as smooth as it does when the wood's spinning, and when it comes to speed... For a long time now the Face-Maker has worked faster than his colleagues, because for the Face-Maker excitement is not an obstacle, but quite the opposite.

No time to think about all that right now, though. Female One Hundred has already lowered her shirt to her knees. The Face-Maker asks her to raise it to her waist, no more is required. But since the Official's visit everything has turned topsy-turvy in female One Hundred's head, maybe now the shirt has to be let down all the way to her knees. The Face-Maker puts on his apron. Male One Hundred sits outside the door. His body is trembling, he's consumed by impatience to continue the operation. But if he was asked why he's trembling and what he's so happy about, then he probably couldn't give the right answer to save his life, he'd formulate his feelings after the Official's visit and his own guesswork in words something like the following: there's success on the way, promotion... serious success too... That's why he's trembling in excitement as he sits there, the way a bull in the slaughterhouse starts to tremble when it catches the scent of blood.

Meanwhile the Face-Maker in his apron has already slumped across the moist, tense breasts of female One Hundred and raised his trembling hand to her eyelid, the third square of the sketch. Working away like a machine he slit the skin and turned it inside out. Female One Hundred stirred under his weight. He pressed down on her even harder and pushed her back against the table. She was in pain from the weight and the knife, but she settled down again — hope makes it easier for us to bear pain and heavy weights. As she felt his powerful body against hers, a wild and impossible thought even flitted through her mind: what if... But the Face-Maker had a name, and it was out of the question. But then again, whatever the law might say, you couldn't control feelings. She shifted beneath him again, and once again the pain retreated. Her body began to feel languorous.

'If you just get in my way, you bitch...'

That sobered her up and frightened her. The Face-Maker sank his scalpel in deeper so that the blood spurted up, she jerked as though she was sitting in the electric chair, and all her languor emerged in a groan. The Face-Maker took another two squares at once, and that meant three times the pain. Her groan became a scream. That was more convenient now, when a patient was completely absorbed in pain she didn't get in your way if only because she wasn't thinking about you or feeling you, and all the Face-Maker wanted today was a body that didn't interfere. His scalpel bit still deeper into the flesh and swept even further across the skin. This is the point at which the purely professional business begins, and that has never really been very interesting. There's nothing to it except pain, habit, the Face-Maker's passion, the self-generated confidence that he will manage it all in time. What point is there in continuing to stand over these two allies: the first of them resistance to pain and the second the infliction of pain? Of course both of them will come out very well if everything should go successfully. Let us return to the street and follow the one person whose life will be completely unchanged by this success. She will simply carry on feeding the Face-Maker and waiting for him, weeping in her love and pity for him and his nonsensical ideas.

XV

The Muse is walking to work.

Look as hard as you like from up above, you still won't be able to spot her in the rain and the mist. But the Muse can see you if your thoughts give you away. She's following the Face-Maker up the hill (her work is just a little lower down than the spot where our *deus ex machina* made his appearance) and the tears are flowing down her face because she can feel that the Face-Maker is already at work and nothing can stop the movement, the wheels of the carriage are already spinning now that it has been set in motion by the Official or, more accurately, by his quarrel. The wheels are poised above two steel points, any moment now they'll touch them and the carriage will start rolling, catching up with the train that is already rolling downhill, because time moves eternally downhill.

The weather is different now, the rain is heavier and stronger, like slim fingers clutching at her cloak, not piercing it, but pressing into her flesh with an indifferent strength, in the same way as the Official inspected female One Hundred. The rain quickly washes away her tears and her eyes see clearly again, and in the rain the cloudy world is damp and beautiful.

The Muse enters the door and finds that once again she has forgotten what she has to do today, something that has been happening more and more often recently. She hardly even thinks about her work at all, but there was a time when she would have found it hard even to imagine that she might forget what job she had to do next. She used to hurry to reach these doors, feeling happy at the thought of sitting at her own desk. She would push in the video button and...

'What have we got today?' the Director asked her in a slightly irritated voice.

She looked at herself, then at the clock. No, everything was okay, he must simply be annoyed with himself. It was silly: all she had to do was say two words about the Director to the Face-Maker in the evening, and the next morning they would change his name for a number, or it might even go as far as Departure.

The Muse never exploited her name, but others frequently did, and they took pleasure in their power, as if they themselves were not dependent on the Official, and they could never understand 'what it was for' when their own time came. The Muse glanced unhurriedly at the control panel. The last program on the list was 'The Immortals'.

'You can watch it on your own, and enter your own code.'

Aha, so that was it, he was afraid. But what was he afraid of? This wasn't the first program in the series. Had something changed in the City? But how would he know anyway? Nobody had any information at all. No information, but...

The entire riddle was contained in that 'but', and the Director could already feel something. Damn him anyway, let him be afraid. She had no problems to do with the Director's level, and no doubts about anything either. Anything that was going to happen could only happen to the Face-Maker, and that meant to her, but not because of some poor broadcast.

XVI

One key pressed, the third, the ninth, the second, and there's the voice:

'Let us review the content of the previous episodes. In one of the regions of the world, separated from the major continent, Immortality became the norm and the basis of social life. By Decree of the Central Council it was decided to limit the size of the population to ten thousand and all women capable of bearing children were exterminated. The ones left were those who were no longer capable of any concupiscent thoughts, and so the ten thousand immortals began to live a life of pleasure in what they had created and the world around them. Several centuries passed in this fashion, and then the people realized that they were ugly, old and repulsive, that their lives were feeble, monstrous and meaningless. By Decree of the Central Council it was decided to make room for a new generation through the enlistment of volunteers who were willing to leave this live, and to bring children into the world so that life would begin to move and change once again.

'Miraculously, just at this time, in the most remote spot of the region a girl was discovered — the very last child in her family. The entire family had died and she was living alone. She was sixteen years old. Many generations of the family had guarded this narrow stream of life, avoiding all the lists and the immortal inspectors. The girl was found and brought to the Council. They explained why she was needed and what she had to do, and she felt the desire within herself. Ten of the very youngest immortals were selected, with ages of about one thousand.'

The introduction was over and the Muse stopped the tape.

She entered her own code in the usual quick manner, then the code of the archive, then the code of the program. That was it, the green lamp lit up on the control panel.

Was the recording clean? Had everything been edited properly? There had once been a case when archive footage of the Choice of the Principal Couple had been edited into 'The Immortals'... all of her colleagues in the Museum had been sentenced to Departure, and after that many others had been moved. Only the Muse had been spared the departure and the change of job — she was the Face-Maker's partner, and she had a name.

Attention.

Several people had appeared before her eyes. They were pleasant to look at — clothes like that weren't worn in the City.

It was twilight and the time had come. The light, white, flowing garments were piled in a heap. They all stood up and bunched together, and their bodies were skinny, flabby and ugly, but washed clean and they smelled pleasant. The bodies had become completely bald a long time before, and all their parts were like babies' parts, innocent and sexless. Even in the twilight seeing it made her feel afraid and bitterly sad for the human race. And the girl was there. She lay down, beautiful, tender, young...

The Muse looked at the scale: ten points of revulsion at a different way of life. Enough, that was almost the limit of what people could bear. But the arrow trembled and crept beyond the red line towards eleven. The Muse stopped the recording. She covered her face with her hands. She wept: 'I don't want immortality, I don't, I don't. God, how wonderful that there is the day of Departure, how wonderful that all of this comes to an end, how wonderful that my body is young, that I can look at myself and love myself.'

But she had to carry on with her work. She began feeling sorry for the people who would watch today's episode. She cut out part of the recording, and that made her feel better. This was her job, after all. The Muse had done what was required. There was no compulsion, she had done it sincerely, voluntarily. Everyone has to be convinced that what he does is either beautiful or just. What she had done was undeniably just — at least that was what the Muse thought. She had moulded every scene and every gesture, she knew the secrets of how to move people and how to persuade them, even so she was convinced of the justice of her work, and for her it was the truth that immortality is sacrilege.

The truth is only what we believe in, even if we have only invented that truth.

She pressed her palms against her cheeks, wiped away her tears and turned on the tape again. This episode was probably the best of all, the previous ones had not generated more than three or four points of revulsion. But this was right at the limit. Her heart was scarcely affected any more by the tortured face of the girl, by the twisted helpless skeletons covered in yellow skin lying all around her — now she looked with a professional eye. The old men would live. The only outcome of this human scrap-heap was loathing, because they had long ago lost the ability to ejaculate sperm and renew life. The Muse looked at the indicator: it was still at eleven points. She cut out a twisted old man lying there with his head thrown back to show a blind wall-eye, pushing back a quiff of ginger hair with his blue hand. She reduced the level of the light a little and then checked the indicator. Exactly ten points. Enough. A good job done, maybe even very good. If she wasn't a Muse, she could have expected a bonus. But she was above any kind of bonus — she had a name.

She checked on the monitoring viewers. Nine to eleven points. Within the limits. Today the City would be convinced yet again of the humanity of its laws. Departure was the highest form of justice. How supremely rational the measure was! If only every person was as convinced as she was of the perfection and rationality of the world around him, how much genuine happiness he or she would experience in a lifetime!

XVII

The Great Face-Maker can manage very well without any illusions. A microbe living in the crater of an active volcano may need to imagine that he is in paradise in order to survive, but for the Great Face-Maker entirely the opposite holds true, sometimes, in order not to be bored, as he picks his nose lying there on his bed, he has to think up something for himself to do, in order to feel like everyone else. But not today, today he has no time to be bored, he has completed his couple, he is entirely satisfied with his work, and in his complacency he has completely forgotten his quarrel with the Official, which really was quite trivial; after all, anything can happen between friends. It should be said that they are each indebted to the other, one made the other the Official, and the other, in turn, made the first the Great Face-Maker. For almost ten years now they have been leading the City in this way, helping each other. But in the City they believe, quite rightly, that the strongest love is the shortest-lived and the firmest friendship is the one which ends when the right time comes. Be that as it may, the Muse's friendship with the female One Hundred is her personal affair, but the friendship of the Great Face-Maker and the Official is a horse of a different colour, because the peace of the City depends on them. But then people all jump the same way, which is a pity, it would be better if the Official and the Great Face-Maker did not jump at all, but were a little less lively.

Less lively? Well, perhaps not less lively, perhaps just a little less human?

Alas, no matter what the line of work or the name, there is always a person inside, even if he is invisible. Is that the reason for all of this? Maybe there is another, but for the time being that's not what I'm writing about. At this moment the Official's inner man would probably gladly have bitten the head off the Great Face-Maker's inner man, even if their numbers were both in the first hundred. But now, on the eve of the following day's Choice of the Principal Couple, as he celebrated with the Great Face-Maker the completion of his most successful operation (just imagine it, a likeness coefficient of minus point zero three; he had probably done nothing like it in all his career, even the Official's coefficient was only slightly higher). Anyway, the last few days had gone very well for the Great Face-Maker, and the result was good, but for a master craftsman the result is not the final consideration. It's the goal, but the future opportunity and the continuing movement are just as significant. You may be thinking the Official is aggressive and unfriendly or else, what amounts to the same thing for an intelligent observer, affectedly gentle and pleasant, but you're mistaken. This evening the Official has persuaded himself (and not everyone is capable of this) that the Great One has no closer friends than him (which is the very truth), and that he made the Official the Official (which is also correct), and that he is fond of this dear man with his huge success and his breadth of vision. So never mind those trivial differences of opinion, today they feel as comfortable to the Official as these familiar rooms and armchairs, as the garden in which you can strangle the birds of your choice, as the City's only pictures — even the Official doesn't have anything like this — in which there are lots of different faces and which, of course, are both interesting and dangerous precisely because of their difference from each other. The Official, who fears doubt like the very devil, would never have hung them on his own walls. Everyone has a lot of pictures and portraits at home, and they all show variations of the

Image: sitting, standing, lying, running, full-face, profile, from above and from the side, and every possible way, and all surrounded by faces similar to the Image, but with appropriate degrees of likeness. The experienced professional eye has no difficulty in distinguishing who is who, and every eye in the City is professional in this sense. It all hardly requires any comment. The Official feels comfortable, at ease, relaxed, free with the Great One! Relaxed, comfortable, free, he repeats to himself at first, and then he begins to feel it so strongly that he stops thinking it and begins to live it. He likes everything about the Great One: his hands (the hands of a master-craftsman) his unhurried manner of speaking, his funny story of how his couple burst into tears when they saw each other today after the final session, and flung their arms around each other's necks in their happiness, when they hadn't embraced once in the last five years. Love had suddenly returned, and it was no pretense, but real, man-made love. And so this is not just a pleasant evening for the two of them, but a kind of quiet, slow-motion carnival with fireworks and masks which are unpretentious, pleasant and humorous. And when the Official reminds the Great One of their quarrel, the Great One laughs and even cries: what fools they are for quarrelling in this brief life, but then perhaps it is necessary. Yes, everything is necessary and everything is possible, in the final analysis it is human emotions which move and create history. Although what has history got to do with it? After all, they know the real value of these puppets which only imagine themselves to be people. They jump and they spin, they are dependent on changes in their number and their place in the City. Both the places and the numbers are controlled by the Official and the Great One, and these puppets have nothing else. Yes, says the Official, emotions are good, and even the fact that we are able to talk like this is not something you come across every day. Trust is the meaning of life, and in this City only we can say everything to each other. The Official actually believes what he is saying, and is actually astonished at his own discovery. They are both pleased with such a pleasant evening, and there are so many more of them still to come. They have to allow that a quarrel is helpful in catalyzing relationships. It is at one and the same time a separation and an occasion for testing each other's trust. Only whatever happens, they both decide, let's not keep it hidden inside for so long, but talk about it straight away. And then these two tender souls can no longer restrain themselves, and they embrace. They say almost nothing about the evening of the next day: what is there to say — the script has been written, the roles have been assigned, the illustrators will show what's required, even if it's not the truth. Not a single hitch in all these years.

'I've got a woman coming round soon,' the Great One announces — even that kind of thing is possible, things are so very simple between them.

'And I still never see any,' replies the Official — even that kind of thing is possible too, because each of them is prepared to drag out his tiniest thought into the light of day for the other to examine.

Then when the Great One tells how his new woman trembles and how she bites the blanket with her teeth in order to stop herself screaming out loud — which wouldn't be decent in the presence of the Great One — the Official asks if he can stay and watch. The Great One is pleased at the idea: of course, that makes it even more of a thrill. They know, and she doesn't. Definitely: neither of them have ever spent such an evening in their lives, they have probably never been more happy together, after all, male friendship is quite incomparable with anything else. The Official is crying as he goes into the next room, and not ashamed of his tears, and poor female One Hundred and Something has been standing in the rain for an hour while our couple have been convincing themselves of their mutual former, unfading, eternal, faithful affection. She came in shivering, chilled to the bone, and the Great One didn't turn out the light, he undressed her and began rubbing her all over, like a masseur, and he warmed her body, but he failed to warm her soul. She trembled and groaned slightly. Of course, in a way that would please the Great

One, after all he was a quite exceptional and unique individual, so that was how she groaned, with her mind alone. Even the Official understood that and he left without waiting for the climax, by another door. They had agreed that he would leave anyway. He wept as he walked along, having forgotten all about the rain mingled with his tears and fell on to the black granite and ran down the invisible incline into the canal.

XVIII

But now the time had come to extricate himself from this state of tender feelings for the Great One. That's not so easily done all in a moment. It's not quite as simple as changing gear. Perhaps the Official still loved the Great One even as he entered his house, and still loved him as he lay on the bed without undressing, and as he crept in under the blanket. Then somehow it seemed to pass off, and gradually their relationship began to creep downhill, like a cart without a horse, slowly at first, then gathering speed. And once again the thought that had never even been mentioned while he was at the Great One's crept out from the cavity in the double wall and occupied the entire space of his cold, precise, quick brain. The couple were ready, the Face-Maker had done a better job than he had thought he could. The Muse also appeared to believe they would succeed once she had seen the Hundreds. The illustrators had been replaced. The hall was ready. The woman of the Great One's candidates had a scarcely noticeable scar beneath the right ear, it would be huge in a blow-up. The penalty for leaving a scar was Departure. The Great One loved the Official. Their relations were better than they had been at any time while they had held office. That was the positive side. But the Great One was still the Great One, and his immediate reaction might prove unexpected. Suppose that by chance, in checking the illustrators, he should discover that they had been changed? But that was not possible. After this evening he would hardly be there earlier than five minutes before the start, as he had been for the last five years. Would you believe it, even the girl the Official had recently found for the Great One had come in useful.

'How amusing,' chuckled the Official, 'I could have sworn I was seeing her for the first time. It's amazing how manageable the human brain is. And the interesting thing is, she likes the Great One as well. Perhaps even more than that, but she is a person of honour, and since she has promised to be faithful to the Official.'

The Official is not very far wrong concerning faithfulness. She could just as easily and convincingly tell the Great One that she loves him more, and then... And then what? That he knows her? Naturally — it was the Official's duty to know the Great One's woman. But the Official had nothing to do with her keeping an eye on the Great One. They had merely exchanged impressions, admiring the Great One's abilities even in this sphere. Even so, tomorrow morning he would have to bring her in. And before Departure, make sure that quite apart from any considerations of duty, she told him absolutely everything out of the sensation of pain. That was more convincing. The girl was very sensual, and that meant she would tell him everything that was needed. Could there possibly be any negative aspect here? No. It could all be done, all of it. Of course, it was not by chance that the Great One was in second place — that is, in joint first place, just like the Official — it wasn't just a matter of professional skill and talent, it was diplomacy as well. Instantaneous and unexpected reactions. Only now the speed and unpredictability were hidden away somewhere inside a double wall because they weren't needed, but the time would come, and then... He had to be prepared for anything, but it could all be done without leaving even a single seam visible. But he would only be able to relax and take pleasure in thinking about the positive outcome after the Departure of the Great One, and a reason was also required for that. That was the Commission's job, though. The Chairman could read people's thoughts at a distance, and as soon as the scales tipped in the Official's favour, his side would automatically carry on ascending. A good

Chairman would do everything that was necessary, and this Chairman was excellent. But what if the Official's pan should start moving downwards? How could it do that? He wasn't the Face-Maker, he hadn't carried out the operation. In the worst case he would be outraged and amazed together with the Great One. After yesterday evening the idea that the Official had been involved would never enter the heart of the Great One or the mind of that little girl, writhing in agony and wriggling her split tongue. In that case the Face-Maker would be the only one caught out. All right then. When all the possibilities have been run through, it's time for sleep. The Official pulled off his shirt over his head, went to the bathroom and washed, lay down without any blanket over him and quickly fell asleep. But in his sleep he whined and tossed and turned, like a dog that's been beaten, like a cat that's been half-crushed. He wept and begged for forgiveness, but that was only in his sleep, and in his sleep a man is not in control of himself. His arms clutched the pillow tightly, and his body turned blue, and it seemed as though someone was trying to strangle the Official, but he kept twisting himself out of their grip, and so the struggle continued without any sign of victory for either side.

XIX

But now, apart from Officials and their like, it's time we remembered the simple people living in this City, for to the Official and the Great One all people are simple — apart from themselves, of course — and to the Official perhaps even the Great One is a simple man.

What are they like, these simple people?

Well, for one thing, today they are celebrating.

And for another — today is the Day of Meeting.

The only day of the kind in the year, for on this day the hall is opened in the House and they can be together without being afraid of the rain, which falls not just some of the time, but always, driving people forcibly back into their dwellings, and the dwellings are narrow and cramped, and there is nowhere for a simple person to see everybody at once.

And so —

Today they almost have equality.

The names and the numbers.

They look forward to the day of the Choice, the Day of Meeting, the day when you can show yourself and look at people. Like manna from heaven.

And this joyful anticipation is expressed in the wild manner (according, that is, to the standards of the City) in which they slowly and ceremoniously make their way towards the House.

If we were to put torches in their hands (reliable ones that the rain would not extinguish) we could look down on them from the height of the House and watch the small flickering lights crawling along, like ants heading for their anthill, up on to the hill where the House awaits them. How merry they are, the simple people, how festive, how triumphant. It's the Choice — and that means they have hope. It's the Choice — and that means the chosen couple's happiness will also be theirs. And then there is the spectacle that awaits them after the Choice!

They walk in total triumphant silence, and more and more doors open wide just as the procession reaches them. And what justice — those who have emerged last become the first as they move along, and those who emerged first are the last, so that there should be no confusion or crush.

Put torches in their hands and you will see an immense tree, with the roots of its trunk disappearing into the doors of the House, and its crown spread out across the entire City, and the tree keeps growing, and its branches appear too large to fit within the walls of the City.

But this is an illusion — just you make them go back and hide in their burrows, and there would not be a soul left on the streets.

Only the street-lamps. The Rain. The Canals. The Stone. Cold, dark, silent.

But nothing of the sort will occur on the day of the Choice, the people are still walking along. What then is the point of these branches which will not fit within the town boundaries? To remind us that they are an illusion. There are exactly as many people as there are spaces and numbers and living units in the stone quarters. And the immense size of the procession is also an illusion, which contains exactly as much truth as the assertion that the earth does not move. But it is difficult not to believe the evidence of one's own eyes. I understand all this, and yet still there are so many torches that they will tear the town apart, and it will burst asunder like a balloon.

'Woe unto me, woe unto me, my brothers...' But it won't burst, even illusions have their limits, and in any case they are most reliably constrained by reality.

Like the magician fire, the wide-flung door of the House silently swallows the tree flowing into it, it is insatiable, it can swallow more than this if the need arises. Let us leave the winding torso of the tree with its blazing flames to burn itself out on the street. And let us watch from within as the crowd enters the City's holy of holies. Here the equality of the street comes to an end once more: out there they all stride with a strict and regular step up the hill towards the House, all wearing cloaks, carrying torches, in the rain. But in here it's the City once again.

For this is no mere hall, it's the City in precise miniature, turned inside out, only instead of houses, cells and apartments there are seats, and they are all numbered too. A semicircle of rows descends on three sides from the entrance towards the stage. How comfortable the rows are, the aisles between them are wide, it's easy for anyone to walk down, find his number and take his seat without inconveniencing anyone else. At the very top and on downwards are the places for those who have a number; around the stage, beyond the wide band of an aisle, are three semicircles of seats for those who have a name. It's dry and quiet, there is a light-blue dome overhead, and a bright yellow light at its centre. So bright that it is best not to look at it. The light makes the blueness so pale that it appears almost white.

The hall fills up silently and slowly, as though wine is being poured into a chalice, first on to the bottom, and then up the sides. First the names, down on the bottom, around the stage. The stream flows in at the wide doors. Not slowly, not quickly, filling up the chalice of the hall, which, if it were enlarged and then put together with the other hemisphere to create a single form — the City above and the hall below — would form an entire earth spinning around its own axis, the point where the Official, the Great One and the Chairman of the Commission of the Choice are presently sitting. If you were to form this earth in this way and analyze its structure you would soon be convinced that a number really is all that a person in this hall possesses. Everything is exposed here — who is worth what, who occupies what place, how many numbers he has moved up during the year. The obviousness even extends to a subtlety such as the fact that the last of those who have a name and the first of the numbers are separated by a bottomless abyss, and in the hall this truth is expressed by a broad aisle — one might call it a moat — which would be obvious to a blind man. Try jumping over this trifling obstacle! How could you possibly do it? You could spend all your life until Departure without ever making it across this space, which is no more than about two metres wide in the hall, plus of course the tears, the labour, the skill of the Face-Maker and, when it finally comes down to it — destiny. If you want to take a closer look at them, do. There are now ten minutes of the greatest collective freedom. The people sitting on the stage are silent and everyone in the hall is thrown back on his own devices.

Ten minutes till the Choice, ten minutes till the ball.

The merriment is at its height, everyone is watching everyone else in silence, seeing who's where now, and what's happened during the year. It's all there to be seen. And there's nothing wrong with showing yourself to others, the only thing that matters is whether you've moved up or not. Well? Then, of course, God forbid that they should mix up your number. It's fine if they've moved you the right way, but what if it's the other direction? And so those who have stood up attempt to move up a row or two, where it's nice to meet people who until recently were with you, but have now sunk down quite a bit. The whole hall is a chalice and, of course, the highest place is the very lowest seat, but 'low' is a word with the opposite meaning to its real significance here. Here all is illusion and convention, but they know the forms of this convention off by heart, like their multiplication tables — and no one would make any mistakes in those. They stand in small groups in the passageways, between the belts and sectors of the rows of seats, talking quietly, half-audibly, in serious and respectable voices, and the numbers have already mingled, and a Five Hundred seems able to insinuate himself quite freely into the Four Hundreds. And there's One Hundred and Thirteen, bubbling over down there on the frontier — look where the rogue's got to, he's bursting with energy, and twisting his face so far out of shape that at times it actually seems as though it belongs to someone who possesses a name, and he is only here by accident, in fact it's quite impossible to understand how and why he came way down here in the first place. As if he's just come over to see some old, forgotten cronies of his and will soon be gone. And quite certainly no one — apart from those who know him personally — even imagines that after the ten minutes of freedom, he will go back to seat One Hundred and Thirteen, to his female partner One Hundred and Thirteen, who is sitting there, like about half of the hall, waiting for the proceedings to start. All of female One Hundred and Thirteen's thoughts are focused on the spot where their gods are sitting, where the outlook is determined by their view of things, and she moves her lips in a daze as she calculates her own destiny. She has no time for the idle chatter of the tiny man who happens to be her partner. She is so absorbed that she has raised her shirt above the regulation level, crumpling the hem in her sweaty palms. And male One Hundred and Fifteen, sitting two numbers down from her, has stretched out his hand to touch hers. Then she comes to her senses and drops her hem, and squints at him so cuttingly that he is convinced his feelings and his guess-work were quite unfounded, and goes off to join the group where the eyes which have long been his are waiting for him — from couple number One Hundred and Twenty Two. It's interesting to stand here like this. There she is, and he stands opposite her; he has studied her and she has studied him in detail down to the last patch of skin, but for everyone else they are strangers, and a dozen numbers around them are discussing the latest news of transfers, and future prospects, and mistakes, and how so-and-so was unlucky, but it won't last long, he's only moved up one number all year, and of course that's not real growth, but then others don't even have that much. And then you hear someone remark that you can't really measure people against others. One Hundred and Thirteen is boiling over with excitement, he's acting as though he's the group's official informant on what's going on down there, where the others are...

He raises his finger, as if to indicate that in a few days' time he will be down there too, it's really only a matter of days, and over the last year he has moved up twenty numbers but that's not his limit, and his face has a higher degree of likeness. The cunning dog has learned to hold it so that you can't tell, even a professional can't tell. Ah, if only the break would finish now and he could go down there, where all his thoughts are directed. Wait a while, my little friend, you have a train-load of time. You will be down there soon enough. And for the present you have your brilliant prospects to look forward to — going way down there and chatting on equal terms in a grave and stately little group. Perhaps you think if they have higher numbers — lower ones, that is — then they talk about something different. That's another illusion. It just feels as if you've not moved at all. The theme's the same. Future prospects. The same eternal, oppressive concerns: if only they had a name. God forbid you should give yourself away, let them know that you should have the right to go down as far as you like, right down to the front row... All these One Hundred and Fives, One Hundred and Thirties, Two Hundreds and so forth — tall and squat, fat and thin — they'll all start going on about how they should be sitting down there in the front rows, and how they are only up here temporarily, in the first place, and not for long anyway, in the second place... Flee to the front rows, flee, thirsting for peace, they, thank God, have no prospects, but they do have this peace, they have no goals to strive towards — listen to what they are talking about, and they're not talking about anything, except maybe women, but they're so experienced in that area that really... and about work — what's there to say about that, they are doers, and everything's behind them now, they even have names, something those higher up in the hall can't imagine even in their wildest dreams, because it's possible to change one's number within the ranks, but as for crossing over into the front rows, people only manage that once in a blue moon, unless you count the women — and they're not people, not in their own right, anyway — but so that even this should not spoil people's lives, they conceal it and record the person who has moved over as always having been one of them, who was punished by temporary deprivation of his name. As much as to say that there is not and cannot be any natural movement downwards, that is, in the only correct direction. Just as the rain cannot cease or the sun — even if it were there in the sky — move from west to east. That is also just. Everything in this City is just. Here justice has very likely reached its ultimate limits. There is a goal, but it is unattainable, so that it should never disappear from a person's life and leave it meaningless. What about the names, you ask? Well, they fit the pattern very well without any further goal, and this is justice too — people like that are necessary (as a fact) for a goal which exists not tomorrow or the day after tomorrow, but today. Do you see how cunningly it all fits together? But quiet now, the ten minutes are almost over...

One Hundred and Thirteen has darted back to his place, grimacing wryly, as if to say he won't be sitting there for long, and the Muse, who was talking with female One Hundred, has also set off back to her seat.

The Face-Maker, having taken a final look at his work, has set off, white as chalk, to join the Muse, afraid to look at the Great One. And the latter has no idea whatever that this perfectly ordinary Face-Maker may bring down the final curtain on his career. But then, even in a world of order, theoretical miscalculations occur, and then, of course, they are rapidly embraced by the theory of justice.

XX

Quiet... Sssssh. The hall falls silent, like a sea that has breathed water up on to the sand in a strong frost which has instantly transformed into ice. All around there is nothing but dead, cold, stony silence. The light in the hall fades, grows dim and shadowy and finally disappears, and now there really is only one face. Without rows or numbers, a face that looks and creates and chooses. There are three figures on the stage, and they are approached by the first couple, who will today become the Principal Couple — for all their own participation in the actual Choice no one ever doubts its justice, or the fact that this couple will be the Principal Couple. The viewers in the hall are divided into those who know the couple personally and those who don't. Each one who doesn't know them shares the same face, he depends on the legend, but each one who does know them, alas, is alone in his knowledge and his attitude to the couple. Think of it — for instance, could male Forty feel the same way as everyone else about the woman in the couple, when yesterday for two whole hours he was whispering their secret words into that finely-shaped pink shell of an ear, and she was using those tender lips like a little girl with a basket, who wanders through the woods and gathers all the berries she comes across. And how many secrets, how many threads there were stretching out from this couple to the people sitting in the hall. If we should lift the couple up towards the dome, the entire hall would hang dangling on these threads, and you would see that the entire City gathered here is woven together by these double or tenfold links, and there is not a single person who hasn't been with someone, and she, in turn, has been with someone else and bound him with a firm, strong thread.

It's a good thing that we can't lift up the main candidates and demonstrate that the City is so tightly inter-linked internally. It's a good thing because it means the people sitting in the hall can retain their illusion — that only the Principal Couple's friends are linked with them, and they have nothing to do with the matter. How should they know that they are also linked through their own friends, and everyone is linked with everyone else? Brrrrr. Alright. We've taken a look and that's enough; or perhaps you imagine that you're not connected in this way with the entire world? Alright, it's time. They're here. Eyes on the stage, where the event they are here for is beginning.

Attention.

The couple ascend the usual yellow and black rostrum on the stage.

Then suddenly there is no one left but them. The light has been extinguished and only their faces are picked out by a ray of light in the darkness, then even that has disappeared, and now, on the screen up above them, their faces are shown side by side, huge and alike. It's not the head, only the face is visible on the screen, as though they've cut out a mask, and it's not important what colour the hair is, or even if there is any, and the contour of the skull has no significance. The faces are so broad and wide that they extend across the screen like a map of the two hemispheres, except that the half on the right is just like the half on the left. At the top of both, in the north, lies the cold white snow-field of the forehead. In the south, below, lies the rounded territory of the chin, smooth as a bay in a sea-shore. In the west lies a delicate bluish ear, shaped like a field carved by a meandering river, and to the right, in the east, another, pink and transparent as mist in the light of the rising sun.

The space across which this territory extends is so immense that wrinkles seem like mountains, and the sweat between them like blue frozen lakes. Only the eyes enliven the wide expanse, but when they too are still, the earth and these faces seem to be as like each other as two birds killed with a single shot. Peeeew — the sound shot through the hall like a bullet, and above the faces of the Principal Couple the Image sprang into sight. The face of the Image had been clearly visible before the evening's proceedings began, suspended, huge, above the entire hall, but then when they extinguished the light and illuminated the face of the future Principal Couple, the face of the Image was also extinguished, so that for a moment their eyes might forget its perfection and then once again see afresh the great beauty of this boundless expanse of harmonious and balanced proportions.

Now there is an ensemble, a trio — the two faces of the Couple and a third, the Image. Like dancers on the stage, in a single synchronized movement, they turned to the right. A pause. Following them, the hall merely shifted the pupils of its eyes to the right, like a conjuror moving a single black sphere from his left hand to his right. A pause. It was clear to everyone how good the work was, a perfect match. Any person out in the hall could do no more than dream of anything like it. If only the Great One had worked on him. How many thoughts skewed through their minds like a skidding motorcycle and span off into the blue distance.

'Aaaah...' the entire hall let out a sigh in which there was envy, and hatred, and compassion, and complicity, and the substance of a dream... Surely it's not possible to decipher absolutely everything?

The likeness coefficient figures have lit up. The new illustrators work like clockwork. The first figure is minus point zero three, the second is minus point zero two. Our Face-Maker could never even dream of such a thing, not even with his latest figures. His heart sank suddenly like a mouse darting into its burrow, and it seemed about to shatter like an egg. But no, it held out, and then the conjuror shifted the pupils of their eyes again, to his left hand, as all three faces shifted to the left. What is this? The mouse has re-emerged, the egg has returned to its shell, although by this time it might already be a chick. The Muse gagged. The couple's friends turned cold, the others blinked as though a hand had been raised to strike them. The light sprang up on the stage, and the projections of the couple were extinguished. Only the incomparable Image was left.

The Great One could not believe his eyes: in the first place, the likeness coefficient had been minus point one, and in the second place, under the right ear he had seen the huge, enlarged image of a crude scar. It could not be — he remembered having painstakingly tidied it up, thinking at the time, as he finished off the neck, that he could have done even more with the face, if he had the time. The Great One glanced at the Official and saw fright and puzzlement on his face. No doubt his own face expressed the same, since the Official was a mirror. The Great One recalled the previous evening and transferred his gaze to the Chairman. He was calm and impassive. Perhaps it was a misunderstanding. Perhaps there was nothing to worry about. The illustrators over there were reliable. And now, when the second couple appeared on the rostrum, everything would fall into place. But no, everything is not alright. The hall is in a state of agitation. Lots of them have a likeness coefficient as good as that. Why shouldn't they be the ones? They've never seen anything of the kind before. Something has gone wrong. Nobody understands what as yet, but something definitely has. The Muse clutched the Face-Maker's hand. The Face-Maker leaned forward and seemed to freeze. It was his Couple now. The scar was obviously added after the operation. It was not the Great One's doing. What for, wasn't it enough that the Face-Maker's couple have a higher likeness coefficient than the first couple? Extra insurance... And what if that wasn't it? What if he didn't do well enough, then his victory would only be a victory for them, but not for him. He hadn't been able to do everything he should have, perhaps he shouldn't have tried it at all, how could he prepare the Couple, with his figures? It was impossible! His head began to spin. Was he really entirely unimportant, and his craft, and his ability, and his sacrifice — of his peace, and his life, and the Muse... And those deadlines he had met by doing the impossible. Halt. Stop tormenting yourself so soon. The Hundreds are up on the rostrum. Their faces are already being considered, they spin like weather-vanes on the screen. Once again the conjuror juggles with the pupils of all the eyes. Once again the trio follow the music in an orderly, synchronized dance. One step, then the second... Ah, how beautiful the Image is. One more...

Figures.

Figures.

Figures, speaking clearly to the hall, and even more clearly to the Face-Maker! Each likeness coefficient is down in the hundreds, but he didn't do his work that precisely, his figures weren't that good. The Great One and the Face-Maker had calculated the outcome before it became clear to everyone a few minutes later. The Great One looked down from the stage at the Face-Maker, whom he had taught without any great faith in his exceptional talent — although he was reasonably gifted — but had taught him nonetheless as though he was an unusually talented person. And then this! In order to eliminate any possibility of misunderstanding, the Great One squinted, so that he could stare into his pupil's eyes more easily. It couldn't be! The Face-Maker turned his eyes away. The whelp! The Great One's lips twisted in a grimace of disgust. Alright, it wasn't all over yet. He transferred his squinting gaze to the Official. His face expressed confusion and astonishment. The Great One believed in his confusion, but he could not believe that he had no part in what had happened. He could not! And this thought slowly stirred in the Great One's brain like some ponderous bird that had always been there, but which in the twilight he had taken for a bush, because now there was light where there had been the tenderness of male friendship. Although his brain believed it, he still did not feel it, but that was no longer the point, his blood took fire, and the bird that had been exposed by the light began to move, flapping its wings, and now it felt cramped there inside and his chest breathed it out... The Great One loved a fight, that was how he became the Great One. What was he so surprised about? He'd done worse himself to get where he was. He knew how to fight then, and how could someone who once knew how to do something ever forget it? A well-fed lion won't break a goat's back, because he always has fresh raw meat. Why should he? But just let the lion get hungry... No pouncing, though. You have to close your eyes still more firmly and hide behind the curtain of their lids, so that the others can't follow your movements. Eyelids are most convenient. Aha, now the Official is getting just a little bit worried, but not so it's really obvious. Here come the coefficients — minus point zero two. Oho, better than his control figures. That's not possible. But it doesn't matter now what's possible and what isn't. The job is an insignificant detail of the past, the craftsmanship means nothing in politics. There are no laws in politics, there is only losing or winning. The festival continued. The principal, the most significant moment had arrived. The moment of superimposition. All the masks were turned in profile. Each one was suddenly illuminated in its own colour. Yellow for her. Green for him. Red for the Image. And now — watch closely. The viewers' hearts stopped, ceasing to fulfill their responsible function of sound-projection. The music stopped. And now there was no air to breathe, but no one was breathing anyway. Well?

Can anyone breathe hanging head-down in water?

Can anyone breathe with his head in a noose, dangling in the air, even if the air has not disappeared?

In such cases one person drowning another advises him: pretend to be a fish when you reach the bottom, before you choke.

Well?

How else can we fill in this pause? Are they really fish? Maybe

they have gills in reserve, sewn under their skin? No, damn it, I can't
carry on like this any more. And I don't understand how they can.
Aha... that's the squeak and the creak of the first heart. And... now
what's happened? They've all breathed out... Pheew... The figures
on the Coincidence panel match. For an instant it was dark. Then
the light came on to reveal the Official, the Great One, the Chairman
and our couple — now the Principal Couple. My God, I've never
seen such wild, intoxicated, terrible merriment; for a long time they
were proudly and triumphantly silent in their sense of fulfillment. In
the first place, they had determined their own destiny. because once
in their life anyone might be a candidate, but not, of course, a member
of the Principal Couple. Things went so far — only please, don't let
this frighten you — that someone's heart actually began to race —
unthinkable! — and beat twice instead of once. It was just like when
a person is hurrying on his way somewhere and he simply stumbles
and falls flat and that's the end of it. No applause, no rustling, the
unthinkable has happened, the second couple has become the Principal
Couple. The Principal Couple of the Choice. That's it, the thought
flashed through male One Hundred's mind. That's it, that's right.
His nostrils trembled and flared slightly, like the nostrils of a dog
that has scented game and then found it. Female One Hundred was
stunned, she still did not know how this would all end, and the hall
was silent, also not knowing how to react to what had happened.
The impossible had occurred before their very eyes, that is, it seemed
as though it still might not happen. And then the Official glanced at
the Chairman. The Chairman rose calmly and smoothly, went over
to the first and second couples and gave them permission to take
their places in the hall. How pitifully they walked, like children after
some serious injury. They don't walk well anyway, and now their
clumsy legs have been damaged too. The hall too was like a toy train
with a broken spring, stranded with its little carriages gently
squeaking.

XXI

The Official cautiously allowed himself to assume that things were developing approximately in the right direction, and his caution was most appropriate, for now the Great One rose to his feet.

He waved his hand.

The illustrators obediently fulfilled his command, and the illuminated figures went out.

Everything was as it should be: they obeyed him. The Great One ascended the rostrum. The Great One was calm. He'd run through worse plots than this in his head.

The Great One bowed his head.

The way a man who is unarmed and surrounded by enemies bends down to tie his shoelace and rises with a grenade in his hand. The only trouble is that when a man loves a fight, his entire mind and will are transformed into energy, and the simple little question 'what for' is entirely squeezed out by the desire to beat and to conquer. It can no more find any space for itself than a cat can live in a rock, even if the cat is small and the rock is as big as a cliff — for inside there is no empty space, but...

Stop, Great One.

Why do you want this superiority, you know what it will cost. It's Departure. What does it matter if your pupil takes your place? He is still your pupil, and your operating technique will remain here in the City, the names that you have created will continue to occupy the front rows, nothing will change after all; you made the City, your people run it, that's your Official who jerks the puppets' hands, heads and destinies, at least that's what you think, and there is some truth in it.

Depart, but leave yourself here in them. And you'll become immortal. Look into your pupil's eyes, full of confusion and shame — his sense of shame will make him faithful to you and your memory. Stop, sit back down, for now you've raised your hand not just against yourself, but against your cause.

The cat thrust its head against the rock, and the pain didn't matter, but there was no way in. It went off, hanging its head.

The Great One raised his head, and each person sitting in the hall heard the Great One's thoughts in his own more or less complex fashion.

The hall's ear grew as huge and all-hearing as the dome, the hall listened to the Great One with all its ambition, aspiration, envy, intemperance, fear of losing and desire to hold.

Their minds refused to believe what they heard — for it turned out that his couple was not like the Image, but like the Original, which was concealed from ordinary mortals, and no one could behold its face. But it had been revealed to the Great One when he was allowed access to the Original. And the scar that the Great One had traced on the Couple, running down from the right ear, was like the Original's scar. For only the Image was permanent and fixed — the Original was alive, and like any living person he could suffer pain and receive scars, the contours of his face could change.

Their minds refused to believe what they heard.

See now what you've raised your hand against, Great One! Against permanence, against the pillars of your own house. The Image is the law of the City. Destroy it and allow changes, and the stone will crumble to sand, and the rain will wash away the sand, and there'll be nothing but desert left, and the water will invade the desert, and this place will become a sea.

It would be good if the Great One could hear this. But resentment has blocked his ears, and his sweaty hand is already winding up the toy train, and already its tiny wheels are jerking spasmodically in his hand.

My God, what kind of idea is this about the Original? How much of it is true and how much of it is self-defense? And yet, if he should prove to be right, it's the end of our Face-Maker and our Muse — and the Hundreds, and the Chairman, and the replacement illustrators. It seems to be all over, and the Great One has out-played the Official, although, as God can witness, the Official had no part in any of this. And on the subtle calculation that the illustrators, aware that they were doomed, would probably want to curry favour with him, the Great One gestured with his hand for the illustrators to show the true likeness coefficient. But the unfortunates were too cowed, and excessive fear is harmful in such matters. No one had told them how they were to behave in such a case, and they lit up the same figures as before — fear like that makes the mind stupid. Now they felt that doom was even more certain.

And the little clockwork engine set off, spinning its tiny wheels breathlessly, like a shadow of the one set in motion by the Official. The hearts in the hall began to race — there were the figures, they knew everything now. The hall stood and burst into applause. At moments like this you only believe the figures, not the person who just a moment before was the Great One, but the Official and the Chairman, who stood facing the hall and returned the ovation. And for a long time nothing could be heard above this expression of unanimity. Although, if you think that everyone was quite unanimous, you are mistaken — there were others too. It wasn't a question of their believing the Great One rather than the figures, they couldn't give a damn for the Great One, the fact was that they had accumulated too much hatred over the years of sitting stuck up there without changing their places, and having the last choice of the women, and wearing the worst colour of cloak — although what really made black ones better than white? God alone knew, nobody could tell you. Probably nothing but the fact that they were worn by the ones with names. And these people, who had waited for too long, suddenly could wait no longer, in the way that a balloon is silently deformed as you squeeze it, until suddenly — bang! The little train skidded on the rails.

'Glory to the Great One?' The people in the back rows exploded into the air like rockets, they burnt on for a while, the fire delayed for a moment, and then the stars flared out, lower and lower... 'Glory!'

They stood up as they shouted, it seemed as though the entire hall would rise to its feet, but rockets are only rockets after all. The Official bided his time until they burnt out, raised his hand and they were caught standing in the light, like a thief when the owner of the house turns the light-switch. They froze motionless, and suddenly all their enthusiasm disappeared. And now a group of people moved in unison along the rows, removing by force of persuasion those who were standing motionless, caught in the light. When he saw this the Great One came to his senses, and his resentment passed. At long last he heard everything his mind had been shouting to him. He went limp.

He allowed them to take him away. Before the stone crumbled into sand, before it was too late.

But the Official is in a hurry — the wound where the pus has flowed out has to be cauterized with a red-hot iron. His mind is also working busily, but he has no resentment, he is calculating. The Official has a task to complete, this is no time for emotions. After the Great One has tried a trick like that, calculation alone is not enough, inspiration is required, and it came: no operating table, no corrections by the Face-Makers, those who wish will occupy the free numbers now.

His lips are already forming the words, and each person in the hall is beginning to understand. The places are free, they can be occupied by force, and they'll set the face right later. And immediately the light blinked out, leaving nothing but a broad beam on the stage, covering it precisely.

So what is happening in the hall?

It's as though no one sees and no one knows. And really, how could anyone make any sense of it? Out there — imagine about five hundred dogs, hungry, fierce and strong, who have been shoved into a cage which is stout and narrow, and where the floor should be there are snakes. From boa constrictors to vipers. So what happens there? Surely it's clear enough? Only one odd thing — there's not a single word spoken. And in the front rows there is silence. They don't appear to hear a thing. Only the unfortunate, wretched couple who aspired to become the Principal Couple have been led out from the front row (what were they guilty of?) by silent people. Everything proceeds in a calm, cultured fashion. The way things are in a cinema when the film is on and the usherettes are showing the latecomers to the free places. In total darkness...

XXII

Now our Hundreds are up there on the stage. He's grinning so widely his face is splitting open round his ears, and female One Hundred's hands are trembling as though she's a vestal virgin who has sinned standing on the edge of the pit into which she's about to be thrown. Above their heads the likeness coefficients are simply too good to be believed. Meanwhile, in the hall they are busy occupying the free seats and they've forgotten all about the existence of the Original. But who could know more than the Great One himself? On the other hand, perhaps not all of them have forgotten, but they can't be bothered with all that right now, they mustn't miss the chance to change their number. Well done, the Official, that was a fine move he thought up. His fingers are still nimble — if we can compare a brain with the fingers and the hall with an instrument — and they played a great tune... So far the puffing and the groans are muffled in the darkness as though it was a pillow, they're like summer lightning in the distance, glimmering like northern lights beyond the horizon. The Muse's heart has shrunk within itself at the victory, as though someone has laid a rose against it. The Face-Maker feels anguish instead of joy — but never mind that, no one ever trusts their first feelings, tomorrow they'll wake up fresh and everything will be different.

And now for the final, concluding act. The Official makes the announcement, then leaves the stage and takes his own seat. Up on the stage only the rostrum is illuminated now, the light has narrowed. Our couple stands there. This is the beginning of the Model

Lovemaking of the Principal Couple for this year, the couple who have been given the names of Husband and Wife.

The Wife's knees are about to give way, but the Husband holds himself erect in his triumph, in a success he could never have dreamed of, even though he foresaw the whole thing. And now, to the accompaniment of heavenly music combined with snake-dog conflict it begins, and gradually everything, even the music and the puffing and panting and the groans, fades into silence.

The little train moves along quietly, braking as it pushes against a heap of arms, legs and heads. And protruding from all its windows there are faces, eyes, breasts, arms.

Yes, the Great Moment! The City waits for it for after year, and every time it is granted its moment of pleasure. An important detail. The Choice has been made, but now, in this too the couple must be no less perfect than their faces.

XXIII

I'm sorry, I must take a break here. The train has only braked, it hasn't stopped. Everything's in order. Silent people have already carefully gathered up the remains of arms, legs and heads, like birds gathering crumbs from a table-top, and they seem to have carried them out of the hall. Have I no right to become distracted? Have I no right to take a break, to go out from this mysterious mechanical butchery into the fresh air? Into the rain? Yes, into the rain.

How bad the weather is outside, how it oppresses the heart. From here, from anywhere, the outlines of the houses are distant and uncertain. Behind me is the hall. In front of me, below, is its enlarged other half. Where shall I go, where can I take a break and draw breath — there is nothing to breathe. Breathe the rain? But you're not a fish... choke on the bottom of the river — no don't, pretend... How oppressive it is. What do I care for them? Every day I have to go back there. How I'd like to stroke a cat right now — mrrrrr! Can you feel it curving its furry shape under my hand? Push my lips into its fur. And that's the end of it? Nothing else to follow? Ah, the fur is wet. And I feel sorry for the cat, all of my life I've felt sorry for the cat, so why do it? I was ordered to, I was, seriously. When you're not free, there's no point in tormenting yourself when you have to do something wrong. But you remember it. And even if it didn't, you'd still have killed it. It's only a cat, isn't it, and there's plenty that aren't cats heaped up back in the hall there. But not me. And not you, and that's a comfort. Microbes die in the crater of an active volcano, you can't do anything to help them either. But they live there. The microbes won't understand your language. Microbes haven't got as far as words yet, so why are you standing out here in the rain? They'll start without you, and you'll miss all the fun. You won't be able to help anyone — every day you go back to the same place, and every hour too. But maybe I will be able to help? No, not these ones. They've already set out on their journey. All that you can do (they're not traveling, they're hurtling downhill with a fierce scraping and clanking of iron) is to describe their journey, to teach others the lesson not to ride like that and not to get on to that train. And that's all? Isn't it enough? What good can you do by sitting there thinking and being logical when the carriage is already flying down the incline? Don't be stupid. The fur is wet, and your lips are wet. What can you do — never kiss again? Then what's the point of living? Why bother to live then? Is it time now? It is.

XXIV

The light became thicker. Music began to play. The Husband and Wife stood up on the rostrum. Immense bluish-white transparent sheets of glass were lowered down on all four sides around them, and instantly the couple grew to ten times their size, magnified so that everyone in the hall could see them, even from the very highest point of the final row. The two figures standing on the rostrum were equally clear, equally visible.

'Get ready.'

The voice speaking was not indifferent, the Official seemed to have a frog in his throat. The Muse trembled. She put her hand on the Face-Maker's knee. He put his hand on her breast. They held each other even tighter and froze absolutely still.

Light as the birds soaring in the indoor gardens, the Husband and Wife moved apart. She curtseyed. He bowed with solemn restraint, then suddenly strode up to her and tore off her shirt with a single movement of his strong, slim fingers. Her exposed, magnified, white nakedness flared up, striking everyone in the eyes, the heart, the body, as though an electric current had run through all the people sitting in the hall.

Phheee-ee-ew — they all breathed out in the hall. And then froze motionless. Up on stage the couple bowed once again, then a second time, a third, a fourth and finally, separately, towards the place where the Official ought to be. That was the ritual. The Wife walked up to the Husband, went down on her knees and slowly pulled off his shirt. It slid down, rustling gently and gleaming in the light. Then the light blazed bright red and the bodies became even more huge, so that every wrinkle and shadow, every fold of skin could be seen, even the little hair growing just above her right collarbone. Without getting up from her knees, the Wife fell back into a prone position, motionless, absolutely still, waiting... Immense, like the hall itself. The Husband stood there with his arms hanging down. The Official's voice spoke again, questioning this time:

'Are you ready?'

The Wife nodded.

'Begin.' The Official breathed out the word and as he did so his fingers felt the Wife's skin, they still held the memory of its coarse, slow, sustained note, and the memory emerged as droplets of sweat on the tips of his fingers. The Official wiped his fingers on his handkerchief. Something was taking place within him above and beyond the range of his will and his mind. His Husband and Wife looked really handsome.

'They really are good-looking,' the Face-Maker said to himself

'Well, well,' thought the Muse, 'all the times I've seen them and I never even imagined they were such a beautiful couple. Why on earth do they avoid each other?'

The illuminators wiped the sweat from their faces. Everything was as it should be. Now at least they had time to draw breath.

'I've never seen her look like that, they must have swapped her with someone else,' male One Hundred and Six thought in amazement. In ten years he had studied every last detail of this body. In reality it was older than this. But male One Hundred and Six said nothing. He merely tensed up as he remembered the sensations he had experienced from that skin.

'My God!' Female One Hundred and Fourteen felt as though any moment something would burst inside her. Every evening for more than ten years she had stroked the face of male One Hundred, that hair, those shoulders, she had even loved them, but she had never seen him like this. 'Oooh,' she groaned, and immediately slapped her hands over her mouth.

Now it was all beginning, and now it began. One steaming-hot, immense red carcass moved up close to the other. The entire hall could probably have fitted inside those huge bodies. Teeth sank into the skin of a shoulder so that the blood ran. 'Ooof!..' the hall gasped.

And now, no longer separating themselves from each other, they turned over, rolled over and over, and their hands began frantically tearing at skin and hair. They growled, snorted and tumbled, huge, like a field swarming with locusts. The pink light was replaced by green, and then by purple — the colour of harmony. The rostrum began swaying from one crest to another like a boat in a storm, and they clung tight to each other. Their embrace and their pain were stronger than ever. The trembling lump of meat was dashed against the side, their heads struck the deck then they rolled away, tumbling over and over, but there was no power that could separate them now, not even death, they had reached the pinnacle of their lives —

the Principal Couple of the City, Husband and Wife, covered in blood, with lumps of flesh torn away, growling, weeping in their hatred of each other, cursing each other, they were happy, and in the midst of this bloody mess, this movement, blood and pain, both of them somehow found time to think about all the others they had seen and the ones they would have liked to have during all those long years spent at work, in the corridors, in the Hall...

'No more... no more... Now!' — it hung in the air, louder even than their growling and screaming. Male One Hundred and Six had lost control, and immediately female One Hundred and Fourteen leapt to her feet, shrieked and sank her fingers into the hair of the people sitting in front of her, and then several others joined the two of them.

They were excited, a single push, a single shout would be enough to bring the entire hall to its feet.

The way the tiny flame of a Bickford fuse vaporizes TNT.

But the Official knew his business very well.

'Lights'

The lights came on.

'Stop.'

They stopped still, covered in blood and sweat, and he merely raised his head slightly — the poor gladiator.

The second time in one evening — it was too much. The first time was already something unheard of in living memory in the City, but this...

Once more he'd have to throw the rowdy bawlers under the wheels.

There weren't so many of them this time, certainly, but something had definitely gone astray in the management of the carriages. Would he be forced to run the wheels over the entire hall? No, this time the sobering-up was instantaneous. Everyone retreated back into himself, and only the poor victims of their own lack of restraint were led out of the Hall, glancing around at those who remained and the figures lying on the stage. The sheets of glass were already being raised again, and instead of the huge, red, steaming heap of flesh, all that was left on the stage was a couple of half-strangled worms which were difficult even to see. Was it all because of them? Glancing round as they were led away, the arrested regretted making their outburst for such a contemptible reason. Silent people dragged the reduced human puppets off the stage.

The festival was over.

Time to get their cloaks and go home. But there were some who no longer had any cloaks or any homes to go to.

In the same identical rows, but this time without torches, in the darkness and the rain, the tree began pulling its roots out of the hall. Withdrawing roots-first, it crept out of the House. But the previous elegant structure was gone. And the ones who had managed in the darkness to grab a number that was a bit better were not all that happy, either. Even though a different house awaited them, some had red-soaked rags wrapped round their hands, and some had a bloody pulp where there used to be an eye. So what was there really to be happy about? The tree limped downhill after the streams of rainwater. Only the front rows had really had a good time, if you ignored that worrying moment during the interval. Even though they hadn't been able to sit through the full show, it hadn't been too bad. They were professionals in such matters — it really hadn't been too bad.

The regular intervals between the people walking along the street were disrupted now, some of them had no hoods pulled up over their heads, some fell down and were helped to their feet. The light in the streets had paled, the street lamps were white, the walls radiated heat. The rain lashed down. The water in the canal was stained that inimitable heavy, dull colour by the greenish streams flowing into it.

But that will soon be over.

And soon it is over. That is what the rain is for, to wash away everything that finds its way into the drains, the blood that sometimes falls on to the stone from injured hands and torn cheeks and the simple tears — naturally belonging to the women. Women are more sensitive to what happens to other people. In a certain sense they are even a more advanced race than their male counterparts, that's why they never really match up, or hardly ever at all. The rain keeps falling and the people trudge along drearily, regularly, quietly. They disappear into the bright apertures where the doors stand almost completely ajar. And gradually they all calm down, which is probably also only fair and just. Night is approaching, and at night peace visits us briefly even in the most troubled times, more troubled than these — but then who has the right to judge which times are the most troubled? And what about insomnia? The happiest of people and the most miserable all suffer from it, and sometimes they sleep soundly — that is true justice, the fact that in the final analysis the world is inexplicable and unexpected. What surprises were possible in this City of ours, after all— and now just look!

XXV

Our Face-Maker is now the Great Face-Maker, in his new house. The Muse is wearing a new house-coat. They have already looked round all the rooms and sat for a while in the garden, he has held her hand like a yellow bird in his own hand, gently and protectively, and she has gazed affectionately into his eyes, unsettled as water still rippling from a cast stone. What happiness it is not to be constantly puzzling over how to move up one more number! There is no place in the City higher than the Great Face-Maker.

What about the Official? The Official has a different profession. The Muse understands that it's different. She moves closer to the Face-Maker, and then she begins to feel sick. She writhes, clutching at her belly and barely manages to get to the sink.

The Face-Maker understands how she's feeling — she's remembered the Hundreds. The Muse weeps, the tears flow and she pukes, the stream of yellow liquid lashes down on to the white surface of the sink. In their happiness they had drunk a glass of wine, but it isn't the drink that's to blame. The problem is the interval in the hall and the bright light — her brain has retained that bright flash, it is still filled with revulsion, and in order to make it disappear, her brain has taken the Muse and turned her inside out.

It's easier for the Face-Maker. After all the skins he has stripped, all that blood and fear, those scalpels and patients over the long years, he isn't likely to be affected, but he still understands. He strokes the Muse's hair and comforts her and explains that if they hadn't interrupted the model love-making, she would have arrived here happy. And even for them everything today would have been better and nicer than usual.

The Muse calms down. Gradually. The Face-Maker leads her to the bed and undresses her. The Muse is still breathing heavily, but more calmly now, because her brain has been cleaned out, and she is already thinking about the Principal Couple, feeling sorry for them, and feeling sorry for One Hundred and Six, who was so brave. Could the Face-Maker possibly be as brave as that? Was it possible at all to behave bravely in the City, where bravery was virtually equivalent to Departure... Bravery was probably when the rain gathered together on the ground, and then rose so high that even the House, standing on its high place, was under water, and then the Face-Maker swam down through the water to find the entrance to his own house, swam along the corridor... The Muse's eyelids stick together, the Muse's thoughts slip along the corridor, trying to find a way in, but there is no way in, and the Muse's soul flounders and chokes, beating against the closed door through which she has only just swum out into the corridor, and above the door there is a red sign: 'No Exit'. But no exit is needed, the Muse turns and pretends to be a fish.

The Face-Maker is too excited to sleep today, everything is still whirling around inside him like a carousel— the figures, the astonished face of the Great Face-Maker, the carcass of female One Hundred spread across the entire hall, sweaty, white, yellow on the outside, his own fear, the calm brown eyes of the Official and the rain, as brown in the canal today as those eyes.

Until the outlines and the original meaning of all of this become blurred, it is pointless for the Face-Maker to go to bed, it all has to disperse and settle and be forgotten in his memory, it has to cease existing today and be transformed into what was (or perhaps what never was), so that what actually happened can be intertwined with dreams and they can swap places and then there'll be a confusion with which he'll have to come to terms so that it will leave him alone until the morning or until some new days that he hasn't lived yet — let it surface once like a fish in the middle of a mill-pond, and smack the water with its tail and say it's time, and the fish will turn into a Maelstrom which has a certain number of metres and a certain number of centimetres to its black, gaping maw, and the Maelstrom will set him whirling and whirl him round the circle the set number of times. The maw is sucking him in. Stop, stop, it's not that kind of confusion, it's success, victory...

Just the beginning? Even so, it's victory, and victory needs to be defended, so he'll have to do a bit more work while the Muse is sleeping — his scalpel will trace its lines on cardboard as thick and heavy as wood, instead of on skin and muscle, before going to bed he will paint in its contours and the Trojan horse will smile at him with its wooden eye, and the sea will draw back to release the serpents without which neither success nor victory can ever exist — and there is no other truth. How many of these pieces of cardboard he has accumulated in his lifetime, but if not for them, how many muscles would have been torn, how many unnecessary fears and pains there would have been. Perhaps that was why the Face-Maker had been able to perform the operation so quickly, why his fingers had not known a single day of rest as they hastened to trace out the serpents, laying out their curves under the wooden hooves, or else without the horse, just on their own. The confusion grows calmer, it hisses and slithers away into yesterday, into a dream. He can follow the same way, but not too soon, only when morning is near, when the rain lashes harder and faster at the stone roof. But that's later, in about three hours, and in the meantime...

XXVI

So many housewarmings in the City, so many happy cripples after today's festival. The most fortunate of the fortunate, the One Hundreds, have already come to their senses. Beat a cat as much as you like, it still comes up good as new. The Husband and Wife are already sitting in their new garden, both of them steaming-pink, tender, happy. He is hastily downing wine as red as blood, not even getting all of it into his mouth, so it flows down over his chin and drips on to his chest (the Husband is lounging backwards), and then on down across his hip, and then into the sand of the garden. People must be jealous of their quiet happiness. What of the Wife? She's even pinker and more tender — women feel everything more strongly — and she's downing her own drink, a red, thick, warm, slightly salty wine that also escapes her lips and flows in narrow streams on to her breasts, then drips down like icicle-water in the spring, filling up her navel until it overflows. Half an hour goes by like that. Then another half-hour. It's good. It's good, and somehow it isn't. She's rested. And it's the usual time, her time. Now all of the time is hers. The Husband and Wife are a professional team. Nowhere to hurry to, no need to get up in the morning. She feels like going somewhere, but maybe just out of habit. She has to give her husband it first. She looks at the door. He intercepts her glance and closes his eyes — the Husband is no formalist. What's the problem, let her go if she wants to. And he'll take a rest as well. They make their rules now. Whatever way they live is moral.

The Wife gets up, opens the door, throws on her housecoat, they're all in the same house now. She presses six doorbells at once, one door opens. Tall, well-built, just the job.

'Wife?'

'Wife,' she holds out her hand and smiles. Of course, everyone knows her now, from the birth-mark on her shoulder to the dimple beside her collarbone.

'Chairman.'

'Pleased to meet you.'

'Of course I know you.' the Chairman's eyes are mischievous, professional, still not calm after the performance. There really is something about the names. They're not the same as the numbers. Here everything is more pleasant, respectful, noble. Must be a different kind of people. That's it, and it doesn't matter if there's a bit less pleasure in it, there's more style, it has that subtlety only the names have. Eh?

An hour later the Husband got lucky too, but not straight away. At one door the man of the house opened up, and he had to apologize. At the second door he found just the thing — the Joint Chairperson of the Commission. Mind-blowing! These women in men's jobs possess such fire. And steel. And God knows what else, too much to mention it all. And above all, it all happens so seriously and thoughtfully, so furiously, like nothing the Husband has ever seen before. The first time with a Name. Nothing more to be said, it's all in that one word — name! He'd never dreamed of anything like it in his wildest fantasy, never dreamed of it, invented it or anticipated it. The Husband staggered as he got to his feet. What, after the model lovemaking, again... What a hungry bitch, the Husband shook his head in admiration at her skill — wasn't it perhaps too much for one man, even if he was the Husband? It was hard to believe that all this time beyond the wall the rain was still falling and somewhere in the night someone else was busy somewhere else with some other business. It seemed to the Husband that tonight the entire City was awake, enjoying life together with him.

XXVII

Alas, not so. The Duty Commission had already been at work for over an hour on the former Great Face-Maker's woman when the Official appeared in the doorway of the office where the woman had said that he sent her to the Great One with the single clear purpose of extracting information, which she had done successfully and then transmitted it to the Official. The Official looked at the swollen, pounded face of the woman and frowned. He didn't like it when the face which he also bore became so ugly. That alone would have been enough to justify Departure, but the Official was, of course, as far as possible humane and just, and only after the woman had erupted in the face of his strange questions about whether she had slept with the Great One and answered him with near-obscenities and a request to let her know what other ways there were to extract information from Great Ones — it was the only state in which everybody spilled out everything, no matter how clever and sophisticated he might be, because the brain was out of control — and that everybody slept with them, even if it wasn't part of their job and she couldn't see any reason why she should be forbidden to do it, that the Official was once again convinced of the cunning and unreliability of women, and he immediately launched into a speech that was probably longer than any he had ever made in his life. The speech made clear to every single member of the Duty Commission, in the first place, that he wasn't interested in what everybody did, there was a law forbidding temporary coupling, only permanent coupling was allowed. Form a permanent couple with someone, and then take your chances if you wanted, only, of course, just don't get caught at it, and in the second place, he had set her to find things out, not to sleep with the man. In the third place, and probably most important of all, his speech made it clear that he was astonished at the tone in which she spoke to him.

The Commission might perhaps have understood the first transgression to some degree, because the gains from her action were quite clear, but as for the tone in which she now chose to address him — at this point the Official simply spread his arms wide in a gesture expressing amazement and hurt and dismay, and even something like sadness; he couldn't bear rudeness in people, especially when it was intentional and sincere and of course (the Official lowered his head) he remembered the reasons why the woman of the former

Great Face-Maker had spoken to him like that. And now of course, after that tone of voice, there was nothing he could do to help her, even though that was the reason he had come, and now he was leaving to think things all over, to come to some kind of conclusion concerning all the people he came into contact with even in the line of work. And he left. The woman of the former Great Face-Maker fell to the floor and twisted and writhed there and set up such a great howling that the investigation was halted and in their unanimous and collective wisdom — oh, how well they understood the Official's noble sadness — they sentenced her to Departure. Two members of the Commission took by the arms and carried her out of the office.

XXVIII

Things were even more simple with the Great One himself — the Great Face-Maker knew better than the Official where his furious ranting and raging had left him. Even the Official, with his swiftness of mind, could hardly have expected such an outcome to the Choice, and now he was too busy with his work to guess what might come next, he had no time for that. In the very best case, the Official's mind would only have time to work out his own fate, and he probably wouldn't get that right either.

During an earthquake there's no time to worry about the order of the household and finding yourself a clean shirt, you just have to get yourself out through the window, naked as the day you were born, and be thankful if you land on a well-clipped lawn.

But the Great One had not thought only of himself, he had lived beyond his own narrow interests after he had grown to his full stature, and there was nowhere higher left for life to take him.

Unity was more important than his own head.

Your cause is more important than you are.

The life of all is a magnitude which remains unchanged when your particular volume of meat and milk is deducted from it — assuming, that is, that you weren't suffering from the plague.

Had the Great One always understood this? Not always, but certainly since he had begun to live beyond his own narrow interests.

'Well?'

'I got carried away!'

It can happen to anyone — a fighting spirit is like fever in childhood, stronger than your own reason.

And afterwards?

Afterwards the person recovers his senses and recants what he said, and asks for his recantation to be noted down in the minutes, and he himself requests Departure. Provided, of course, he's an intelligent person who regards his cause as higher than his own interests — if it's the Great Face-Maker, for instance. Does the Official understand such exalted arguments? Of course not. But since this Departure suits the Official just fine as a way out of the situation, the Official agrees even though he doesn't understand: it's less bother.

The Official is not the Great One, he can never understand what the former Great Face-Maker is feeling now. At this moment the latter is like a man who has somehow found himself in a house of high rank and accidentally tipped over a vase, then tries to catch it in mid-flight and knocks over a stand of crystal-ware, and finally, as he stands there surrounded by all that scattered porcelain and crystal silence, only carries on breathing at all because he wouldn't like his dead body to cause his host any more bother — like a father who doesn't know his own strength who pushes his own child and then sees him go tumbling down the stairs, like someone you suspect of something, who can't bear the suspicion and sets a belt around his neck, and as you remove it you already know that he wasn't guilty after all.

It was no vase the Great One had smashed — it was the unity and the faith of the City. And what did his recantation mean, now that the words spoken no longer depended on the speaker? And what good were the futile efforts of a man smothering the flames on the chairs, the table and the divan, when the fire was like a flood that had filled the entire house and the roof was on the point of caving in?

The Great One's conscience was writhing like a worm on a hook, and he was repeating the worm's movements. But the Great One was not suffering because of those who had been given Departure for supporting him, or for those who had been torn to pieces in the attempt to seize a higher place: faith had been shattered into a thousand fragments, and each piece was as different from all the others as death is from life. It isn't just that the Great One is ready to recant, ready for Departure — life is painful to him now, and he feels only one desire, to make an exit from life somehow — the way a wild beast will come rushing out of a burning forest straight into the arms of the hunter. The way a fish leaps out of poisoned water in order to die on the land.

The Official comforts him. The Official loves him. The Official understands him. The Official weeps over him and strokes his head like a mother caressing a son who is distraught over the loss of a favourite toy. It doesn't matter now how everything looks to each of them or what they might say to each other — the toy can't be glued back together, no matter how much they want it to be.

The Great One suggests a public Commission in the same hall, with his own confession. The Official is convinced that the slightest reminder of what has happened will be fatal to the City. The Great One nods — that's right.

The beast comes running out of the burning forest.

The bird comes flying out of the burning forest.

There stands the hunter, gun in hand, and he looses both barrels into the burnt fur and the scorched feathers.

But the Official was kind, he personally walked with the Great Face-Maker to the door of Departure. The Great One embraced him. He sympathized with the Official, for he knew better than anyone else what he would have to go through. If only he hadn't pushed him so hard, better not to have pushed at all, then the forest wouldn't have caught fire, and he could have taken Departure differently.

The Great One would have taken Departure like the autumn

forest falling into sleep, dropping its leaves in slow, lazy indifference, like a bird dying on the wing, without folding its wings away, like water dying when it is calmly covered with ice, like grain dying when it becomes bread... like the founder of the human race dying when his time come, leaving the imperfect wheel of life behind him to turn regularly, creaking monotonously through the centuries, like a wheel that is not imagined but actually made by hand, and yet it carries man safely along a well-worn track.

He would have died the way the ice dies in the spring, he would have died in the wisdom and peace of the Great Face-Maker, almost the only person in the City to live to see a natural Departure.

The Official looked at the Great One, who had already stepped on to stairway. The stairway shuddered and began moving downwards, the doors opened, there was a glimpse of the blue dome, and then the doors closed again, leaving only the steps of the stairway hurrying on downwards and on through the stone.

That was one more worry off his shoulders, now he could be himself for a while. The reason the Official had started the entire blaze was behind him now, there was no Great Face-Maker. The whole business was finished, he ought to be glad.

But just you try feeling glad when you find the shoe that was lost after they've already sawn off your leg. Are you happy now, Official?

XXIX

The Official, poor man, came home, sat at his table, sank his face into his warm, white, slim hands and sat there without moving for an hour, or perhaps even longer, and during that time many thoughts raced through his head like horses galloping across a meadow. And as many decisions as there were riders on the horses faded and disappeared from his memory. Probably it was the first time there'd been so many in all the long years of his difficult service, a service which seemed unnecessary to some, but was actually not only necessary (the Official laughed at the memory of the naive expression in the Great Face-Maker's eyes), but essential to the safety of all, and only he understood why — the warring boundaries of the human spirit and flesh, to which no proper limits could be set, would not only give rise to dissent within a man, not only would they destroy him, which might at least be lived with and accepted, but they would destroy the City itself. The Official had always reacted calmly to a man's attempts to escape his influence, to do what was forbidden by the law and justice, and he had not even always sent him to the Commission, he had not even always accepted the Commission's decision — one example of that was our own Face-Maker. But when it was a matter of the City! Then the Official forgot the very meaning of the words magnanimity and humanity. Magnanimity had no plural form as far as he was concerned, it could only be applied to a single individual. In this sense (damn the former Great Face-Maker for being so tricky) everything had turned out well: only a few hundred numbers had been actively involved in the revolt. To a certain extent they could be regarded as a single individual, and everything had been fixed — that particular plural individual had already been given Departure.

While the City was snoring and sweating and seeing its prophetic dreams, the sinners' poor souls were pursuing each other through the air, like balloons full of height, hurrying through the rain from here to there. And their bodies? In a City where it is always raining, how could that be a problem? Everything is soluble — including the body.

And so, on the one hand, this plural individual had disappeared, but on the other, it was quite obvious that the words and actions of this individual extended beyond the bounds of Departure: they had not been dissolved, they had not disappeared into the canals, flowing rapidly down from the hill and out of the City, and in order to put a reliable end to the action of these words, he would have to appoint Departure for all who had heard those sacrilegious words. Infection is cauterized with a red-hot iron in order to leave the body healthy, but the problem now was that everyone sitting in the hall had heard, and that meant almost the entire City. While it was undoubtedly possible to destroy the cause which was leading to the destruction of the City, it was not possible to destroy the entire City, because the Official's existence and the law were justified in the very name of its preservation. But the City would have had to be destroyed in the name of its own preservation. Of course, none of those who didn't even have a number had been in the hall, but they had no concept of the City's trades or the basic obligations of its citizens.

And so, either what was would remain — which meant himself, the Official and the City, minus that plural individual, but then the law would be transgressed in the course of its own fulfillment — or the entire City would be exterminated, that is, the law would be fulfilled in the course of its own transgression.

XXX

Yes, it was a vicious circle.

The Official stood on the border of power, power over people. But he himself was subject to a superior force, a force higher than his knowledge and his ability to control himself. A force which easily overpowered his refined intellect, the way fingers crumple a piece of paper, the way an elephant's foot crushes a sleeping python lying in its path, the way buckshot rips a sparrow's tiny body to shreds.

But unlike many who stand on this borderline, he knew of the existence of this force and dealt with it extremely cautiously, and when events occurred on this border territory, he was in no hurry to act, and he didn't act out of conscious deliberation, but out of his feeling for this force. He hadn't made a single mistake for many years now. But today's event required more than guesswork — it required some assistance. A man can drive his car, despite the fact that the body-work is dented and full of holes, and the whole machine rattles and shakes like an old cart: he can keep going when the air hisses out of one of his tyres — slowly, but he can still keep going. But when one of the wheels goes rolling off to the side and circles on the spot before it settles down on to the surface of the road, even though the engine may still be working, there's nothing to be done — he has to stop.

And now the Official stands frozen over a wheel that has come adrift.

The Official needs help. But help is expensive, it is a sign of your powerlessness.

Those above us do not like to perform our work for us. It's better to find someone else capable of doing it for himself.

Help has to be paid for.

But what with? With a name.

That's acceptable.

With Departure.

The Official is not prepared for that.

Even he, who controlled the life of every person living in the City, was terrified at the thought of Departure. The Official was prepared to agree that this was a terrible failing for someone who bore the name of Official, more than a failing — a weakness, more than a weakness — it was pitiful. But what person living, even the most eminent of names, was not pitiful in some way, at least sometimes? And anyway it was the only thing he could do. God alone knows what should really have been done, but the Official was only the Official. Like a tangled mass of string that comes free when you pull one end, and you can wind it into a ball, all these tangled and confused thoughts in his head suddenly untangled themselves and formed themselves into a clear and simple decision. After all, for so many years he had served the supreme power, standing on the border between that power and the City.

Between the law and the person...

Between freedom (or rather, in the Official's view, permissiveness) and the Law.

He had the right to venture this step, one unknown to himself or his predecessors.

Yes, yes, his thoughts sped along, only He-Who-Stands-Over-All knows the truth, in the final analysis, even if the outcome is the worst possible one, the Official still has an option — just himself and the non-numbers, and Departure for all the rest. Although this would break the law, it would not destroy it, because he — the Official — and the Law were one and the same in this City. And now life was simpler and easier, and the thoughts, like rows of awkward figures, were already forming in his head, like birds hurrying on their way south through the sky in autumn, calling to him to follow. And the Official took fright again, for this was doubting his faith, why should he listen if it was enough to know that he existed? And he changed his mind again, and began once again to run through the option of destroying the City... and he submitted totally to the cogency of the idea of preserving himself and sacrificing the City, without breaking the Law. And something happened to him, perhaps intuition, perhaps illumination, but the thoughts were not part of him, and he picked off each bird with a precise shot, and finished each of them off with the butt of his gun, and he even stood and watched for a little while to make sure they weren't moving any more, and they weren't. Then the body performed what reason had just rejected in such a cruel fashion.

XXXI

Now it must happen. How much fear, how much doubt the Official has gone through. An ordinary inhabitant of the City could scarcely have borne it all, but then the Official — at least this was the way he had finally formulated it for himself, and convinced himself of its truth, and was quite sincere about it — was concerned for the inhabitants of the City, and this had protected his sanity from exploding into space, the way a meteorite explodes and then falls.

But what business is it of ours how a man deceives himself in order to make it easy to do something vile or dishonest which saves him at a particular moment — we know this technique only too well. The answer is simple, we must do it, and we have to feel, in the first place, that this is voluntary, or this is noble, or this is not for our own sake, or we were forced to do it and are not to blame, and in the second place, there is no other way out, and in the third place, we are doing all this in the name of some good greater than the evil accepted and employed by ourselves.

The Official was able to do this better than the others, and he really did have no other way out.

XXXII

Blasphemy was the name for what the Official intended to do. To hear Him-Who-Stands-Over-All, to receive the truth at first hand! Of course, the Official was closest of all to the border of Him-Who-Stands-Over-All, he even actually stood right on it, but to hear meant to cross it, to set foot for a moment on alien territory, where the law was different and unknown to anyone, where each step and each breath was unknown, where perhaps the body, like a scrap of paper, is instantly consumed by fire and reduced to ashes, where there is nothing to breathe, from where, perhaps, there is no return, and if there is, then will you be the same, what form will you have?

Mysterious alien life — is your name death?

Is your name fear?

Is your name emptiness?

Do you exist?

The Official suddenly began to shiver, as though his body had become a shadow on a wave, and a wind had swooped down on the water, and the shadow was shattered and twisted by the rippling surface, and it shattered into drifting fragments, and the former reflection ceased to be visible, and only certain lines, which did not even resemble a human being, were spread over the water, driven by the wind.

Yes, his body had become a rippling image; in just the same way one can pour out the sand from a glass — only a moment ago there was a precise form, compressed inside the glass into a strict, perfect cylinder — and now there are only a few small yellow heaps mingled with the grass, which has bent beneath the weight of the grains of sand falling on it, but is drawing itself upright, for the wind is blowing the grains from each blade.

The border between body and thought has been passed.

Does fear drive a man to that place?

Curiosity?

Profit?

The Official crossed the border in order to survive. Flesh and bone no longer hindered his thoughts. Thought was diffused, like the light of camp fires through the rain. Here, beyond the limit of its own power, it could not speak and ask questions, but it could hear what was audible to it, or rather, apprehend it, for it was not in words. Bushes in the darkness, which could be taken either for a man or a bear. Or for fear. Or for salvation, or something that had no name, for it did not exist in knowledge or experience, but he could touch the branches, and feel their rough bark washed by the rain and realize that something living had frozen motionless beneath his hand, that if it would not help, neither did it conceal any threat.

But now thought became looser. The Official attempted to hold on to this bush, but there was nothing to grip it with, and then there appeared a sensation of height, cold and loneliness, which had always been there within him, but was only now known for loneliness.

The height was also divided into territories, beyond the border of loneliness it was warm, steam drifted in the air, white and yellow, it smelt. There was no border in the smell, but there was a customs-post there — without any border. The feeling of hope in salvation was left to lie on the shelves of the customs-post, like confiscated foreign currency and weapons. And yet the movement still continued.

Consciousness, like the soot from a lamp, slowly took wing and drifted away behind his back.

It seemed as though nothing could happen if there was no means of apprehending the surroundings. The body is washed away, feeling is left behind in the customs-post, consciousness is nothing but the smell of burning, one more step and it is the track of a rocket across the black sky, it is gone!

No-thing!

Nothing?

None of those things which merely hinder listening, hinder understanding, hinder seeing.

Clarity was independent of everything, there was nothing left. And now the Official existed in general — he would have ceased to exist if it was as simple as that! Simply because there is no limit to human possibility, to what a man will do to test his limits and see at what height (or what depth) a man ceases to be a man, and who he becomes at this limit, and then beyond this limit. But the Official was all why, this was not a test, and not just idle amusement, and it wasn't done out of excessive strength or pride: need and fear can do what is beyond truth and strength.

Shoot an arrow into the sky, or fire a heavy bullet straight up above your head, and somewhere up high height will come to an end, for an instant the arrow and the bullet will hang in the air, and like an over-ripe bunch of grapes, like a shot bird, it will fall to the earth beside you.

One instant — and the Official was suspended on high, beyond the border of his own self and facing the border of Him-Who-Stands-Over-All.

There it is. Help? Advice? Command?

The whole messy business was for his sake. He had wagered his life for his sake. He had gone beyond his wit's end for his sake.

So today the one-minute coded transmission will contain twenty printed pages. But there is no means of hearing, of apprehending, let alone of comprehending. He seized it with his future memory, like an apple seized with a leap. And then there was emptiness, what he had seized, or been given; and then thought, like a snowball made of sticky snow, gathering sensations and memory, came rolling back. Not like an arrow or a bullet, falling like a stone through the air, but down an inclined staircase, narrow and dark.

The steps were badly chipped and scattered with shards of broken wine and acid bottles that glinted briefly a dark green mouldy colour, and where his shoulder should be there was a sudden blow, and blood came, and the pain struck at thought, and his ripped shoulder tumbled on over the step, and its edge came up against the sharp blade of a scythe protruding from the wall — and now the pain of the regained body flooded the brain just as sharply; a rusty knife was thrust into the empty space where an eye should be, and the knife twisted, because the speed of the fall was great, and the Official still had no eye, he felt it on his palm, which had squeezed it together with a fragment of glass, and the acid splashed up and burned the eye and the wound; his body was growing heavier, and hurt all over, it was gathering inertia and constantly impaling itself on knives and scythe-blades, glass and rusty iron hooks, smashing against protruding stones, and as it tumbled down it was acquiring form, and the eye transferred itself to its slashed socket, and his spine began to be where it is in living human beings, and the Official even felt himself growing accustomed to this falling, but then the staircase came to an end, and his body somersaulted and jangled like a bag of coins, and lay on the floor. The Official raised his aching head, and the Official saw with his eye that he was sitting at a table and his body had its previous form and nothing about it was changed, and he would never understand the fact that life had left it, and he would even fight, more than once, to survive, but that no longer mattered.

The Official had become merely the executor of a quality which had previously been absent in him, and now, with his memory — which was no longer future, but past — he recalled that out there, before he began to fall, he had received a message without deciphering it. And he had no present memory, for nobody has such a thing, present memory is a descent through hooks, broken glass and knives, an uncontrolled and defenseless descent.

XXXIII

Yes, the Official had become an executor.

Why this strange turn of events?

It's not so very strange — having betrayed himself and transgressed his own limits, even for the most important of motives, a man will never return to his former condition.

Betrayal is irreversible. Betrayal is one-way motion, and even when it moves backwards, it's still forwards, only under the delusion that it's backwards. For a man moves not only in relation to the earth, where he can walk in any direction with an accuracy of a degree, or even a minute, thinking that his road is the only one. Lucky man, walking in his ignorance, when in actual fact the main road extends throughout space relative to eternity. The earth is a fraud, she has our heads spinning in confusion; we walk along — as we think — in a forwards direction, but in fact going nowhere: what deceit and power of illusion there is in the tiny spinning globe beneath our feet. The road leads forward, up and down, but the blood within runs independent of our road, and our road, independent of the countries of the world, leads round a closed circle to death.

Melt a tin soldier and try to cast the former figure into its old soldier's shape. The same shape, the same word. But if you've overheated it, then the colour's different, and the elasticity, and the whole thing has changed. If we are to be really precise — even the bubbles of air inside are different. What can we say about a human being, if this is true of a lifeless tin toy?

The Official, having discovered himself through pain, became an executor — you could say he now had a new biography. And a new fate. But I think that an executor is, after all, more of a participant in the events that concern all people than a ruler, a commander or a rebel, who all bring destruction, for entirely opposite reasons, to everything around them. But then they are also participants in everyone's lives, tragic participants, while even the very best of non-participants are not subjects of life, and consequently not of attention either — they are manure, or mould, or worms who see themselves in the mirror of their own imagination as dark-eyed knights.

What executive act had the Official to perform in his new function and his old position? If he were to recall to consciousness what he had apprehended out there on high, before the fall?

He had to test our Face-Maker's readiness for work of which the Official knew nothing, but which he was obliged to carry out.

And where are the twenty pages of coded transmission, if there is nothing but this test? Instructions! For an executor instructions are a more serious business than a command or an idea.

For an idea without a command is a fantasy. And a command without instructions is unbounded amateurism, stupidity, senseless freedom, the opportunity to act as you think best, according to your own understanding, but always within the law. But when there are instructions... And with his past memory the Official began to decipher, recall and learn each line of these instructions, which our Face-Maker will bear the full weight of in saving the Official.

XXXIV

So the City, which might have already ceased to exist, awoke early the following morning: the new beds had been well tried, dampened, scattered and crumpled, and life continued along in its customary rut — the way a car that has skidded out on to the grassy kerb on a corner creeps backs into the two ruts on the road, the way a passenger train that is about to smash into a row of oil tankers after the points have clicked over at the very last moment goes hurtling down another track in another direction, and the passengers sitting calmly in their seats will never know how close they came to death, and only the driver's hair will turn gray that night.

And this is still not the final station.

The Muse rose calmly in the morning and began to shake the Face-Maker because it was time for him to be going to work, but he had only fallen asleep when it was almost morning already and he didn't want to return to the worries of this world. He wanted to finish what he was saying in that other place, where he was standing in the hall in front of the inhabitants of the City and speaking — he couldn't say enough about the sense of faithfulness to his chosen path that he had carried in his heart since he was a child, and everyone in the City could experience happiness in any position that he or she might happen to occupy. For happiness lay within us, and the people sitting there before him should not imagine that he was simply repeating what the evening broadcasts said — everything in the world looked the same from the outside: intelligence and cunning, nobility and self-interest, coercion and desire. But that was only from the outside. It wasn't just a matter of different cities where there was or there wasn't a limit to immortality. It was a matter of what was inside us. All he had to do now was to wake up and he could convey all of this to everyone in the waking world. He tried to force himself to wake up, in order to reduce this mystery to the form of a slogan and change everything in this City, to manage it without any revolt, so that even the Official could understand him and become a different person — there, inside himself. At this point the Muse finally managed to bring him back to this world and he left his solution behind, and tried painfully to recall it, wrinkling up his forehead, that was just like every forehead in this City, and screwing up his eyes that were just like the eyes of the Image in the Hall. It seemed to him to be more important than his own Majesty, more important than the fact that the Muse was staying at home today, because now she was obliged not to do anything. Her very life was her work, for it consisted of service to the Great One, and every glance and gesture would be taken as a word by those around her. Even more important than the fact that today once again he would hold a scalpel in his hand and his eyes would be fixed on the exposed muscles of someone's flaming red face.

XXXV

The Chairman had other things on his mind when he got up in the morning feeling rather ill. The Wife had only gone home when morning had almost arrived. She had her freedom now — she was the Wife! The joint Chairperson had put in the same amount of time too, in fact an hour longer, but she felt nothing except tenderness and a pleasant, entirely wakeful fatigue. As though she had been keeping it inside herself through all those years of stern work, and now her turn had come and everything had come splashing out, but there was still plenty left over, enough to last all her life. She was ready now to live her life without ever closing her eyes or folding her arms — if only it wasn't for her work. When she let the Husband go home she had cried and kissed him all over — there was a meaning to life. He didn't really want to leave, either — they had found each other — but the Husband didn't have to be told the meaning of obligations. It was funny, yesterday he'd been afraid even to look at her. How many of them she had sentenced to Departure, more of them than he'd had women, but he... And now she was kissing him, down on her knees, weeping. There was some kind of resolution in that.

The Husband had never been bothered by that kind of nonsense before, and now it meant absolutely nothing: it was her business how she felt about him, why she felt one way and not another, like all the other causes and reasons in the world. The Husband felt that he was tired, and it was time for him to go home, because now for the Husband going home meant going to work.

Chapter Two

The Trial

I

The entire city has already crept out into the streets and redistributed itself around its places of work for the day, so that in the evening it can unredistribute itself and creep back home again. In fact it's only an illusion that it becomes any different when it's dressed, businesslike and at work, in reality it's still just the same old hands and the same old hips, the same old cheeks and the same old hair, the same old lips and the same old eyes — they may all have been turned inwards for the time being, but they're all still the same. Even now, just try scattering them around their bedrooms again and you'll see soon enough that there's nothing else to them at all: the very same life that existed yesterday — in public it's turned inwards and hidden, at home it's all out on the surface. Unfortunately, it would simply be too much to expect for it all to be permanent and unchanging — there are periods when everything gets jumbled up, when people lose all definition inside themselves and on the surface, and that is how the Face-Maker, instead of sitting in his office, surrounded by helpful, silent, inwardly concealed hips and hands, now finds himself walking along a corridor. He himself has no idea whatever as to why this is happening, why he is being led along like this by the man on his right and the man on his left, but that is hardly surprising — after all, he wasn't present at the moment of contact between Him-Who-Stands-Over-All and the Official, and he doesn't know that at this very moment the Official is involved in an attempt to save the City's life, or more precisely, to save the Official's life — at least that is the way the Official sees things.

They had come to fetch the Face-Maker in the same way as they came for him once before after an operation the previous year. Only recently he would have hunched his shoulders, tensed up and pulled his body in tight around himself, but now he rose lightly and nimbly to his feet, as though he simply felt like going for a walk. He washed his hands without hurrying. He looked at his own face in the mirror and ran his hands over it. He rinsed out his eyes. He went back to his desk, poured himself a little water from the jug and took a few sips. Then he got up again. The Commission might be serious business, but he was the Great Face-Maker now.

Ah, how lightly, precisely, unhurryingly he places his feet as he walks, for, indeed, who in the City has his body under better control than our Face-Maker? In any case, it's quite impossible for him to walk in any other manner. They say that face-makers never make more than one mistake, and that's why his steps are as precise as a cat's, he walks over the soft carpets as though with every step he is preparing to spring and the only reason he doesn't is that there is no victim. Has he forgotten the corridors of the Commission? No, he hasn't forgotten them, but surely he didn't walk along them like this then? Things are different now, but even so his heart might easily stall within him at any moment, stop beating for a second and then start hammering afresh at the air with its wings. Right here, the Face-Maker remembers, there was a door, and now there's the beginning of a new corridor leading off to the right. And now to the left. The men walking on his right and on his left move in a respectful manner, also like cats, but of course, like cats of an inferior breed and obviously no longer in their first youth, already just a bit flea-bitten. Finally, there it is in front of them — the door. And above it is the name — Chairman.

The Face-Maker entered the room alone and the occupant sprang to his feet to greet him. That meant everything really was all right. Last year he hadn't got up, he hadn't even bothered to look up, and when he did eventually look up, he kept his eyes narrowed so that his soul couldn't be seen through the crack, and the face that had been such a close likeness of the Image was instantly unfamiliar, even alien. But this one got up to meet him, gave him a seat, then sat down facing him and spread his feet on the floor. His eyes were a bit red — that meant he was tired. It wasn't important to the Face-Maker just why he was tired, but showing such politeness even when he was tired — now that was important. He became even more sure of himself and once again his voice became soft and velvety, not like the rotten, squelchy falsetto that had been prepared to come slithering out. He set aside the voice that had been prepared and released another — his own voice, or perhaps even a bit more impressive.

'What can I do for you?'

The Chairman didn't even have time to answer. The door opened and the Chairman jumped to his feet — it was the Official. The Face-Maker rose to his feet too. The Official nodded to the Chairman without even extending his hand and then, smiling, dashed across to the Face-Maker and embraced him, as though the Face-Maker was the closest friend the Official had. The Face-Maker responded awkwardly and clumsily at first, then he laughed and squeezed the Official in return, perhaps even tighter than the Official had squeezed him.

'Oho, what hands you have! Sit down.' And then to the Chairman: 'Give us something to drink.'

'Water.' The Chairman poured out two glasses and handed them across.

'Thank you. And now you can go.' The Official nodded. 'What hands you do have, after all.' The Official eased his shoulders up and down. 'You almost overdid it. You should come and join my people, you'd be quite invaluable over there. How do you manage to work with a scalpel with those iron fingers of yours?'

As though he's talking about one thing and thinking about another, his eyes flash and then go probing to and fro shamelessly inside you, like a thief who has permission for his stealing.

'Are you ready?' At last a question that means something. The

Official rapped his knuckles on the low table, set down his glass, ran a hand over his face from top to bottom.

'For what?' the Face-Maker also tapped his fingers on the low table and, ah — what fingers they were, twice as slim, and so beautiful to look at.

The Official gaped at him in such apparently genuine astonishment that the Face-Maker actually believed in his surprise. The Official gathered up his smile like a table-cloth from a table, rolled it up, tucked in the ends and spoke through the tight bundle with his hard eyes narrowed to slits:

'There's a little job that needs to be done, I'm just not quite sure whether you're up to it.'

'In what area?'

The Face-Maker readied himself to listen to the Official's intonation, he didn't believe a word the Official said, but the intonation was different, he could probably trust that. Of course, the Official was no novice at such conversations either, he could probably even put the Chairman to shame when it came to driving people into a tight corner. But not the Face-Maker. Perhaps he really wasn't the best face-maker in the City, but the Face-Maker had spent a lifetime preparing himself for more than just work, and after the Commission he'd learned his lesson so well that he remained on guard even in his sleep.

'In yours.' — Don't ask any more questions, don't try feeling at my intonation, it has no pulse. — He smiled, lie a wolf yawning. 'In yours.'

'Are you deceiving me?'

'Half and half.'

'Which half?'

'Either of them.'

After that the conversation moved on to the Muse and how the Face-Maker was such a lucky man and so on and so forth, and how yesterday the Muse had been the first lady at the evening of the Choice, and how the Official had admired her and probably everything would work out fine and the Official chuckled as he said that he himself would 'serve as his messenger boy'. Out of all of this idle chatter the Face-Maker registered nothing definite internally. He knew well enough what these good relations were worth, this happy, open, jolly attitude had been tried out on him often enough at the Commission. The Official was a virtuoso performer, of course, but the model was still the same.

But now this is closer to the point:

'Do you know how they got on to you at the Commission that other time?'

The Face-Maker says nothing, listening, concealing his own intonation.

'It was my doing. You accidentally moved my partner from my pre-Official days back down two numbers, and that was enough for me. So it was me that started things between us. I owe you.' The wolf yawned again.

He's probably lying, but what's the difference? If the Official didn't think the Face-Maker or the Muse were needed any more, he'd condemn them to Departure without so much as batting an eyelid. Just as long as they were still playing his tune, he must be needed. The Official stood up and embraced him again

'Alright, if we talk all day there'll be no work done.' He called the Chairman, who came in. The Official kept his arms round the Face-Maker's shoulders. 'If so much as a single hair on his head...' this time without any smile, not even a wolf's smile, or perhaps this time he's pretending. The Chairman watches — he wouldn't want to miss anything, after all, or it would be like in that old joke: 'We're not going to arrange Departure for you, we'll think of something worse.'

'What could be worse?'

'We'll keep bringing you back and organizing it all over again, and again and again till the end of your life.'

No, the Official and the Chairman had lived so many years

together, now, they'd worked and joked together — naturally with considerable caution exercised on the side of the Chairman. The Official had never once spoken in quite this manner. This was no trick. He smiled.

'Of course, d'you think I don't understand?' But he doesn't understand why the Official's bothered about a single hair on the Face-Maker's head if the Face-Maker's carrying a load that would crush an elephant.

'Well then,' the Official says before he leaves, 'it's up to you to decide, don't just carry on playing the fool, you've got to do a bit of work for your Name.'

The Chairman has lost the thread now, and the Face-Maker has nothing to feel particularly happy about either. Just what kind of little job is this? The Face-Maker has to be prepared for it, too. That hair on his head business was a pretty convincing sign for any one who heard it said.

He tensed himself, sweeping away the cold patch that was creeping down his spine with the power of his will, as though he was melting away snow with fire. He was prepared to bear anything, but so far there was nothing to bear. The conversation had to come first. General information that everyone, including, of course, the Chairman, was well aware of. Even including the fact that the Great One's pupil had traveled uphill faster than a downhill bob-sleigh. The Commission — what needed to be said there, the Chairman knew better than the Face-Maker. The questions about the Muse whistled past his ears like bullets — pee-eew, and they were gone.

No matter how hard the Face-Maker concentrated, no matter how hard he tried to control himself, he still clearly gave away something he didn't want to reveal, above and beyond the words that he spoke. But how could he understand what it was, if he himself didn't even know when it happened? A master craftsmen knows his trade, and no one could ever doubt the Chairman's mastery.

It was a pity when the Chairman stood up. It was already the end of the beginning, he had no more to ask. The master craftsman hardly even seemed to have begun working, he was just coming to grips with the job. He'd been just about to pin the Face-Maker to the wall like a butterfly and then squeeze himself down to the size of a flea and climb in through the Face-Maker's eye and down deep inside him, down to the bottom, where his soul lay in its shell. He would have found out everything that the Face-Maker himself did not know, he would have seen everything, written everything down: but more than that, simply out of curiosity, for his own amusement, he would have slit the soul into two halves with one stroke of his sharp little knife and poured the yolk of the soul out on to his palm or on to a microscope slide.

And now they would part, and the Chairman wouldn't be able to pin him to the wall. Instructions are just the same as traffic-lights for a car. Whether you feel like it or not, you brake.

'Come into the other office, please. We'll take a look at what your compassion's like.'

The Face-Maker remembered about compassion, and he smiled with one corner of his mouth. Yes indeed, how was his compassion doing nowadays? As a person with a name, wasn't he supposed to be devoid of that particular quality — after all the people who had been taken from behind their desks before his very eyes, after all the people who had squirmed and screamed and wept under his knife, and all the other things as well... Work and compassion, life and compassion were incompatible. Otherwise, who would have any right to live? As for half-hearted compassion, compassion at the level of mere sympathy — that was a game others could play at... The Face-Maker was really only aware that compassion of that kind actually existed from the terms of the law forbidding compassion. Perhaps when he was still a child, or during his first years at work, or that time at the Commission, he might have been a little bit upset when he was peeling off the skin from the face and the patient was crying from the pain, unable to close his eyelids — those red and juicy eyelids — or when he was listening to the screams of the person who had gone into the office of the Commission ahead of him, and when he had gone in and seen him sitting there with his mouth open and a trickle of blood running down over his chin. But now — now they could put the entire City in that chair in front of him, and he wouldn't shed a single tear from either eye, he wouldn't even blink, he could be perfectly sure of that, the Face-Maker reassured himself, as he stepped out towards the next office. Take yesterday, for instance, after they turned on the lights and carried out all the hands and heads and hundreds of people were just left sitting there in the chairs, what had he felt? Tenderness for the Muse and joy that the operation had produced such an enthusiastic response from the hall. He was like everybody else. The Face-Maker walked on feeling calm, even happy.

II

The door opened. It was a wide door, extending half-way across the wall. It moved away from him like a kitten moving across a carpet, nimbly and noiselessly, and it closed just as noiselessly. The armchair, please. The person who greeted him was wearing dark glasses, and his hands were as slim and flexible as the Face-Maker's own. The Face-Maker always paid particular attention to people's hands, and these looked as though they might also be no less skillful than his own. The Face-Maker somehow felt more sure of himself. As a test of what a man could be sure of, a good pair of hands was no small matter, they helped him to feel calmer when he needed to be calm. The chair they sat the Face-Maker in was soft and comfortable. He felt even calmer. He felt the warm, light pressure of fingers touching the skin of his hands, his neck, his forehead, and he even felt as though he could simply doze off. He hardly even felt the belts as they were fastened round his body.

The hands brought him a piece of paper. On the top was the initial data. Female One Hundred and Five — face and weight normal, corresponding to the number. Everything corresponded to the number. Condemned to Departure. One Hundred and Five, thought the Face-Maker, that's a familiar number, and then suddenly he remembered: of course, she was that friend of the One Hundreds. It was her the Husband used to go out to visit before he had a name. The Muse had talked about her so much and said how female One Hundred and Five loved male One Hundred, and sometimes she missed him even more than the Muse missed the Face-Maker, and in some ways the Muse would even like to be like her. At one time she had even known her herself, but then she'd fallen outside the range of the numbers it was possible for the Muse to associate with. In fact, at one time in the past she'd been her very closest friend. She'd been brought up with her... — Aaaagh!

What a repulsive scream, even muffled, the Face-Maker thought with a grimace. He turned his head and the door slid open quietly and gently, as gently as tiny snowflakes dropping on to the palm of your hand. The two men who had brought him to the Commission an hour ago were dragging female One Hundred and Five along by the legs. What a repulsive face, beaten to a pulp, a mass of bruises and blood, a face with almost no skin left at all. The head was hanging to one side, but the woman was still screaming. Something inside the Face-Maker squirmed ever so slightly. Quiet, now, he thought. Right — the silhouette of the body is quite normal, with the hips just a bit on the full side. They've already ruined the face, and now she can hardly even be recognized as One Hundred and Five. How rapidly a person's destiny can change, the Face-Maker thought with deliberate force. But then, how can you call it destiny — she's been condemned to Departure. He wondered whether it had been the Commission's idea or the Official's to show him precisely female One Hundred and Five.

They tossed female One Hundred and Five on the floor. They lifted up her head, and the woman began to stir. She groaned. The man standing on the right took hold of a scalpel and slashed open one of her legs from the bottom to the top. She jerked and screamed.

Quiet, now, thought the Face-Maker, tensing, I myself open up the neck and the cheeks. Quiet, this is nothing more than a test for compassion. You can stand this — it's nothing, the Commission's at work every day of the week. And what about yesterday? In the hall. Enough to drive you insane. But you just thought about something else. His hand twitched very slightly.

The person conducting the test leaned down towards the Face-Maker:

'Is there anything you would like to say?'

The Face-Maker shook his head and pressed his hand harder against the arm of the chair, and then immediately felt afraid he might have moved too abruptly and if the Tester didn't notice, then the machines and the sensors might.

At this point the man standing on the left picked up a scalpel.

A fine job they do, the Face-Maker forced himself to think, professionals. No doubt about it. Then he noticed that he was having difficulty in forcing himself to think. Am I really not able to remain calm? After all, my testimony has no effect whatever on her destiny. Exactly the same thing would have happened whether I was here or not. And if I don't hold out, there won't be any new work, any Muse, maybe not even any me.

Probably that was what betrayed him, the fact that he thought about the Muse. The thought that she had once known female One Hundred and Five somehow got jumbled up with the thread of thought about the pointlessness of interfering, and they wove themselves around each other, and what came out was that it could have been the Muse, his own Muse, and not female One Hundred and Five. But once again the Face-Maker took himself in hand, and his hands didn't even tremble. Well done, he thought, and the idea that he could survive it all after all must have been what fatally relaxed his will — he was too quick to assume that the victory was his.

The woman didn't scream, she just clenched her teeth as the man standing on the left raised the scalpel to her right eye and then supported the back of her head on his hand and lifted it up. If the Face-Maker had not already experienced that sense of relief and victory, he would probably have taken this in the same way as all the rest — after all she had already been condemned to Departure. The Face-Maker jerked quite involuntarily, breaking off all the sensors and throwing the chair over on to its side. He groaned in a low voice as though he was suffering from some dull pain, and he clutched at the belt in an attempt to tear it open. Then he felt a hand on his shoulder.

'Stop it.' He looked upwards sharp as a knife, a wolf with all his fur standing up on end in his fury, and he saw the Official standing over him. But now there was nothing in front of him, no table, no woman, nobody at all.

The Face-Maker went down on his knees and burst into tears, his voice a pitiful howl, and he couldn't give a damn for the test, or the Official, or the City, or for anything else in the world. There was only one thought swirling and skidding around in his mind, like a car that has fallen into a swamp — It could have been the Muse. It could have been the Muse. The Official placed his hand on his shoulder again. He squatted down in front of the Face-Maker.

'I'll come when you've finished with your howling.' He unfastened the Face-Maker's belt and went out.

The Face-Maker lay there for a while, then he got up and set the chair upright. He sat in it and closed his eyes. His head ached, but it was empty, there wasn't a single thought in it, except 'It could have been the Muse'. Then that thought was squeezed aside in his mind as another came creeping in like a cowed, guilty dog: 'You didn't pass the test, not even when nothing depended on you.' The Face-Maker opened a door and released a bird into the emptiness: Damn you all, you and your tests. Curse every last one of you — he began to laugh. He got up. He lay down on the floor. He laughed and his tears ran down the way they do after the anesthetic, when the feeling's coming back to the face. He stood up, hammered his fists against the wall and gradually became calmer, and now there was probably only a single thought left in his head — I couldn't hold out, but I don't give a damn, at least now I can feel I'm my own man.

'Feeling better?' the Official asked, glancing in at the door. 'Or not yet? It'll pass off all right.' He went out. And soon the Face-Maker actually did feel as though it had all passed off. The Official appeared again, in a jolly mood this time. 'Congratulations — you passed.'

'Don't lie to me, d'you think none of it means anything to me any more?'

'Look at the board.'

The Face-Maker looked up and he saw the text light up above the door: Assessment — Positive. Normal.

The Official put his arms round the Face-Maker's shoulders.

'You see, that means everything is in order. Now you've got something to celebrate,' the Official held out a glass. 'Here, drink to your victory.'

The Face-Maker drank without even feeling the taste, and he suddenly felt safe and at ease. The test had obviously been conducted according to rules he didn't know and his natural reactions, which contradicted the City's normal standards, had been assessed positively. All he had to do, without any faking, without any attempt to show on the outside what was not there on the inside, was just to be himself and believe in himself, and he said to the Official:

'I thought the trial was already over at that point, and you know, I really have no wish to be tested any further.'

The Official nodded, he was pleased at the Face-Maker's words. The warm-up really was over and done with.

'You're a swine,' he said to the Official, 'vile, despicable scum.'

'That's right,' said the Official, as though he was terribly pleased at the Face-Maker's words.

'Well,' he said, 'and what else?'

'What else?' said the Face-Maker. 'If you ever end up on my

table, I'll do exactly the same to you as those butchers did to female One Hundred and Five.'

The Official was simply delighted at this.

'My God,' he said through his tears, 'if only you knew how your words touch my heart, how very dear you are to me. How beautiful a sincere man is, even in his rudeness, there really is nothing higher than sincerity.'

This caught the Face-Maker on the wrong foot. He'd prepared a great many things to say about the Official, about the City and about the general vileness of this lazy, indifferent mechanism of laws and the injustice of Departure. But when he saw such happiness on the Official's face, the words stuck in the Face-Maker's throat, and he lost momentum. He fell silent and retreated into his own thoughts. He recalled his first Commission and the Muse, who could have been in female One Hundred and Five's place. He made no attempt to say anything else to the Official.

III

By this time the Muse was already waiting for the Face-Maker. The normal working day was coming to an end, and she was walking back and forwards across the room, from one corner to the other. As she waited, she remembered the first touch of the Face-Maker's elbow against her skin, she remembered how she loved to take off his cloak. She reorganized the events of the day, then put them back in the old order. She sat down and folded her legs up underneath her. She watched every minute as she counted it, and if a minute was a cat or a dog, she would surely have forced them to run faster. The Muse had definitely made up her mind to go back to work the next day. She could even do that if she wanted. Today she had realized that she couldn't go on spending the whole day and goodness knows how much longer as well just waiting around like this. When the door opened and she went dashing towards it, she saw it was the Official. She wrapped her housecoat more tightly around her and pressed her hand to her lips, and suddenly she felt something running across her palm — she took her hand away and saw blood, and she dropped her hand again. But why blood, she thought.

'He's alive, and all is well,' said the Official.

The Muse was grateful to him for saying that straight away. She put her hand to her lips again and then took it away again. She had bit her lip. But when had she managed to do it, and when had she begun to worry like that? She never used to do anything of the kind, even when she was waiting for him after the Commission she hadn't been that nervous. She wiped her hand and then pointed to an armchair for the Official.

'Why isn't he home, why hasn't he come himself?'

The Official gestured sympathetically with one hand as he sank into the armchair and fed her three reels full of talk about the difficulties of his new work and in general about the importance of the first few days in a new job, especially after the events of the previous day. Yes, yes, the events that she herself had witnessed — and the consequences, which would continue to make themselves felt for another few days. Everybody had to pull together to put everything back into shape, there were three times as many operations to be done as before — there were a lot of changes going on and he, the Official, would not be able to leave his office at all for several days. And of course, the Official immediately agreed that the Muse needed to work, and that an exception could be made so that she could return to her old job, only, for God's sake, she had to be careful, because any annoyance or disagreement would be taken to mean... He couldn't even imagine how they might be taken, and after all, it wasn't possible to explain to everyone why a woman would want to stay on at work after such a vast advancement in her fortunes. The Muse agreed with him, and her mood became pleasant and happy. Tomorrow she would go back to her chair and once more she would submit 'The Immortals' to close monitoring (the episode that had been postponed until next week because of the recent events) and she was already wondering how many points the members of the viewing panel who were still alive would award — and the new ones as well, of course.

Everything's fine, she tells herself. But no matter how hard the Muse tries to dispel her thoughts, like pigeons swirling high into the air they sweep back down to the dovecote, flapping their wings noisily and cooing as they settle themselves down. Why isn't he there really? And why has the Official come, and is what he said the truth, and can she trust him, even though she believes absolutely that nobody in the City can be trusted — but then that's the way a woman is made, she wants to believe.

But that's enough of the Muse — the Official is up to his eyes in all sorts of problems without her.

IV

'Are you ready?'

The Face-Masker had only asked whether it would involve any experiments on other people, and he had relaxed when the pleasant woman had shaken her head and said, of course not. It was just that the warm-up couldn't possibly have been carried out without an additional subject, since... The Face-Maker had grimaced — enough.

'Where will it be, here as well?'

The woman smiled and explained that no, it wouldn't, and she led the Face-Maker into a room which he remembered being in from that other time during the first Commission. The same lamps on the walls — he'd noticed them before, a human hand emerging from the wall, holding a torch. The fingers seemed so slim and vibrant, that at the time he'd taken them for real fingers, he'd thought the hands were genuine hands, and they'd told him that the hands were really genuine, but since at the time he hadn't believed a single answer from anyone, he hadn't believed that either. Remembering his question, he asked the woman whether the hands were real. No, said the woman, it's not living tissue any longer. It was strange that the reply was a matter of indifference to the Face-Maker, he was already living in the knowledge that knowledge of what is true and what is false changes absolutely nothing in life. Enough, he broke off his own train of thought, it's time to concentrate. It's time. What was the content of the first trial, and how was he to behave: should he be natural again or entirely the opposite? That was the most important thing right now.

'Come this way, please.' The woman pushed open a glass door that was virtually invisible, it was so transparent.

Suddenly there in front of the Face-Maker was a cube which only a moment ago had been invisible to him. He wondered why he hadn't noticed it sooner — after all, the torch and the hand at the junction were slightly distorted where the boundary line of the cube cut through them like a fine thread.

'I'll explain the most important points to you. If you begin to feel unwell, then you should... see over there, on the right of the chair — it seemed there was a chair and a panel of switches inside the cube — press the red key. The Face-Maker sat down and fastened on the sensors. She showed him how to use the key for halting the Trial... but the problem there is — and the woman raised her finger in a mocking childish gesture.

'What's your number?' the Face-Maker interrupted her.

'Forty-One,' she said with a smile, then smiled again, this time without any words, filling out the pause — did the Face-Maker have any other questions to ask? — and then she continued with her line of thought. 'The point is that we have to wait for as long as possible before we press the key, and you should only press it when you feel that you are losing consciousness. The result of our trial will depend on when you react and how long you can stay in the chair.'

'And that's all?'

'That's all. You'll have nobody to deal with but yourself.'

The woman went out. She closed the door and sat down on the

far side of the cube at the control panel. Then she disappeared from the Face-Maker's view.

The walls were less transparent now. On one of them an object traveling at incredible speed appeared, moving straight at him, ponderous and inexorable, closer and closer, until he could see it was a train with a headlamp protruding from its forehead. The floor was trembling under the Face-Maker now, and he felt a laughable desire to stop the trial already. He even reached out one hand with a smile. It went rushing past him, almost touching his body, the wind lashed painfully at his arms and his neck and stroked his face, but the Face-Maker didn't even flinch. He understood the Official had meant it when he said not a hair of his head was to be harmed. What if that was really just another deception? What if he and the Chairman had just been acting out a game, what if... but now the walls had begun to move in on themselves, they had turned black, and although almost nothing seemed to have changed yet, the air had begun to press against the Face-Maker's body the way it sometimes did when it was raining. The walls moved closer and closer, soon they would close in completely. No, somehow they must have come together without touching him, and he was left in some kind of air bubble — the switches and the 'off' key had been squashed flat and thin, like the smoke from a match that's just gone out. The Face-Maker was calm, but even so he raised one finger before immediately lowering it again. Maybe that was all part of the trial — the fact that it was impossible to put an end to it. He'd had cases like that himself, when a person had lost consciousness on the table, and the Face-Maker had never stopped his work — there were revivers to deal with that. A few hours later the person would be up on his feet and quite well again — not actually quite as well as before, but that was a mere detail. He had no right not to make the fullest possible use of the operation time, he couldn't possibly waste it by giving the patient a break. There were always thousands of people in the queue, they were waiting for him, and the Face-Maker's every minute was already divided up among the inhabitants of the City. But it wasn't like that here, he was the only one they were working with here, he was the only one who would be able to carry out the work required after he had been through this trial. Or perhaps he wasn't the only one — that would mean yet another deception. The squashed bank of switches fell to the floor, clanged once and lay there. The Face-Maker decided not to bother asking why they'd taken away the switches, in the final analysis that was no tragedy. Still it was a pity that he couldn't see the woman's face, perhaps he could ask, but then he changed his mind again — the walls of the bubble had burst into flames, he could distinctly smell smoke, and the bubble had begun shrinking. The flames were already right up close beside him, and he was enveloped in fierce heat. His body broke into a sweat. 'Future causes' — that was what he thought it was called. He laughed. A man being burnt on a fire sweats in order to restore his body temperature to normal, and for just a few seconds he is able to do it. There were no switches under his hand, his fingers clutched at the chair and he gripped it tight, then his fingers opened again. He sat there calm and relaxed. The tongues of flame crept closer to him across the floor, climbed upwards and went out, while new ones sprang to life... Suddenly his brain began to register alarm signals. It wasn't the fire, it was the smell of burning, not the tongues of flame. Somehow, somewhere he sensed where the main danger lay. He shouldn't have taken everything so lightly, it was all mere camouflage. He shouldn't have paid any attention to it at all. He should have simply prepared himself for the most important thing to come. Some kind of animal had slithered into his throat, it was tickling his throat, scratching at it and preventing him from breathing. The Face-Maker began to feel sick, he stroked at his own throat in an attempt to squeeze the animal out, to force it out into the open, and a stream of liquid came spurting out of him, gleaming a cloudy yellowish-green in the light of the flames. He felt a bit better, and then again he was choking... Wait: asphyxiation begins when there's no oxygen in the air, or when there's no air entering the lungs. Coloured circles whirled and span inside his brain: what was the answer to the riddle? If he could find the cause, he could fight it. Curse the damn flames — there was nothing left for him to breathe. His throat was clear, but there was something wheezing inside him. Suddenly a suspicion flared up and the coloured circles scattered into a thousand fragments and faded away to nothing — they were pumping out the air from under the cube. Calm down. Stop breathing. Not a single movement. There's still some air in the bubble, it's up at the top. You have to get up. Now you can take a careful breath. He felt a feeble stream of air enter his throat. The wheezing inside him stopped. Aha, you were right. Higher. You can get higher by climbing on the chair. But then they'll notice that you're on to their game. Never mind that, when it comes down to it you easily could have done it unconsciously, but then climbing on a chair is already an action of thought. It's even harder to breathe now, but there's no more hysteria. And most significantly, for some reason the thought of the next trial flitted through his mind — there must be no hysteria there either.

He felt almost certain that the trial was not all that difficult, and the whole point was (he could drag it out for as long as necessary) that he could halt the trial at any moment, when he felt he couldn't breathe any more... but there were no controls any more, the key had been flattened. That meant his thought was no longer controlled by it. It was painful to breathe now, but still he would go on standing here for another minute. The Face-Maker began running through the various possibilities. Move to the right and there was a wall. To the left — a wall. Backwards — a wall. Upwards? He reached up a hand and it was burnt. He pulled it back and tried to lower his arm. He couldn't, it was held fast. He tried with his other hand and the same thing happened. Never mind, he could stand there just as well with his arms up. At moments of disaster you have to think and act instantaneously. He tried to sit down and he managed it. But there was nothing to breathe. He tried to stand up. No. Hands up in the air and can't stand up — the red circles began spinning again, everything around him was black now, not a scrap of light anywhere. It was only now that he realized the fire was gone, it must have stopped ages ago. Remember: fear disengages consciousness, and consciousness seeks contact with fear, it's like an anchor or a harbour for a ship in a storm, it's like... Wait, the brain isn't taking any part in solving the other problems, of course, this narrow concentration that can lead to destruction is fear. Now it's the end. Now you have to stand up somehow. It's time. Halt the trial. The non-existent stop key is stuck. No response. The wall's just as dark as ever. As though they've welded him into the chamber, or into a diving suit, then lowered him into the water and cut off his air. His heart stopped. His lungs hung like limp sails seeking wind, and only his brain kept working for another instant. In that instant, he heard himself begin to rattle, then he struck his head against the rattling sound and went tumbling smoothly all the way down to the bottom, and he hardly really felt anything at all, there was no more than a fleeting shadow of feeling that some force was ripping apart his lungs, his brain, his heart — the pieces were all flying off in different directions and there was a light approaching him at great speed.

Aaaaaaagh, creaked his body.

V

The Muse opened the Principal Couple's door. She was still in a higher position than them, although, of course, the gap was not as great as it had been before — a fact she was reminded of soon enough. The Wife was not home and the Husband was extremely glad the Muse had come. He immediately started babbling about how glad he was to see her, that life had been so boring because she hadn't been to see them for so very long, that the only thing he had were his feelings for her, but he had never dared to touch her, because there was such a distance between them, but now it had been swept away, and even though her position might still separate her from him, he wasn't just any old One Hundred any more, now he was the Husband, and he kept going down on his knees, leaping back up, trying to embrace her, weeping. The Muse stood there in total and absolute confusion, like someone who was walking across a plain and has suddenly found himself at the bottom of an abyss. She had often seen the Husband when he was calm, crushing birds, telling her the touching story of his tender feelings for female One Hundred and Five on pain of absolute secrecy from the Wife, who was still female One Hundred then, and the Muse couldn't set their old relations aside so quickly and re-orient herself to this shift. She could never have said that she found the Husband repulsive or even unpleasant, no, she liked him in a general human kind of way — or perhaps that was another little falsehood she had permitted herself in order not to feel any sense of shame for these visits. The Husband, emboldened by the Muse's silence, was already embracing her. He'd already hung himself on her neck, and her knees had begun to give way. Probably that was what roused from her state of amazement — the way a car will spin its wheels for a while when you step on the gas, and then instantaneously accelerate away. She went down on her knees herself and began laughing, and then chuckling and guffawing — she chortled so loudly that the Husband leapt to his feet and began straightening out her shirt in his fright. The Muse tumbled back on to the floor and roared and roared with laughter. The Husband took a startled step backwards. The Muse went on laughing. She had just imagined him lying there.

'What an idiot, what an idiot. Why did I ever bother talking to you, if you simply didn't understand a single thing I was saying?' That was how the Wife found them when she returned, the Husband pressing himself back against the wall with wild staring eyes and a face blotched with red, the Muse stretched out on the floor, pealing with laughter. The Wife took it all in immediately. She screwed her forefinger into her forehead.

'As they say in the City, bite off more than you can chew and you'll choke.'

The Husband suddenly rushed at her.

The Muse stopped laughing with equal suddenness and got to her feet. Her eyes were still filled with tears of laughter and revulsion. Without even bothering to look at either of them, she went across to the door.

'Please don't think that I'm in the least bit offended or that I'll tell the Face-Maker anything about this.' She didn't bother to wait for any answer.

Very often we don't really need a reason to do what we've wanted to do for a long time, but don't, because without a reason it seems awkward. The only answer she heard behind her was the resounding smack of a hard slap to someone's face. Whose? Judging from the double sound, both his and hers. It was followed by the scream of a cat that has just been stepped on with a hob-nailed boot.

VI

The Face-Maker was lying in water. He opened his eyes and couldn't immediately understand where he was. It was like an aquarium in which they keep fish. The Face-Maker looked at his hands. Everything looked okay. The fingers? He tried them and they worked just fine. Sitting and watching him from behind the transparent side of the tank that ran right in front of his eyes was the smiling Official.

'First class.' He said, and raised his thumb. 'Fifty per cent above the norm. With reserves like that, we've doubled all the basic indicators for you.'

'I don't want any more of this,' said the Face-Maker.

'Of course.' The Official had never expected anything else.

He, the Face-Maker, was right. There was no point in getting himself into this kind of state. It was all voluntary after all — the Face-Maker simply wanted the job he had been waiting for all his life, a job that was impossible unless he'd gone through the trial. But enough was enough. Afterwards, if he felt like it, if he changed his mind or came to a different decision or a different conclusion, then he could continue with the trial. The Official helped the Face-Maker climb out of the water. He undressed the Face-Maker. He rubbed him dry with a towel, and he did it all himself, on his own. He brought fresh, dry clothing and again carefully, very carefully, he slid the Face-Maker in through the wide sleeves and the wide neck. He sat him in an armchair. He poured water for him, scooping it straight out of the aquarium. He drank half himself, then gave the rest to the Face-Maker. He certainly needed it — his throat was completely dried out, yes, he needed the water, and he thanked the Official. He chuckled to himself, the only clear thought that still remained in his head now was that he'd exceeded the control figures by fifty per cent. It seems a man is still a man, no matter what you might do to him. He had his name — the Great Face-Maker — and the Muse, and the prospect of new work, and... he'd almost croaked (if he really was still alive, that is) and yet for all the monstrous ugliness of the definition, he was delighted, genuinely delighted at the idea that his personal figures were actually fifty per cent above the norm.

In much the same way a man who has lost his wife and son in an air crash might be delighted in his hysteria that at the last minute he decided not to send his cat off with them.

In much the same way a man burying the woman he loved might be delighted that the coffin is so fine and dignified, scarlet and silky.

In much the same way a man who has lost his arm might be delighted that he still has his cufflinks.

In much the same way a man who has been walled up by an avalanche in a cave where nobody knows about him and he can never expect to be rescued might be delighted that he is still alive, until he remembers that to die from hunger is far worse than to be crushed to death.

Maybe the rocks will fall away, maybe they'll dig you out, maybe they'll remember about you, but until they do dig you out the main thing is that your loved ones mustn't know the position you're in, or else they'll suffer because they don't know what they can do to help, and that will simply be unnecessary suffering, and you have to explain to them that things are not that bad yet, this is still only the beginning of your life without bread and water and you're ready to survive as long as life can maintain its hold on your body, you're not afraid of hunger, but time is still stronger than you are, you know that too, and the only thing you can try to impress on the one who loves you is that everything is all right and nothing has happened and life is carrying on as it should.

The Face-Maker lies on the bed and smiles, he tells the Muse about how well things are going at work — the new laboratory, the office, the new duties and the remarkable people. And how he couldn't come home any earlier today and yes, of course, he'd sent the Official, the Official ran errands for him now. Why was he breathing so heavily? Because he'd been in a hurry to get back to her. Why were his hands so weak? That was tiredness too. The Face-Maker tries to protect his Muse. He's a noble individual. The Muse is noble too, she takes good care of the Face-Maker. Not a word about the unpleasant part of the visit to the Principal Couple, but of course, by all means she mentions that she's been there. Everything's fine with them. They're still just as nice, but something in them has changed, especially in the Husband, and she doesn't think she's likely to go and visit them in the near future and later on there won't be any time. The Muse is intending to work, because waiting is so very hard, and she's fed up of visiting people, and she's very concerned that the Face-Maker gets so tired. The words tumble over each other, they gather together into flocks and arrange themselves in straight lines, like an arrow-head of birds that has launched into the sky. The Face-Maker is overcome by drowsiness. He really is tired.

And now they're washing the dirty laundry together in a thawed patch on the frozen river. The dirty water runs down and the ice-cold linen cuts at their hands, and the Face-Maker needs his hands, but he feels sorry for the Muse and he squeezes out the cold heavy sheets, his fingers turning red in the wind as the water runs back into the thawed patch, and all around them the sun is shining on the blinding white snow. They are surrounded by the black marble headstones of graves, that is by houses, and below them in the drain a long, thin ribbon of yellow is winding through the current, and sometimes its tiny curls cling to the side of the channel for a brief moment — female One Hundred and Five is on her way out to the outskirts of the City, mingled with the rain, and then on further still — perhaps she'll even end up in this little stream where the Muse is washing her laundry. At last they have both fallen asleep. Words... Words... Nothing but words, yet see how it helped. To hell with it all, curse the lot of it, all the pains and troubles of the world, all the horror of this black stone, of this rain, of this laundry-washing. The cold. Female One Hundred and Five's eye. The Husband with his eyes goggling in lust. Their care and their deception in the name of protection. It helped. In their sleep they see dreams, and perhaps they're not actually as terrible as this life, perhaps they're even better than it is, because she needs to have her head lying on his shoulder, and he needs to have her head lying on his shoulder. How he wants her to sleep until morning, and what does he want with any trials anyway, there's nothing else he needs at all. But the Choice is already behind him. The Face-Maker has no way out.

When the train's flying along, just try getting out — it'll just plaster you along the wall of the tunnel.

The plane lifts up its head and goes slicing through the sky like a knife through butter — get out if you like, there's the door. But the very idea's enough to set your shoulders twitching.

The choice is behind you, and even the night is only granted to you for a couple of hours out of kindness, but any moment...

They came for the Face-Maker when the night was scarcely half over — that was what the job was like. The Muse agreed that was what the job was like, only now she can't get to sleep again, and she's already beginning to wait for the Face-Maker, and she's happy to remember that this morning she's going back to her 'Immortals'. When the Muse has something to do, it somehow makes the waiting easier.

Not a trace is left of the Face-Maker's thoughts of yesterday. He'll go through with it, because if all there is to live for is to keep your place among the Great Ones, what's the point if you've already made it, and only dead people carry on living without a purpose.

VII

They get ready. The Official is there beside him. When the Face-Maker came in he was already there. When he could have got any sleep was a mystery. The Face-Maker's in the water. It's really quite pleasant, the water's warm, about twenty-five degrees. It's no problem for the Face-Maker to tell the temperature of the water or the air. It was well worth going back home as well. His thoughts are quite different now, and his sensations are different, morning thoughts and sensations, even though it's still night. Yesterday's events have already been pushed aside somewhere to the very outskirts of his brain, they're wreathed in mist now, nothing but a silhouette against the dawn, a fleeting half-shadow, and somehow even the terror seems beautiful. And that feeling again — he was right after all to have wanted more than anyone else, one stage was already behind him now, and it was scarcely going to get any harder from now on, he wasn't a machine, after all, they had to take care of him. They were training him for his work, not trying to turn him into a cripple. The water was pleasant. The idea of 'pleasant' and the word 'trial' once again provide some kind of familiar impulse. The Face-Maker is splashing in the water now, snorting as he swims and shaking his head about, and already on his guard, the way a cat might seem to be just lying there, with his eyes closed, dozing, but all the bird has to do is come within range of a single leap. And when they fasten the sensors to his body, he manages to experience the contact an instant before it happens, so the reaction scale stays at zero.

Meanwhile, the Official carries on talking about the Face-Maker, about how marvelous it is that the control figures have been exceeded, and he honestly doesn't really know what to think about it. In passing, the Official explains that he's there all the time, and this is a trial for him as well, and it's still impossible to say who's suffering the most and what the consequences might be for the Official, because he and the Face-Maker are like communicating vessels, sharing a single destiny, and God forbid that the Face-Maker might not survive it all, there's no way to guess the exact limit... They're trying to guess it by putting ten control groups through the trial in parallel with him, and they've had to replace all the control subjects twice already, but he still doesn't have enough data for what he needs, and in order to protect the Face-Maker, the others are one trial ahead of him, but very often the controls are no help in explaining how the Face-Maker behaves or what he's capable of. And that little deception the Official permitted himself with the red key wasn't actually his own idea, it was an improvisation of the trial manager's, and the Face-Maker would soon see that was really the case, because the trial manager was only material for conducting the experiment, and now the Official would deal with him in the same way as he had dealt with female One Hundred and Five. Even though he understands everything perfectly well, for some reason the Face-Maker begins to feel a certain liking and trust for the Official, for there is not a single word in what he says that arouses any doubt or revulsion in the Face-Maker. We are basically made very simply, no better bait exists for us than nobility, sympathy and magnanimity, and we climb on to the hook ourselves at the very first word of kindness. Once again the Face-Maker attunes himself to the Official's words, and at this moment he realizes that the wall of the aquarium has turned dark, and his head has already been pushed down into the water by a lid that is just as dark, and then he realizes that he is under the water... The very first thing you have to do is to stop breathing, while your head is still working. You have to think about the fact that the Muse is waiting for you, and that you have to come home this evening and tell her something that will cheer her up, such as: I had a very good day today. He even begins imagining how the Muse will press herself against his cloak, and how she'll start to cry, because she understands anyway, only she doesn't want to upset him, even though maybe not everything's all right at work, but then, what does 'all right' mean when she can leave any time she likes, she doesn't depend on anybody there, for the Muse leaving doesn't necessarily mean being given Departure.

There's nothing left to breathe. Nothing but a little mouthful of water. Yes, yes, maybe, the reaction was unconscious, a reaction of trust that went beyond reason — it was intuition: he simply had to transfer his body into an unconscious state, almost to die. To stop breathing and hold out was not easy, but he would hold out. He wasn't a man at all, he was nothing but dead tissue that had been put into the water, he was a striped robe that had been thrown into the water, he was a bird that the Official had already crushed in his strong fingers. There was the pink foam already, and there was the film glazing his eyes. No, he had to wait for the Muse. Muse, I have to wait for you, you live in fear now, yesterday you saw the way the scalpel went in. Oh God, now his body was swelling up and he was being drawn upwards, but no, it was ice, a thawed spot on the river with a thin crust, he simply had to hit it harder with his head, that was all — dark, fragile, half-melted spring ice, right, here we go at top speed, with the head. Again and again, like breaking through a wall with your head. It's broken, he's alive, a gulp of air and then no more. Another layer, another one — blue, he can already see the sky, he can already see the tree up there, like in his childhood, another thin layer and then it looks as though he really will be able to breathe. His head hurts, there's something running down his face — his brains — but he needs to hit it just once more. That's the sky up there, get on with it, then, you freak. Okay. It didn't work there, so now try here. Ah-ah, a black shape, so you can't do it here, it's the bottom of a barge, that's happened before. Female One Hundred and Five is waiting for you. Stop. This is really hard now. It's harder for her, of course, but you're a master at sewing up an eye so that it sees your fingers and your body — the barge has gone past. Hit it.

It was just somebody's joke. It wasn't the bottom of a barge at all — just the soft vague mushy form of an inverted house. But then why the feeling of the blow? In order to bring you round, so you know you're still alive? What a good thing you spent the night with female One Hundred and Five, she loves you so much. But then why is there a woman lying beside you with the hem of her shirt pulled up, laughing? It's the Muse. Why is the Muse lying there and laughing? Of course, how could you possibly compare with her — she's the Great Face-Maker's partner, and what would you want with Great Women anyway? They're all old, because while their partner's clambering up the ladder, they grow old with him and they have dangling breasts and bellies that hang in folds. One Hundred and Five, my own little smooth one, I wouldn't change you for anyone, do you hear me, I don't need anyone else at all.

The body slowly sinks to the bottom of the aquarium, turns over and remains lying there with its mouth clamped tightly shut and its eyes closed, motionless and lazy, with its legs spread apart and its crushed arms jutting out in different directions.

Is he ready or not? Should we wait, or might we wait too long? The Official pressed up so hard against the glass that his face seemed to have fused with it, and if the Face-Maker had seen that image, looking as though it had been squashed flat by a caterpillar track, he would certainly have been filled with compassion for the Official, the same compassion that the Official attempts to win from everyone, even the people he processes personally before Departure. He sincerely wants people to understand his pain and just how difficult it is for him to be the instrument of God. Unfortunately, in the present case, unjust though it may be, the Face-Maker is unable to satisfy this permanent craving, for there is no Face-Maker, there is just a striped robe swaying at the bottom of the aquarium, rippling its long blue sleeves with the white stripes like a fish rippling its fins, without the slightest relation to the Face-Maker.

VIII

The night continued but the Muse couldn't sleep. She got up and there were strange thoughts in her head, not like any she'd ever had before. Yesterday evening with the Face-Maker they'd set out the previous day on the chess board and recalculated all the moves as they played them through once again, not rushing things, but taking everything one move at a time. And the difference had been demonstrated quite clearly between thinking slowly together and thinking alone instantaneously.

But sometimes (and perhaps not so very rarely for the Face-Maker) the instantaneous decisions were absolutely accurate, the only possible ones. The Muse didn't need to be told that was how things sometimes were, because she herself was like the Face-Maker in this way. But afterwards, later — and there was a certain satisfaction and unhurried inspiration even in this — a new decision could emerge, and sometimes three moves were all equal, as though uniqueness had tripled itself without becoming any less convincing or real.

It was probably really a great happiness — living every day as hope. Just a little bit higher, now. And all those times when a day replayed over again, the way they did it every week, had helped the Face-Maker and the Muse to behave more kindly, more generously and magnanimously, and at the same time more intelligently. And even in the most specific of actions there was scope for inspiration, and then it became the only possible one, because some detail or other made it more unusual than the most intelligent decision reached in advance.

Now the Face-Maker had withdrawn into himself, probably

because there was no Face-Maker any more, there was only the Great Face-Maker, and beyond that for her, the uninitiated, there was only the Day of Departure, and that was by no means the best thing to look forward to, push it away, as far away as possible. There was no need any more to resolve every day in a new and different way, everything had already happened anyway, what else could happen? Now there was nothing left but ordinary weekdays, which were all cold and empty, and the only concern remaining was not to lose what they already had.

The Muse must be nothing but a stupid woman after all, just a dumb bitch. She can't even begin to imagine that everything's just beginning. She regrets all the good times that are past and she shakes her head as she thinks about all those gray weekdays, and every now and then she gives a little shriek or a groan, but why, God help her, she doesn't know herself. Just now when she went over to the shower she was very nearly sick. What's going on? She always used to love the warm rain rolling down over her body. It's like being out on the street, only you've got nothing on, and the rain is just as strong and it kneads at your body and the steam rises from your skin, as though it's earth thawing in the spring, and your entire body becomes light and fluid, and you can raise your hands, throw back your head and close your eyes and stroke the falling streams with your skin. But today as soon as she even went close she almost puked.

Okay, if there's no way, there's no way. The Muse sat back down on the bed and pulled on her housecoat, her hands stretched out on her knees, tired and feeble. She tried to get up. She felt she was about to faint. She stood up. It all seemed to have passed off now. No, you have to go to work. It's time. Too much idleness and waiting and you won't even be the Muse any more. It's time.

She should at least splash her face with water. The nausea rose in her throat again. Okay, damn the water anyway. She got dressed. She went out early, in order to leave behind the alarm that was growing inside her here, in the house.

Probably when you've overeaten — too many rooms, too much quiet, too much waiting — you just have to open the door and get out. And then think about home again when you're at work and long to be there, but you can't go. And then the longing for quiet will return, and you can love it once again. And everything will pass off, she decided, all by itself.

The Muse went out into the street, and the rain embraced her in its usual manner, tensed her body and drove her along, pressing her down towards the earth.

IX

Lord God, how infinite is the space you have placed between 'too much' and 'too little'. Like meat — too little fire and it's raw, too much and the meat's tough, you have charcoal instead of reddish flesh... Or like coffee — if it's boiled, if the foam has risen beyond a unique, mysterious point, then it's spoiled, and if the foam hasn't reached that point, the taste is wrong too. But no matter how infinite (or tiny) this space may be, there is still a way to squeeze into it, like settling yourself into an armchair, and then to stretch out your legs and take a breather.

And that is what the Official does. Eyes turned inwards, eyelids lowered, hands on belly, legs — long ones — stretched straight out, feet collapsed outwards. From time to time, like the pointers on weighing-scales, they perform circular motions, as though somewhere inside himself the Official is placing something on the pans of the scales and his feet are showing whether the weight is excessive or trivial. A coarse mechanism, the human weighing-scales, without any divisions or precision. But what does that matter, when you're taking a breather that's quite good enough. The dressing-gown is striped white and blue, and through our half-closed eyelids we observe it keenly. In general it's the stuff of fairly ordinary life, the usual weekday. What person condemned to Departure has not endured harsher trials, only to come to an end, to break off abruptly on one of them? Not everybody survives even the Face-Maker's operations. But on the other hand, it must be said that the Face-Maker is being treated gently, because this is not just a trial, it's training as well.

Today, to put it in more precise terms, was a 'happy trial'. It contained the meaningful element of 'what for', it wasn't simply meant to keep on bending someone until they finally broke, so it wasn't important to wonder whether he would survive or he wouldn't, because in every person there is a point beyond which he will break, like a rubber ball under a steam hammer, like a bird in the palm of the Husband, like a copper pipe in a vice, the rubber insulation between two wires — squeeze, press, stretch, and even the most flexible...

Aha, it seems the dressing-gown has begun to stir. Raised its head. No, it's gone still again. Still too early.

In his many years of work the Official has observed so many of these people condemned to Departure, that he has become able to tell in advance at almost exactly which stage in which trial a person will come to his end point.

The Official stood up and approached the glass. He actually felt sorry for the man lying there. A humiliating kind of word, that: sorry. Or perhaps it wasn't humiliating, if he assumed that it was himself lying there on the bottom and quietly flapping his blue-striped sleeves?

The Face-Maker just lay there, not even existing, not knowing that as from today the time allowed for the Trial had been halved. There was unrest in the City. They had to move faster. It was an order.

X

The Face-Maker didn't feel them lift him up, lay him out on the table, put the mask on his face and pump the water out of him — the pleasant, warm water at about twenty-five degrees, the temperature that he could tell simply with a touch of his fingers — then put an instrument on his chest that made his heart move and cover the Face-

Maker with a sheet, so that when he came round he wouldn't get a fright and take the top of the table for the bottom of the aquarium.

And about four hours later, exactly at the time when the Muse went to work, the Face-Maker began to come round.

'My gills hurt', was the Face-Maker's first complaint.

What came after that made even less sense: when the familiar eyes of the Official appeared leaning over him, he stirred his fins and wanted to get up, but they wouldn't let him. The Official wasn't really there. It was a woman he'd never met before.

'I'm your doctor,' she said. 'In fact, I'm actually the Joint Chairperson of the Commission.

'Joint Chairperson,' the Face-Maker took the name in with unexpected understanding. That means their own people are dealing with me. It means so far nothing's changed.

Then he complained about his gills again, and demanded that they move the instrument cupboard in his office from the right side to the left. Because the flames had to be on the right, and although the cupboard was transparent, it prevented the flames from roasting the patient's face properly. And the patient (the operation was in full swing), was not just anybody, it was the Official.

He asked for something to drink. He took a sip and was immediately sick. His organism simply rejected the water. You can't give a dog a piece of poisoned meat twice.

The Face-Maker couldn't remember what had happened to him the previous night. The last event retained by his memory was leaving his former office. Then how was the Official tied up in all this?

His memory began reeling back to an obvious absurdity — the combination of the Face-Maker's office and an operation on the Official. The Official's happy-looking face emerged out of the fog.

'You're a woman,' said the Face-Maker, 'the Joint Chairperson — I know you.'

'Of course,' said the Official, 'definitely a woman, most definitely. An excellent idea,' said the Official, 'a woman. A broad, to put it in simple terms.' And the Official winked at him and looked around him in fright. 'And every broad,' — it was clear that the Official was telling the Face-Maker a terrible secret — 'is the Official.'

At this point the Face-Maker finally realized that it really was the Official standing in front of him, and from that moment his memory slipped back into place, the way a dislocated joint slips back into place in the skilled hands of a doctor.

'I'm ready,' the Face-Maker said immediately, and he tried to get up. He tried to help himself by pulling on the edge of the blanket that was covering him, and the blanket shifted, but the Face-Maker was left lying there. The lower edge of the blanket stopped exactly at his knees.

'Of course you're ready,' The Official-Broad had never for a moment doubted his unusual capabilities. She picked up the Face-Maker herself and stood him on the floor. And then she said: 'Walk!'

The Face-Maker began to fall. Then suddenly his body remembered the feeling when the Face-Maker was standing in front of his own desk after the Commission, and his knees had suddenly begun to give way, and then the Face-Maker had laughed and told himself: 'Don't be stupid, you're perfectly alright!' He repeated the phrase, and just like that time, it helped. Because the Face-Maker took a step, clutching the blanket, and moved in the direction of the armchair, so that everyone would simply understand that he wanted to sit down for a while. The way it is in boxing after a powerful blow: so that your opponent won't know that you're feeling groggy, you carry on throwing seemingly perfectly correct and logical blows, and you even move about, although your head has gone soaring off somewhere like an artillery shell and is spinning round and round over there with the rest of the world. And then, still spinning like a billiard ball, it comes back to its pocket, that is, to your shoulders. Your opponent is astonished when you thrash the air in a place where he no longer is, and it must be said that this astonishment or sympathy for you may often not go unpunished. You've already managed to gather your wits, your head is sitting there firmly in the netting of its pocket. And you...

The Joint Chairperson is humane. The Official even more so.

'He needs a rest. He needs sleep.'

An injection. The Face-Maker falls asleep right there in the armchair. And he doesn't hear the Joint Chairperson telling the Official about her night with the Husband and both of them hooting with laughter. It doesn't bother the Face-Maker in the slightest.

XI

What, tell me, could possibly bother the Face-Maker, the finest greyhound in the City, as he rushes around a long, long, circular road, as fine a track as any you could possibly imagine — uphill or across a ditch, downhill or across a vertical wall, and his stride is easy, his body stretches out, and every paw finds a foothold in the air, and they move the body along like oars in the water pushing along a boat. A single jump. A hop. Run on. A leap. A jump. And it doesn't matter if there is a shot to the right or to the left, and somebody's shadow has twisted in the air. Up ahead, to the side, beyond the bend there is a popping sound, a squeal, a brief struggle, then rain and more rain. His body stretches out on the air, seeming at least twice as big as the Face-Maker himself, it seems about to expand even further, and his paws shoot out ahead of him like arrows from a bow, they fly on, his belly scrapes against the air and grows hot from his speed. Speed, there is nothing in his head except speed, because he knows the condition of success is more speed, faster than speed itself, use the road to define your possibilities and ah! How well he pierced the air, how well he has leapt that ditch without even noticing it. Ahead of him around the circle almost all the days have begun to spin and fuse into a single leap, a single flight, and the only thought in his head is — faster, faster and you'll win the race, just one more circuit. Only one thought, and somewhere up ahead maybe not even one, maybe he's forgotten, maybe a barrier will appear (or maybe it won't), just like that, out of nowhere, right across the road, and then — stamp on the brakes, stop dead as if you're suddenly rooted to the ground, until they lift you out, because... but what is this 'because', what is this knowledge, this caution, when the Face-Maker can feel it — just one more effort and there it is! It really is — more speed, more, more, teeth bared, saliva flying through the rain, the goal — there it is across the road, howl! howl! and sound the horn — and that's it already, bigger and faster than he imagined it, smoothly now, even higher and more thrusting and more ineluctable — onwards to victory! And he flew on through something white, light, rising gently into his face all at once from around a bend, without even feeling the leap, or anything at all: could that really have been the barrier? Everything inside him lit up brightly in joy, it was that easy and he hadn't been expecting it, and now there was nothing left around him, everything was light, and everything was flight, only the light was somewhere there behind him now, and everything was still there ahead of him; with his paws jutting out and his triangular face with the teeth bared in a spiral along the throat on the outside of the crushed, broken animal, like a raw, fresh hide pulled inside out, his body flopped down on to the grass in the rain. And then skidded on by force of inertia, without stopping.

'It's time.' The Official is shaking the Face-Maker by the shoulder.

'Stop it.' The Face-Maker answers by rubbing his face with his hands.

And instantly the dream evaporates from his memory. Has something really been happening all this time, has it happened or not? Why is his body shattered? His hands? His fingers? As nimble and flexible as usual. That means everything's in order. That means really not a single hair on his head... That means part of the trial is already behind him, and perhaps the greater part... But could it really be the greater part? And immediately a new steel ring clicks into place in the chain of the conversation. Find out from the Official — what comes next?

'Will you go home now or shall we carry on?' What freedom, the Official has even leant down over the Face-Maker, as much as to say, whatever you wish.

'No, whatever you want to do,' the Face-Maker said, baring his teeth in a grin.

'It's really quite an easy trial, perhaps even the easiest of all,' was what the Face-Maker heard the Official say.

Well, of course he would be strong enough for an easy one. He wiped his face with a hand that he had dipped into the water and his eyes began to see more clearly. His hands touched the skin, and they began dancing such a lively dance, that if you were to put a scalpel in them...

'Well then?' The Official winked. 'Shall we get down to work? Soon there'll be real work to be done.'

There will, thought the Face-Maker. What are all your doubts by comparison with that. Yes, the Face-Maker is in no fit condition, of course, to carry on listening to every intonation in the Official's speech, to listen and compare and study it like the detailed map of the circulation of the blood in the body which he knows off by heart and which probably, even during the test for compassion, even at the most terrible moment, he could have imagined quite clearly; he even remembered that when the scalpel entered the leg he had seen in his mind's eye which muscles had been damaged and which had been destroyed. In just the same way he had heard every word and every phrase not just as certain signs possessing an external meaning, but as material for a reply to many questions, as signs of what was invisible to the eye. But now he was deaf, now all he could access was that external level of the sign, its primary meaning. Now all he heard was that there would be work to do, and that was the end of it.

What condition the Official was in, the degree of falsehood or inaccuracy in his information, the Official's attitude to him at this particular moment and his attitude to him in general, all of which only yesterday the Face-Maker would have extracted instantly from the words he heard — it was all inaccessible to him now. But then what attitude could the Official have to him? His personal attitude was one thing, and his working attitude was another. Oho, thought the Face-Maker, I may be falling a long way short in analysis and knowledge, but I still seem to be thinking in the same old way.

'An easy one? All right,' said the Face-Maker, 'I think we can manage just one more easy one for today, and then take a breather.'

XII

The Joint Chairperson sits the Face-Maker in an immense copper chair and fastens on the sensors. We've seen this before — it's the usual beginning, but then, of course, it's not entirely usual. The tall, white room is usual, but this is the first time for the copper chair with the high back and, just look, there are curtains that close right in front of the Face-Maker's nose, like in the theatre. Again he finds himself alone. Bright light. Confess, now, you were really scared when that wheezing began, and what if it had been glass again, you hate being inside glass now. But you shouldn't be thinking about such nonsense. No doubt repetitions are possible, but only on a different level. Anyway, never mind, let's try getting a bit more comfortable in this chair.

Aha, so now the Official and the Joint Chairperson have gone, we're all on our own. But then how do I know? Just because I can't see them, it doesn't mean they're not here. Think! Think! Reason. Aha, so here's a model... If I'm not here, then everything that surrounds me will not be here inside me, and if it's not here inside me, that means... To judge from my thinking technique, the effects of the shock clearly haven't passed off yet, but then, on the other hand, I can already think about the impossibility of the complete perception and analysis of the information provided by the Official. How's my brain coping now? Better... It feels like it's beginning to move, like a car starting from a standstill, like a stone falling into an abyss, like a dog from under a wheel. My hands? Wiggle those fingers, each one of them fastened tight to the armrest with a ring of copper so wide that you can still wiggle them. Still, it's not that easy.

The Face-Maker felt his fingers come away from the copper with some difficulty. It wasn't because of fatigue or cramp. Inside himself he could feel his fingers quite as well as during his very finest operations. Could everything that he had been through really in some sense help him and even prepare him to some degree to tolerate excessively heavy workloads? Perhaps there really was some wisdom in the sequence of the trials, perhaps the Official himself really was dependent on the outcome of the trial? Stop. The dog dug all four paws hard into the sand and came to a total standstill. Small blue sparks had begun passing between his fingers and the copper. No sooner did his fingers come away from the surface of the armrests than they were forced violently away from the inner surface of the rings. An invisible spring unwound from his fingers and struck him in the shoulder. His shoulder swelled up. It hurt. The Face-Maker grimaced — that was the first time he'd been hurt externally. No reaction. It hurt, but even so, it was easier than the trial for compassion. In general, it's quite useful to experience pain yourself, because afterwards, when you're fixing up your patients, you're protected against compassion by your own pain. In this case it could be regarded as payment for pain inflicted, and that's fair as well — for some reason he recalled the fact that the operations, even for those with a Name, were carried out with almost no pain-killers, so that the results would be valued all the more highly, and for half of the second and final part of the operation the face was already fully sensitive to pain. Probably it was really painful; he wondered what degree of pain he would tolerate himself, after a lifetime spent causing pain in the name of the patient's improvement. Generally speaking, almost every one of those who had acquired a name or a high-ranking number, and especially those whose naturally-given face bore little resemblance to the Image, had something in their heads, will-power, for instance, but you also needed to have a body that would tolerate repeated Operations of Likeness, and there were people who had operations almost continuously in order to keep on moving up the social order. Brrrr... What was his pain, the Face-Maker's, compared to that! A rough stone with pointed edges tumbled down the Face-Maker's shoulder into his belly. Aaaaagh — but the scream was somewhere inside, because the stone, or perhaps it was nothing but a ball of glass splinters, began revolving even faster, and the pain moved higher, into his throat, his eyes, his brain. I can't take any more — I want to keep my eyes... And externally — yet another layer of thoughts concerning the scream and the pain and the blood. The blood flows with every word, and the pain is the very simplest thing that they have in this trial. The upper layer is already soaked in blood, now it has flowed down into the lower layer, and everything down there is screaming and there are other thoughts above them, this is still not all there is, I can have more, I can have more. We've all had a name already, or perhaps we will have one, perhaps the sweat springs out on the palms of our hands when we want to listen to music... but now you can't deceive it any more, you can't weave any more spells with delirium, it's got you now, and the glass has exploded and every fragment is stuck there inside you, but thank God, after an instant it has come flying out. Now it's shaking the walls, the walls get bigger and smaller in turns, like a pendulum, the sheet of paper on the table is as big as a cathedral, and then it's no bigger than a speck of dust, and your heart is swinging to and fro beside it, and the splinters have moved over there, and so has the Mu-u-ussss... I'm not swaying, it's only the glass that's swaying back and forth like that, my eyes aren't swaying. Is he screaming? Ah, I've already screamed, you're wrong if you think that I haven't screamed, I can scream inside myself. And up here, at the beginning of my throat — all right, on my tongue — there's a small featherless fledgling, but it's not a bird. Squeeze it for me, Muse, ask someone, Muse, ask someone else quickly if you can't do it yourself. Let him squeeze it, let him hold it, let him crush my scream, let everything be wet with blood, only stop these walls from moving, I can't stand my foot growing so huge that it steps on itself, I don't want to be crushed by my own foot, ah, my bones are already crunching, stop this bird, this splinter, it's only blood and... But I thought I hadn't held out, I thought I hadn't held out, the walls came together and choked each other, the big ones and the little ones, and the sheet of paper, and the foot turned over on it, and my head cracked under my foot like a nut, where did I get such heavy feet from, very odd, that, when I walked here I moved so lightly.

Very odd, that, I walked here, and now I'm sitting here, and the final splinter's got stuck somewhere close to my throat, I have to spit it out, that's all, and then I can open my eyes. What else? There's no pain, somehow. And my fingers don't hurt. They're simply shaking. What a pity I haven't got any head. But then a smashed head is less important than my fingers. How lucky I am my fingers didn't end up under my feet and get cracked like nuts, but then they probably wouldn't have cracked like that, they'd have broken more quietly. Go to the Muse after that, and she wouldn't understand that you used to have beautiful slim fingers, so you wouldn't be able to go at all. That's interesting, now, a squashed head pronounces 'o' like 'i'. And 'f' from the side, like 'i', and all the other sounds, like a car under a heavyweight press, from the side, like 'i'. And the eyes see everything differently — a house looks like a sheet of paper, and a sheet of paper like... it doesn't see that at all. The blue sparks don't hurt at all — it's actually quite beautiful, it's even good for me in some ways. But then this trial is good for me too, this trial... stop, but you said, thoughts covered in blood. This is a trial in blood, and it's not over yet. They promised you it would be easy, and now you can see it really is. Ah, you idiot, and you were so nervous about it, as if there wouldn't be anything more difficult than this, as though everything would come to an end and there wouldn't be anything at all any more. There will be. And it will never come to an end. The trial is endless and eternal, just like work. Hang on there, a trial for work? Yes! And eternal? His deliberations entered a layer which contained the knowledge that this was still not pain and the thought of blood, as though the bloody rag had rung itself out and turned pink — of course, you fool, first the trial, and then work. And then work. A trial for work.

XIII

'You're looking well.'

The Face-Maker hadn't noticed the curtains parting. He hadn't noticed? The sheet of paper trembles, it's not moving, but it's only half at rest.

'Your four hours are up and you look just fine. Of course,' — the Official shook his head and pursed his lips — 'I have to tell you that you were right at the lower limit of the norm. The only thing that evens things up a bit for you is the fact that you came out of the trial yourself, which is something even you haven't managed before. And so, you were saying you're ready for the next one, there's only...'

'I want to go home.'

'Home? Now just you listen to me, there's no question of going home at this stage, we're all in a hurry and everybody wants to get this over with. I'll tell you all about it later, as a friend.'

'As a friend,' the Face-Maker smiled heavily, like a corpse, 'perhaps, as a friend, you'll take my place in this chair?'

Then the Official explained to him as though he was a child that even if he did take his place, that wouldn't change a thing, because it was the Face-Maker who had to do the work, not the Official. With his capabilities and professional experience what he should be doing was getting on with his own job, and if the Face-Maker was interested to know whether he'd ever received a dose of these sweet pleasures, then yes, he had! And it was hard to say whose figures were higher, although, of course, that had been a rather different kind of trial, it had been more psychological in nature, but then, who could say what kind of pain was the worse, moral or physical, and he, the Official, couldn't understand, that's right, he couldn't understand the Face-Maker's tone or what he was saying. And if tomorrow it turned out that he could help the Face-Maker and take his place in one of these trials, then he, the Official (the Official pulled himself up to his full height and seemed to change into someone the Face-Maker didn't recognize) would certainly sit in that chair — and then he laughed: I'm joking, I'm joking. I won't sit in it, except perhaps for the sake of friendship. See what an act I've just put on, I'm just playing the fool. But you note that the Official has stuck close beside the Face-Maker all these days and has no intention of leaving, even though he, the Official, has a lot of things to deal with, even on an ordinary day. He has no intention of leaving and he's going to spend the entire trial here with him, the Face-Maker, and by the way, one of those who were tried to the limit and thanks to whom the Face-Maker can now chat with him, the Official, and ask to go home, without bothering to wonder how many lives his success and his salvation today had cost — one of those people, who no longer exist, was a genuine friend — yes, yes, a friend of his, the Official's, to whom he owed this very face (the Official's finger prodded cautiously at the skin of the cheek slightly below the right eye) and his name. And he, the Official, owed his friend much more in his life than he owed the Face-Maker, and he should have been there to see the last few seconds of his friend's life, and at least lend him a glance of support, if not halt the trial, but!.. He had stayed here with the Face-Maker, and not because the Face-Maker was dearer to him than his friend, but because the truth was dearer to him, and today the truth and the Face-Maker were one and the same. And perhaps he was suffering in his heart just as much as any other man, perhaps in his heart he was still a man too.

The Official lowered his eyes and the corners of his lips and grunted like a piglet, and a single tear crept down across his cheek and fell to the floor. Strange, thought the Face-Maker — it fell on the floor but it didn't burn through it. The blue sparks touched his hand again. He didn't even flinch.

'You're talking me round again.'

'It's just that we have to hurry.' The Official dried his eyes, for at this moment his eyes had swollen up and another drop had fallen, like water dripping into a toilet bowl.

'I want to go home.'

The Joint Chairperson pressed herself very hard against the Face-Maker and unfastened a sensor. The Face-Maker stood up himself, and he felt infinitely light, so light he could probably have flown — he had no body at all. He set down his right foot, the one he had crushed himself with, and flinched at his own thought. His leg was trembling, and so was the other, but it felt light, like a broken arm when the plaster is removed, lighter than the other one.

'Take me home.'

The Official gestured hopelessly. The Joint Chairperson brought cloaks for herself and the Face-Maker.

And then his consciousness was abruptly switched off. When the Face-Maker came round, he saw that he was lying in a strange room and the Joint Chairperson was sitting opposite him in an armchair and watching him. She was wearing nothing but a dressing-gown. He looked at her, then at himself...

'Did we do it together?' the Face-Maker half-asked, half-stated.

She shook her head:

'In the state you're in, people die, they don't sleep with anyone.'

Then the Face-Maker tried to pull the blanket up over him, and with her help he managed it.

'If we had, you wouldn't be pulling up the blanket now.'

'I wouldn't be pulling up the blanket,' said the Face-Maker, 'and you fasten your robe and close your legs.'

'Anyone would think I excite you. At the Commission every one of your female patients has told me that when you lean down and press your chest against her on the table she starts to go wild, and there's no need for any anesthetic, but you always act as though you were made of wood.'

'D'you think I don't know all about that? But when a woman's aroused she forgets about pain and she doesn't get in the way of my work.'

'I wouldn't get in your way either.' She dropped her dressing-gown to the floor. It lay there at her feet, and it looked as though she wasn't standing on the floor, but had risen above it, and she might fly away altogether, and she had to be held.

'In order to make love, I have to feel love.'

'That's all very fine for you, you have a fine life altogether. Unfortunately, the most I can count on is sleeping with someone just for the sake of it. I'm sorry.' She bent down to the floor, pulled on her dressing-gown and fastened it. 'I simply didn't know that your heart is so pure and virginal: it's like goat's shit that's been lying in the sun for a week, like a knife with the blood of the murdered man wiped away, like a gob of spittle that's been spread across a face. A thick scum for which everything is going well and which can make love, so it seems, only if it loves, and then exceptionally, and will never permit itself to lower its face to a face lifted up to it. What do you know about us here, who spend the night slaving away after the nightmare of the day, watching souls and bodies twitching in agony before your eyes, when the foam covers the lips and the arms break and the tears and the blood come out with the eyes and fall on your eyes in the darkness, flow into your mouth and trickle across your belly and your arms, and you twitch together with them, and it goes on not just for a day or an hour or a night, but for all your life, and in the meantime you're rocking your well-adjusted spinal column regularly backwards and forwards — go on living in your repulsive state of holiness. It's a pity we have to take care of you, or I'd be the first to stick a piece of rusty old iron into you, not into female One Hundred and Five, but into you, like a knife into a rubber ball, with my own hand and then twist it there with both hands, so that at least once the blood would come gurgling out of you, and the life with it, and you'd die slowly — the way people die when they've been badly beaten and then dumped somewhere, unable to do anything about it.' While she was speaking her eyes opened wide and large and then they began to spin, as though someone was waving a torch in circles right under his nose, and there was a smell of burning wool and scorched flesh.

The Face-Maker trembles violently, his pain returns, the pieces of glass come flying out of his skin and they scratch the hand clutching at his heart, the floor has turned upside down, and the earth has followed it — and now the Face-Maker is falling upwards, clutching at the door-handle, and overcame by fear at the thought that he might not be able to hold on. The Face-Maker pulls the handle towards himself as hard as he can, and his hands rip off...

The blanket has been thrown off on to the floor. She is lying beside him.

'If only you knew how wonderful you are. if only you knew how wonderful you really are,' — and the Joint Chairperson weeps and weeps, and she caresses the Face-Maker with her strong, sensitive fingers.

Now the Face-Maker is flying again, in order to come to his sense in his own bed and not know whether anything happened or it didn't. Because he's dressed and he's lying here, in his own bed. The Muse isn't here yet. She's at work. But how does he know that she's at work? How does he know that She's at work? The question is asked in turn by the Husband and the Wife, standing there in front of him, and the Official and the Joint Chairperson, and the Chairman asks disapprovingly:

'But how do you know that she's still at work?'

'I don't know,' the Face-Maker confesses quite sincerely, 'I haven't got the slightest idea. I know that...' Stop, stop, stop. What about the trial? They haven't told him anything about the result, have they? He goes back to the office himself. After feeling lost for a while, he manages to find the door he entered the first time. Inside it's quiet, there's nobody there. But then, out from behind the curtain, the white curtain, a woman appears. She knows, of course, why he's come. She asks him to calm down. She'll tell him everything. They warned her that he was bound to come back. The results of the trial were within the normal range, except that it was ended by his deliberate return to consciousness, but he already knows that, because they've already told him. And the Face-Maker is surprised that she knows all of this so well. Perhaps he really has been told everything already, for instance, the fact that the Muse is still at work.

'Didn't they tell you about where I'd been after the laboratory: at home, at my place or somewhere else?' The Face-Maker watches her face, as though he's thrown a stone into water, to see whether there will be any rings on the surface or not. If he's thrown it into a bog, there won't be any. Not a single ring. Not a single excess sound.

'At home.'

'Thank God for that.'

He believes her, but perhaps that's because he wants to believe her. Okay. He stood the test, and that's more important than anything else. It's not worth spending the rest of his life wondering whether he slept with that woman or not. He stood the test, and that's the certain truth. But why does he think he stood it? He didn't really do too brilliantly, if he had, his heart would ache differently. Differently? Wait, what data have you got on what happened? Memory. But why couldn't it be a dream? So she removed the sensors, and she pressed herself against me harder than usual, or perhaps I imagined it and all the rest is nothing but a dream too. But is the other version possible? It is. The wall sways, It sways again. God preserve us from not knowing something. But what do you need to know for? Simply in order to know what really happened and what is happening.

XIV

Today the Joint Chairperson wouldn't even see the Husband. The Muse came home a little later than usual. But one event has nothing to do with the other. The Face-Maker also came home, in the company of a female laboratory assistant. He could hardly make it. He went straight to bed and was half-delirious again. He half-slept, and the Muse walked around quietly, looking at him in a way that was new.

Maybe I should give it all up, thinks the Face-Maker. Move back down out of the Great Ones to my old name. But no, not now I'm already on the way. You can't stop a landslide half-way down the mountain. Or maybe you can stop it, and you can choose a different mountain. Go on then, choose one. But for me it's not simply a mountain, it's the only mountain. It's the reason I'm alive. And instantly there was no more delirium.

'I don't want anything else.' The face is fierce, harsh and sinewy. The Face-Maker has never called out in his sleep before.

'Hush, hush.' The Muse stops him. 'I'm not arguing with you. You said yourself that whoever suffers is right. You're suffering. That's the main thing, and everything else has to be measured against that. And against the fact that we have seventeen years of life together behind us. The fact that you're suffering is in one pan of the scales, and the seventeen years are in the other. Or the other way round, the fact that you don't suffer is weighed against the seventeen years, and whatever is heavier, more important, more enduring is the truth. And no word means a thing if it is smaller than life and less real than life.'

The Face-Maker grows calmer and forgets that a moment ago his face was not the Face-Maker's face, but his brain has already been wound up and it needs movement, and he begins thinking to himself about their seventeen years, now that they've been tossed into his thoughts and they're jutting out there as obvious as a wall right in front of your eyes, as obvious as a vast moat in front of a horse, as obvious as a flame in front of a moth, and the Face-Maker's thoughts halt in front of this wall and start running on the spot, like the wheels of a truck that's stuck in the mud, you take stock of the situation, then take a break, take stock, take a break and then step on the gas again, and the lumps of mud go flying out from under the wheels, and the truck sinks lower and lower, until you can hardly see the ribbed black rings whirling around underneath there, and there are hardly any more lumps of mud, and the truck seems completely motionless, even though inside everything's humming and whirring, and there's more energy being spent than on running along at top speed. But it doesn't budge, and there's so much energy being wasted, and the wheels of his thoughts carry on spinning.

XV

My Muse, you were faithful to me when I had nothing, no skill, no experience, no ability, when I was still a student trying to learn what can never be learned. You told me then that you were right and I shouldn't study. But I learned what could not be learned, and you said that you had been wrong. You were faithful to me when I forgot about you, when I stopped thinking that I was living to serve you, that everything I did was only for you, not for others, not in the name of some idea I had invented, not in the name of the salvation of these little people. I killed myself within myself in order to serve you, but it didn't happen straight away. You were faithful to me when I lost my way and forgot that people really do need help, that people really are waiting for the appearance of the one who will save them, and they believe that there is some power on earth that can change everybody's life some time. I hadn't realized that yesterday's experience of error makes them no longer capable of believing even in the truth; they're right, you can kill a lot of people and a lot of things, but you can only believe in resurrection once, and that's already happened, and they don't believe in it any more. What should I do, I wondered. If people don't need you and if you don't believe in what can help them, or you believe that it will only help for a certain time — two thousand years or a century — and then everything will be confusion and chaos again. And then I thought up a funny little idea: I hid the most important thing away inside myself and, no longer hoping ever to reveal it to the human race, I began to serve you, the Muse. Perhaps when they saw you, the people might understand something, perhaps one happy person means far more than any words about happiness, perhaps one person who has found peace means far more than any words about peace; and I began to think that this was the truth. Be faithful to me, Muse, or else how shall I help people if I can't save humanity through you!

The Face-Maker said all this to the Muse because what was happening to him today was making him feel like a beast facing a row of yawning pits that had just been uncovered in front of him, with sharpened stakes thrust into their bottoms, and a row of traps with their jaws gaping wide and sprung ready to close, and crossbows pointed at his face and wire nooses curled up in the grass like snakes. All of this could be seen, it was all separate from him — and it could all be avoided and overcome. But the trouble was that this was the path that had to be followed, and there was no way the beast could fly over it through the air, all he could do was to shout to those following behind him: 'Turn back, go and cut down the trees, but don't follow me'. Or he could bar the way of those who were following and fight them, in order to turn them aside from the road, because the gaping pits had not been opened for them yet, and the rainbow-shaped cross-bows had still not been set up for them. The Face-Maker revealed all this to the Muse, because tomorrow he might not be able to say what he had said to himself, or say why he was crying the way people who are bound hand and foot cry over a child which is being worried by a dog, when all that's needed is a good kick to make it creep away, baring the teeth in its mad muzzle. Any day, and therefore any trial, held power over him as well. All these endless weekdays that tugged at him the way hungry wolves tug at a living bird, and the spine cracks and the feathers fly and at any moment the torn-off head will cover the eyes behind the clenched jaws like a shroud, and the body will give a final couple of flaps with its wings and become still between the teeth. But he's still alive, still alive, and so much is behind him now! Not simply a lot, it's an entire piece of life, the usual — or almost usual — life of an inhabitant of the City. Perhaps he isn't a bird at all, but a worm who has been set on a hook and is not twisting and squirming because of the metal point inside him, but out of his concern for humanity, his understanding of its woes, because humanity itself is squirming on a bent spike, and it can see how it's tormenting its own like — by squirming itself and simply by being humanity itself. His thoughts tried to change direction, like a herd of stampeding sheep at the edge of a precipice, with the ones behind pressing the others on, but ahead there is the void, and the ones at the front, the ones who have nowhere to go, manage to hold out on the edge of the precipice, and they turn and run along the edge at the same speed, at the risk of tumbling in and down at every step.

Of course, he wasn't a bird and he wasn't caught on teeth that were about to close, he was a worm, a smooth, slithering, obsequious, repulsive creature, and if you pulled him apart you'd get your hands covered in shit, if you ripped open this huge white, fat, spongy body from the top of the head to the tip of the tail, although how can you tell where the head is and where the tail is without bending down close to this huge trunk of a body, let it croak there if it can't set itself free. That idiotic babbling about the Muse — that was all from facing that electric chair every day, from having nothing to breathe every day, from seeing scalpels pushed into eyes every day so that the blood gushed out into a red wall-eye, like a geyser, like oil gushing up out of the ground into your face, into your eyes. Agh, you can't see, and you go back to the electric chair again, because you're obsessed with the idea of creating a new face that will save the world. All lies. Pharisaic jesuitry, and you know it. Take the Muse by the legs and smash her head against the wall, And then smash your own brains out against the same wall, so that they run down the surface, more beautiful than all the marble in the world, for brains are beautiful, they are the worlds of the stars if you look at them through huge lenses. Where are you, saviour, protect this worm, unhook him, put him gently to bed, say that I am losing my way and that I don't understand anything about pain. Pain is noble and things have always been like this and they will never be any different. There will only be this fire, this splendid curved hook and this fish that will swallow the barbed hook, and then a man will rip out the hook and eat the fish, and distribute the left-over and feed humanity, and in their gratitude they will crucify him, exalting him above themselves, and they will be saved by their sin. Worm. Hook. Fish. Man. Crucifixion and then the worm again. That is the entirety of history, and there has never been anything else, do you hear, you worm that looks as much like a Face-Maker as rain is like water, as much as an icicle dripping from the roof is like water. As much as fresh steam is like water. Oh Lord... What is the point of all this passion, if soon it will be morning again and the trial again. And nothing will change in anybody's soul, except perhaps that life will be a little kinder to others, think, think now... you little fool, you need the hook too, as if you were any different from the others.

XVI

Once again the Muse calmed him, for what he was saying was merely fatigue and the need for confession, the need to cry out his pain, to scream it out, the need for liberation, and that is not the only truth in a man, there is also work and its faithfulness, there is tomorrow, when it will be possible to do that for which the Face-Maker has carved out his path and followed it, and though he may not have done it yet, and though time may propose the form that exists within him, the Face-Maker, or it may never happen at all, today at least, she, the Muse, is with him, and today she believes that his time on God's earth has not been wasted, and it was not mere chance that brought their lives together. The Muse speaks in such a way that he doesn't have to answer her, and he can close his eyes and listen to her, resting his over-wound brain, and he comes slowly to a halt, like a top in which the movement is becoming exhausted, like sheep that have unexpectedly exhausted their running. And putting his arms round the Muse and turning her back to him, the Face-Maker begins to fall asleep.

XVII

The streets are deserted at this hour, as though the rain has washed away every living soul and every step rings hollowly, like a single blow on a bell. The copper boot-tips clink against the granite, and the granite rings inside itself, but outside the rain rings even louder, faster than the eye can follow it smashes against the stone and goes swirling away into the stream. Ah, the rain of the recent changes has been thicker and denser, it's harder to breathe now. The Official never used to feel that it was hard simply to walk along the street and breathe, but now he can feel it in himself. How man times in the night, since he became the Official, has he taken his own woman, his own partner, through Trial and Departure so that h wouldn't be dependent on anyone else and wouldn't be weak through her, so that she wouldn't get in his way at night when he thrashed about in his bed (that came with the name — screaming and choking in his sleep and waking at the sound of his own scream) — so that he could wake up calmly and there'd be nobody there, and he wouldn have to explain anything to anyone, something that he mustn't explai but which he couldn't refuse to explain either: how many times in the night had he wandered like this along these streets, but it seemed to him that the rain on them used to be quieter then. Or perhaps inwardly the Official used to be calmer and simpler, and he could hear the sound of his steps more clearly in the night, and he used to relax, the only person in the entire City with the right to walk the streets whenever the fancy took him

Once there was a man who, during the first half of his life, when he was happy, used to come to a room in a house and stay there until the calm and the tenderness in his soul had melted and trickled out and settled on the walls of the room, so that it was comfortable, beautiful and quiet. And then during the second half of his life the man would come back to this same place when things were difficult and he was struggling, and the room would heal him and return what it had borrowed from him, and in returning it, the room saved him. That was how the Official had calmed and comforted himself during these nights — but now the scythe had run across a stone. There was no more peace in the night of the City; the rain and the quiet and the steps were all the same, but there was no peace. After the Choice everything had shifted places, as though he had disturbed some invisible equilibrium, but where and how he couldn't tell. Maybe he should call on some old friends, wake up one of those who had survived, some female One Hundred and Two, press himself against her and then go to sleep? Then see the wheel start to turn the grindstone, and the sparks fly from the knife, always more and more of them, until the steel is about to come to an end and there's no more point in the stone whirling round, and now his hand's tired — the stone splits in two and the knife flies off to one side. The rain quenches the steel, and it hisses, and is covered in a blue sheen, and then his foot kicks the stone into the water, so that the flood will carry away the fragments... and his soul is barren and dead.

There is no need to go anywhere in order to avoid feeling even a moment's dependence on your weary longing and your former human attraction to living beings. The noise of the rain returned, it began drumming against his cloak as though it was knocking at a door, stronger and louder, more and more of it. And what does the rain care whether the cloak covers the Official, and whether he is the first citizen of the City, or whether every single inhabitant of the City depends on him — it lashes at his back, at his face, flowing as indifferently down his body, as it flows down the walls of the houses and the palace, as indifferently as it flows down the walls of the canals and along their channels and through the City, out there beyond its limits. The water is green and yellow. The Official thrust his hand into the water, and it burnt him. Of course, all that work. The canals were full. The water flowed along almost up to the very edge, on a level with the pavement. And still more work lay ahead.

The Commission was working round the clock. The laboratory assistant dipped his hand in some solution and the pain eased. The Official himself became calmer as well, in some ways that kind of pain was convenient, it was probably even a better distraction than a woman. The Official stood up and put his arm round the back of female Fifty-Five, the same hand that had held the whetstone for the knife, he remembered and chuckled briefly: there she stood before him, all his, to the very tips of her fingers and toes, by right of duty and friendship, and she didn't know what to do. Sometimes the Official would caress her, and sometimes he would look at her, give a chuckle and strike her a swinging blow, not too hard, so she wouldn't actually fall. She stands there, not knowing what to expect today. But it's alright, he doesn't hit her, he doesn't caress her, his mouth just twists into a grin, like a pair of a rusty doors that have crept apart — off you go. And she goes back to the chair at her desk, to doze until the morning — she might have as much as an hour left before the beginning of the Face-Maker's next trial.

XVIII

An hour before the trial the Face-Maker is sleeping and dreaming that he can't wake up, and he's struggling and hammering on the door and beating his head against it, because he has to wake up, and he only forgot for an instant how it's done. But any moment now he'll remember the secret, it was just the resistance of life that made him forget everything. And he has to wake up, he absolutely has to, because he might be late for the Commission, and he won't be in time for his trial, and he'll never find out what comes next. But the Muse has already woken up and jumped to her feet. She watches him threshing and flailing as he tries to wake up, and then she tries to wake him, and she slaps his cheeks and pours water on him, and they've already come for him, and the Face-Maker struggles even harder out of his sleep towards the Muse. Now the Muse and the man who has come for him shake the Face-Maker together. Anything but that, don't let the Face-Maker become ill with sleep, or everything, absolutely everything will have been in vain — herself, and their success, and life — don't let him fall ill like that. The Muse kneels in front of him and weeps, but the Face-Maker is already snoring, he's already squirming like a worm cut in half, as though any moment he'll join himself back together again. Another shudder, then another, stronger this time — wake up from that accursed sleep! But there's nothing he can do. He just keeps on squirming inside and outside. The Muse stopped and wiped the tears from her eyes, and sent out the man who came for the Face-Maker. She lay down beside the Face-Maker and held him tightly in her arms, and first she began squirming together with him on the floor, and then she gained control of him and imperceptibly, invisibly, they grew still. She began kissing him when his body stopped moving, and she began caressing him, as the Face-Maker had often caressed her, she began speaking to him in the same incomprehensible fashion the Face-Maker used to talk to her.

'If you're standing in your own way, throw your body to the dogs, they could use a piece of willing meat.

'And then carry on along your way.

'If the road runs into a blank wall, don't argue with the wall, break your body indifferently against the stone.

'And then carry on along your way.

'If the earth crumbles beneath your feet and the wind scatters your shattered body with the earth, submit to his power.

'And then carry on along your way.

'If you're standing in your own way...'

The Face-Maker heard the familiar words as they squeezed themselves crookedly into his dream and tied their meaning in crooked knots before they settled down in his head like a dog that has found a home, like a cat after its long time away in March.

The Face-Maker woke up, and realized that the door in front of him was not a door, but a wall that only looked like a door, no point in charging it with your shoulder or beating your head against it, just take a step to the right or a step to the left, or turn back — and you're free. And the Face-Maker saw that he was not the only one standing facing this stretch of wall that might be taken for a door, and he shouted: move aside, the way out's close by. And nobody listened to him, because the people were deaf.

'But look, it's a wall!' he shouted for a second time, and he began dragging away the people standing close to him, and then he saw that each of the people standing there was clinging tight to his own door, because they were afraid of the void and of freedom, and the Face-Maker was unable to tear them away, and when he turned and walked away, the Face-Maker could still hear the dull blows of shoulders against the wall. That was exactly how he would have gone on battering against the wall for the rest of his life, if not for the Muse. He took a step to the side.

The Face-Maker was five minutes late for work. But nobody reproached him for such a tiny transgression, which might have cost another person Departure. Only when he arrived, the Official was shuddering with tension. The Official was in a hurry. The Official knew something the others didn't. The Official knew what the deadline was, and it was tomorrow.

Chapter Three

The Operation

I

Tomorrow — that means all the time in the world. Tomorrow is a whole day and a whole night, there's a whole lifetime before tomorrow, there's enough time to die before tomorrow. But on the other hand, no matter how much you cram into one day, it still passes, leaving behind it as much done as would fill some people's entire lives. Only don't think that if there's not much time you can skimp on something, or miss something out, you won't be able to explain afterwards that when you were building the house there was no time for the roof. People have to live, and with or without sleep, you put all you have into that house and spend all your energies, all your life if necessary, but give them a house with a roof, and on time, with doors that don't squeak and wake them from their sleep, so that they can sleep soundly. Let the rain keep on pouring down, but at least in your own home there must be a roof to keep you dry.

The Face-Maker and the Official managed things in time, without skimping, they did it all. One used the other to get it done, and the other just did it for himself. Everything living in the Face-Maker has been sponged away, he stands now with clear, calm eyes, his hands precisely controlled and no longer trembling, the light shines above him, the scalpel in his hands is absolutely still, as though held not by fingers, but in a vice, and the vice is attached to a work-bench, and the bench has rooted itself in the earth and spins round with it.

He-Who-Stands-Over-All lies there before the Face-Maker on the table. The body up to the chest is hidden from sight beneath a white cloth, only the head is visible. What it is really like is hard to say, there is nothing to compare it with — in all his life the Face-

Maker has never seen a head or a face like it. It seems to be larger than any human head, and the face cannot be compared with anything at all, it's not even a face, nothing more than the material for a face, inflated and swollen, as though it's not an operation that's needed, but the creation of an entirely new face. If he had seen it before the trial, the Face-Maker would have gone mad at the very thought of it, seized the semblance of a door and clung there so that not even the Muse would have had the strength to pull him from it, but now — put a god in front of him, and he'll raise his scalpel and calmly carve out everything that's required and possible, from A to Z.

However, decisiveness and preparedness are all very well, but the Face-Maker lacks knowledge, and therefore he is careful. An incision from above. Slowly. Not too deep. What on earth was this? He had only made the one line, and only removed two squares of skin, but the material of the face already looked different to him, he had caught a glimpse of something indefinable but familiar. The Face-Maker bent his head down closer, and it all disappeared again. Another incision, there where the eye should be, one square up — it was amazing, a cornea appeared under his scalpel and then disappeared again when he withdrew the blade. Careful. More careful still. Forceps. Incision. The corner's lifted, there it is, a cornea. Very good, now the next square, a little higher — that's enough. That's already an eyelid. Now a square lower. The Face-Maker is not there, he is entirely focused on the tip of the blade. Amazing — he got the eye at the first try. That's real luck. Gently. A crack opened in the face, and the Face-Maker thought that some words emerged — what were they? He didn't recognize them, but he understood their meaning. A break was needed. The Face-Maker felt as though he had only just begun, and he could go on working without a break, and right now, the very next minute, he could do something really important, the most important thing of all. But in such matters He-Who-Lay-Before-Him remained He-Who-Stands-Over-All even at a moment like this. The Face-Maker moved away and carefully put down his scalpel. He attempted to recall the words he had heard and couldn't remember a single one. And he immediately felt that he was tired, that yesterday was still not over, that he had passed its boundary physically, but his soul, his thoughts, his sensations and feelings were still back there, where today would only come tomorrow, and only tomorrow would he take up his scalpel and approach Him-Who-Stands-Over-All and make his first incision.

Your real life is where you need to be most badly, most importantly, but externally you live where you walk, where you work, where you talk, where you are bound by obligations and the cares of the world. The Face-Maker sits in an armchair with his legs stretched out, his feet set like the hands on a weighing scale, repeatedly coming together and separating. And his face is calm, and his hands are still, and his feelings are there, in yesterday, which is actually today.

II

It was raining, and the field was infinite and empty as a marble wall, and the line of the horizon could not be seen, so that the Face-Maker didn't immediately realize that he didn't know which way to go, and that he had nothing to cover himself with, and he was hungry. At first he had the sensation that his body felt the rain differently, that his fingers had stopped feeling water, and his legs could scarcely support his body, it was too heavy for them — the way a man who has set an excessive load on his back walks along on yielding legs, realizing that in a few more metres he will have to set his load down, and there is no one around to help him raise it back on to his shoulders, and this load is his very life. But the greater part of the road was now behind him, he could breathe here, no one bothered him here, and ahead lay work and the Muse. And again the Face-Maker dragged himself along, through the pathless field, forwards.

But everything comes to an end, even strength and desire and limits. Even those who play games, hanging over a precipice, first by two hands, in order to astound their companions with their fearlessness, then by one hand, and then removing the four fingers one by one —even they reach a limit beyond which they don't have the strength to replace their fingers on the rough warmth of the stone, and they go hurtling downwards, aware for just one instant — between the sensation of intrepid security and their fall — of their own majesty and immortality. But the Face-Maker was not playing games, and therefore the one hand still voluntarily holding up his body continued to serve him, when from lying on the sour, newly ploughed earth in the soaking water and mud, he raised himself to look, not forward this time, but around.

He saw that he was not alone: women, children, old men and men with bodies like children's — their faces identically shriveled, their eyes identically hungry and defenseless — were floundering in the sloppy mess. They recognized the Face-Maker, and they all came crawling over to him. Closest of all came an old woman, and she looked at him with her dead, sightless wall-eyes, and ran her dead, cold fingers over him, raised her blank eyes to the sky and said indifferently. 'It's Him.' They were all overjoyed, the way someone with a slashed belly might be overjoyed at being shown a healthy, pink-bodied child. Then the surface of the field floundered about once more, an old man appeared beside the Face-Maker and held out to him some bread and meat wrapped in a rag.

'Here, eat,' said the old man, 'we've been waiting for you, we believed in you, and now you have come to us.'

The Face-Maker looked around, and saw the wild eyes of the children watching the bread and meat with tears running down their old, wrinkled faces, and the Face-Maker shook his head, even though he was already sitting on the ground holding the bread and meat, with his head raised to the sky, trying to catch the flowing water to assuage his thirst. Having spent all his life in ceaseless rain, it was only here that he realized what a blessing it is, and he was horrified to think he could have forgotten that rain is water. The Face-Maker shook his head once again and said:

'Your children are hungry, and you yourselves have nothing to eat.' He could not take the last scrap of food from people who were dying of hunger.

'...And cold,' the old man said to him, and he pulled the oilcloth from his own shoulders and held it out to the Face-Maker. 'We knew that you must appear among us, and we prepared food and clothing for you. Do not look at us, at our eyes and our bodies and our children, you must go on further, to a place to which we know the road and will never be able to reach, but if you take everything that we have, then you will reach it.'

'Do not deceive us, you have to go,' said the old woman, and she fixed him once again with her blank eyes, and he saw the joy in that face.

'But you'll die here, and I won't be able to help you.'

'Yes, yes, we'll die here, and you won't be able to help us, but you'll get there, and we'll get there in you, and that is very important to us. Perhaps even more important than getting there ourselves.'

'But I can't,' said the Face-Maker.

'If we're bothering you, we'll crawl away, but we want so much to eat what you hold in your hands, even if only through you — we saved it for you.'

Never, in any way, was the Face-Maker able to explain to anybody why he did as they asked. But sitting in the rain, watched by the people who surrounded him, he ate and cried, and the rain and the tears mingled on his cheeks and flowed down on to the earth. The Face-Maker could see the children dying as their mothers held them in their arms, he could see the mothers dying before his eyes, and he saw that the old woman with the wall-eyes, who had been so happy at his coming, was a young girl, and the old man who had promised them the Face-Maker would come, the only one who had known the time of his coming and known that it was inevitable, was still a youth.

'But I will not save you,' said the Face-Maker to the youth.

'You will not save us,' said the youth to the Face-Maker, 'but you will see those who will surround you at your destination with different eyes. You will understand this, and so will they, and you will not have to tell them everything — they will change and they will be happier than us for us.'

As the Face-Maker left, the black field was still floundering in the streaming rain, and several hands were raised in the air to wave him farewell, and one hand was motionless, pointing the direction in which the Face-Maker was walking. What he had seen, and the bread and the meat, gave the Face-Maker new life, and his legs bore him along firmly and quickly, ahead of him instead of empty space he saw the eyes of children watching his hands as they held the bread and meat and watching his mouth moving as it chewed the soaking bread and the tender meat. And something began changing in the man's soul, and his eyes gazed more keenly in response, because he was beginning to see the earth with their eyes, and many eyes see further and see more than the very finest couple.

III

He saw a green meadow ahead of him, where the rain came to an end. The sun shone there, and he saw the beautiful clothes on the men and women, and he saw the beasts playing with them peacefully, and the Face-Maker began to walk more quickly, because he hadn't gone all that far, and he could ask these people to help their brothers who were still out there in the rain in the ploughed field. The Face-Maker was almost running, if a man can run uphill over sharp stones or up a sheer cliff-face. They grew closer all the time, and the Face-Maker had already prepared the words which would gather the people together, and then, having collected a lot of bread and warm clothing, they would go to those who had sent him, and their waiting and their faith and his coming would not have been in vain.

The Face-Maker drew closer and became convinced that his eyes had scarcely deceived him at all: the women were young and lovely, the men were nimble and strongly-built, and the beasts were large, powerful thoroughbreds. But there was one thing that the Face-Maker had not seen from a distance: the beasts were not playing with the people, they were eating them, and what had seemed a game from a distance, turned out to be killing. One beast, noticing the new arrival, dashed up to him, licking up its hind legs in a funny manner, and curving its velvety spotted back, and he caught a glimpse of a white dress rushing to head it off.

'Muse!' cried out the Face-Maker.

The woman looked at him, and then the Face-Maker saw that it wasn't the Muse at all, but he saw that she was the one he needed and she was more lovely than the Muse. He realized this was his destiny and he had been making his way here to her, and the people in the black field had died for her sake, in order to save him, the Face-Maker. He rushed towards the woman, but before he could reach her the beast broke her back with a blow of its paw and with professional skill snipped off her head with two movements of its fangs, and tumbled it along in front of itself, kicking up its spotted, velvety, rounded hind quarters in a funny fashion. The body continued writhing on the green grass, and red spots appeared on the white dress, and the Face-Maker ran over to her and put his arms around her, and then the body grew quiet in his embrace, it grew calm and was still. Then the Face-Maker raised a heavy stone over his head and threw himself on the beasts, and when the beasts left their terrible games and, nipping each other playfully, dashed off into the grove of trees standing on the edge of the field, the Face-Maker realized that these were only the beasts' children — funny, jolly, good-natured and pitiless in their naivety, like all children. And the Face-Maker also realized that there was no one he could summon to the help of those who were left in the black field. For a long time he laboured with his hands, his nails and a sharp stone to dig a deep pit, in order to place in it the bodies that lay in the field and cover them over with earth, together with their heads. The last one the Face-Maker put in was his destiny — he had not been able to match her head to her body. The beasts were probably herbivores, they didn't feed on human flesh, the killing was mere amusement for them. The mound of earth rose up, and the Face-Maker evened it off into a regular square, like the House. He finished his work, then pressed his lips to the earth, took his leave of her, rose and went on. And in his eyes the eyes of the black field were joined by the eyes of the green meadow and the eyes of his only beloved, whom he had seen and loved for only an instant. And the flesh of her body, was now living in his body. But this was only the beginning of the road, and it was paradise in comparison with what he saw further on.

IV

And it was truly like paradise when the Face-Maker finally reached his own city and began to knock at the doors of the houses in which his patients lived, those who owed him their future and their present, and they came out on to the street without fear of the rain or the law against congregating, and they were kind, and they nodded their heads in response to his requests for help for those who were back there in the black field, and they picked him up, probably to help him, and all together in friendly silence carried him off to the square before the House. Yes, yes, they agreed with him, they had to go now, straight away. They looked at him tenderly, the women stroked his hair, the men held the wings of their cloaks over him, because the Face-Maker was wearing a pitiful oil-cloth which scarcely covered him against the rain, and while his patients were agreeing that the Face-Maker's wishes were correct, and expressing their admiration at his nobility, some of them had already been into the House and brought out a huge roll of cloth for cloaks. They stretched out the cloth high in the air on four pillars, and immediately there was no more rain above them, it fell to the right and to the left, in front and behind, but where the patients and the Face-Maker were it was dry, and the Face-Maker thought that this was prudent foresight, and the awning would be useful for the people his patients would carry back from the black field in their strong arms. He was overjoyed that the salvation of those who had sent him was already beginning. He smiled and wiped the water from his hair, pressing his fingers close in to the back of his neck, and the water streamed down his face, and his eyes saw clearly, and then the Face-Maker saw that he was surrounded by the lumber that he had once seen in the basement of the House —fragments of old armchairs, chairs, tables, gilded frames — and they soaked all this with a thick black liquid with an unpleasant smell that stung his nose, and his patients were already standing on each other's shoulders and raising up the Face-Maker higher and higher, and there, high in the air, they bound the Face-Maker as tight as could be to a stone pillar, with ropes damp from the rain. Stone has no fear of fire, neither do wet ropes — for a while. They bound him there so that he would not fall, so that he might see everything around him for as far as possible, and then, having fulfilled their task of kindness and justice, they left him — for what sense was there in dragging themselves off to save people like themselves, at the risk of their own death. And so that he wouldn't embarrass people, the pile was ignited down below, the fire flapped its wings and hid the Face-Maker and the lumber from sight, and the black soot began to stain the centre of the awning, and it instantly disappeared where the flame struck it, and for these few minutes, in the face of the fire, the rain, which was omnipotent, was lost, it was overwhelmed and obliterated by this elemental force, and the fire spread its wings generously and swept them in ever more wide and powerful arcs, and there was no more soot, and the Face-Maker felt and saw what he had already experienced once on the eve of the Choice, and he recognized it now, and he was glad, because he knew how it would end.

But this was paradise in comparison with what he saw and felt later. If at the Final Judgment he had been offered forgiveness of all his sins simply for recalling what he experienced later, the Face-Maker would have refused, for without being aware of it, he still carried within him a living sense of the truth, and this had become the only measure by which the Face-Maker now judged his own actions and what he saw around him since he had returned from that place. And in this truth his life was a paltry price to pay, and his pain was a joke, and his suffering amusing, and his success insulting, because the eyes of the black field and the green meadow — the great censor — watched him constantly, they scrutinized the Face-Maker's every action, his every attitude to himself and those close to him.

V

The Face-Maker worked calmly and precisely. A new face, with which he could help people, was the truth that dwelt in him now. It was as simple and constant as the rain in the City is constant. It was simply a human being who now lay before the Face-Maker.

And for the first time the Face-Maker thought calmly and with gratitude of the one who had made him undergo the Trial, made him undergo the sufferings of those who lived around him and with him. If it were not for this, the Face-Maker would scarcely have been capable of creating the face of his own suffering, a face to help himself and his own Muse. And other people? He would have forgotten about them, just as he had never thought of them while he was engrossed in his work, his hopes and his misfortunes, and living only in them.

Yes, no matter how lovely the face might have been then, it would have been strange to everyone.

But today this would not happen. In the Face-Maker's hands there lived those hands that had been stretched out to him imploring help, which had clutched at him in the attempt to survive, the hands that now lay still in the black field or the green meadow, because the soul controlling them had quit them and settled in the Face-Maker's hands, and it controlled every movement of the scalpel.

The Face-Maker was now the debtor, the pupil, slave and creator of what he had experienced — not an artist in the name of ambition and change, but in the name of help for the living and those who had yet to appear on this earth.

As he worked the Face-Maker created a Face which he had not seen and no one alive had seen, but it was everybody's face, for its features were those of the time.

The words moved in an unaccustomed and therefore clumsy manner, attempting to be like thoughts. They were like blind people feeling each other with their fingers, so delighted to find familiar faces in the crowd that nothing can persuade them to let go of each other. Although the strangers standing close by might in fact be dearer and closer to them, in their fear of losing what they have already found, they make no attempt to seek out other people like themselves.

By this time his fingers were already performing their familiar work on the third square of the face. It was strange: the more the Face-Maker removed of the old, coarse skin, which had long been untouched, the less familiar became the face that was slowly emerging beneath his fingers. The head was just as immense, but as the features appeared they became steadily more intelligent and hideous than the original formless mass. He had a momentary suspicion that even this face that was emerging had been uniquely lovely for someone at some time, and that meant, didn't it, that even beauty was temporary and relative? No, that could not be. Beauty was permanent, and this face had always been hideous to everyone. But either his eyes were growing accustomed to it or his soul was, and when the hour and the moment arrived to remove the skin of the first face, the Face-Maker felt sorry to part with what he had uncovered, because these swollen blue wrinkles, narrow eyes and motionless grandeur contained their own truth, they bewitched the Face-Maker and subdued him, and probably, if he had been doing this in his laboratory, not under any pressure to complete the task rapidly, he would have left this face, because there was an answer in its power and wisdom, which he came to know better the more he worked with it, but it was an answer only for a few, and probably a long time ago, and not for anyone now. There was no sense in changing the face of any person living in the City for this one, it was uglier and more primitive than a city-dweller's face. And nonetheless the Face-Maker delayed things a little and set his scalpel aside more frequently than he made an incision in the face he had uncovered. Probably he needed to fix his work in his memory before he could part with it, he needed to see in it as much as possible of the meaning and truth which exist in every piece of work and which are sometimes invisible even to the artist himself, because genuine truth, like a pea in the pod and the yoke in an egg, is concealed within — what can there be in common between the chalky shell, dead and lifeless forever, and the life of that yellow colour that hangs down over the edges of the teaspoon and later, flowing across your tongue and mingling with bread and butter, supports life by its own death? So what of the shell? It was time to remove the skin he had opened up, because the truth should lie beneath it. Once again the Face-Maker ceased thinking, and his work began to think for him. But the skin under the scalpel was fragile, compressed and thin, and he had to be careful. When it finally lay in the broad white basin like sausage-skin, no one would ever have recognized it for what it was a few hours before, because a few ragged scraps bear no resemblance at all to wisdom and authority. The Face-Maker gathered himself and saw the result of his work.

VI

'What great master made this face that has been uncovered?' the Face-Maker asked himself in his astonishment. 'After all that has happened, how is it possible to think of beauty and craftsmanship?' And realizing that nonetheless he was thinking of them, he was horrified at the fact that it was possible. It meant that there was something greater than suffering — beauty. Surely there could not be beauty in what he had seen? His mind recoiled from its own thought, for there was... But is there anything higher? What can overshadow beauty? Perhaps the man who created it? When was that, and what great artist was it? He worked almost without stitches. What material is this? It isn't skin. Yes, it's some unknown material. But how lovely this face was, he could not begin again, he could not tear his eyes away, he cursed himself, as he had cursed the City and its people up there on top of the fire, for being deaf, and for being so busy, for their indifference, and he himself was unable to tear his eyes away from these wrinkles, the entire radiant, white face, the holiness of each feature, line and fold. Only the eyes destroyed this impression of beauty and light... but one could avoid looking into those eyes. They had scarcely changed, anyway. Something came to life in him. And the Muse also came to life, and her hands and her body came to life. Once again he wanted to work as he used to work, performing an operation on the Muse, after all today he had the right to create any face he liked, any face he had seen in his imagination and his suffering, he wanted to express in this face what he had experienced, and what still existed out there, and what is constantly going on today and tomorrow, so that this face could save them all and change everything in the world, so that this face would be a reminder to everyone that they should not struggle to get their numbers changed, that they should not kill each other, that they should not keep beasts except in cages, or let people go near them, unless they armed the people so that they were not defenseless. And what if some day a master-craftsman should remove a layer of skin and reach the face created by the Face-Maker — then let his hands be filled with the power of the desire to save people. And he realized that this face had revealed to him the desire to save people and to create a new face. But the eyes... the eyes would be the last thing. He would be able to change them, he would do what the masters who worked before him had not been able to do. Yes, yes, the Muse, and the City, and the suffering, and the pain, and everything that lived and died within him, and lived on in him even though it was dead — it was all in order that he might create a face which would save people.

The Face-Maker sat down again, in order to give Him-Who-Lay-Before-Him a rest. Because He was once again deadly tired.

VII

The Muse had work to do as well. She watched 'The Immortals' once more and restored all the scenes that had been cut, she added more blood to the body of the young girl, she inserted an episode with a ripped cheek. But no matter what she did, the level of revulsion at another way of life on her meter was zero. It no longer concerned her, in the same way as the horrors of a painted hell are forgotten at the sight of a human being suffering agonizing pain when you are quite unable to do anything to help. She thought only of the Face-Maker, of what he was like when he emerged from That Place, and that she was ready to do anything at all if only he would become the old Face-Maker again, just for a minute, let him fall sick with his dream, and she would nurse him, let him lose his Name, she could work for them both, if only he would come back to her. And every time the Official came to her and reported that everything was going well, the animal terror she could see constantly in his eyes — after all, he couldn't be afraid of her — made her believe the Official, or at least, she believed that the Face-Maker was alive and working. If he wasn't still working, the Muse would have faced Departure. She checked the broadcast with the panel of viewers and was unable to understand how such trivia could induce a revulsion level of eleven points. She left the next episode of 'The Immortals' exactly as she found it.

VIII

But the Face-Maker didn't feel like working any more. As he rested he looked at the face of Him-Who-Lay-Before-Him, absorbing and memorizing every line, every movement of the master's scalpel. Deep within him a kind of misty white veil was drawn across his memory, and the beast-children became harmless and innocent, and the people became more beautiful, and it seemed to the Face-Maker that they were approaching the City, where he would be able to help them. The smell disappeared and was replaced by silence and clear, misty air which no longer held any fear or pain. A man can survive any experience. Give him the opportunity to go back to life and experience the miracle of work, and he will rise from the dead. Nothing is ever lost, a man can rise again from the cross, after the death of every living thing, because he is able to forget, because he is able to desire, because he is able to live in what will make him happy and — believe me — it is never too late for this to happen; even in death one may feel within oneself the strength to forget, not to remember, but not through the oblivion of hatred, only through the oblivion of love, and the desire to save everything that remains after you. The Face-Maker rose to his feet.

What wonderful hands nature had given him, what a wonderful time he had behind him, when each day there had been work, with the Muse beside him, each day new sheets of paper which his fingers decorated with the patterns of forests, and mountains, and seas, and gods, and trees which shed their golden leaves in the autumn: and then once more the first square, up on the summit of the forehead, where the grey, soft hairs, light almost as air, come to an end, thinly scattered silver running away and back, the first square was in there amongst them. Millimetre by millimetre the line of the former face disappeared, the eyes softened and became kinder, the oval of the lips was drawn out and flattened and transformed into a narrow thread, the face changed, and the eyes changed — but the face became harsher, more predatory, and a smile emerged on the lips, and the cruelty was hidden in this smile, but could not entirely disappear from view, it was almost exposed. It was strange — the eyes were kinder than the obvious cruelty. Evidently the eyes had not changed at all, only one face ago they were harsh and overbearing, and yet now, in comparison with this cruelty, their hostility seemed like kindness. Where was the truth? In the eyes? But they were so different in appearance. In the face? But it changed to suit the time, which looked like it. It seemed as though nothing could be more terrible than these narrow lips, these wrinkles threaded with reddish-blue veins, this cruelty which pretended to be a smiling tenderness, attentiveness, compassion and concern. Nothing could? Yes it could! This was still a kind face — if it pretended, that meant that sometimes it was not itself. It was even in some ways a beautiful face — not, of course, like the second, which was white, kind, wise and perfect. But when this face also lay on the white surface of the basin like sausage skin and boiled potato parings and mingled with the first two so that it was difficult to distinguish what skin belonged to what face, the Face-Maker, having seen and experienced things which would drive the reason from the soul, leaving it to die, stayed his hand and threw the scalpel into its solution.

He had seen and recognized a face which was like the face he had felt within himself when he wanted to be the Great Face-Maker, unique, the one who turned the world upside down and saved it. He recalled his hopes and his choice, and the face was similar, but still more terrible than the one which now lay before him, and was grinning crookedly, glad to have been recognized. Like a thief who had only intended to steal, not to kill, but is so afraid of being caught that he kills the person who has grabbed his arm and then flees, and glancing around him, buries the knife without even wiping off the blood, the Face-Maker grabbed his scalpel and thrust it in just below the chin: he seemed about to slice off the flesh, together with all the accumulated faces, like slicing an apple in half because the top half is infected with rot, and he saw the pupils of the person lying before him grow wider and wider, till they seemed about to burst out of their black orbits and explode, unable to bear the pain, and now the dark blood would come gushing out. And... One Hundred and Five immediately cried out in his memory. Something inside him slowed his hand, and the will disappeared, and the Face-Maker stopped. The one who had sent him to be tested knew that anyone who had drained the cup to the dregs would spare any living thing, because he possessed that experience. Even when his own salvation was concerned. And the Face-Maker was immediately calm. He wiped his face with a napkin and transferred the scalpel to the first square.

Would he have carried through his choice now as he had done when he believed in his exalted destiny? In the right to stand over people? Of course not. But then would someone else now be standing here? Hardly. The Choice of the Couple would have gone through calmly and there would have been no changes.

But why argue now about whether it was possible to live differently yesterday, when you are already living today? There is a good reason — if you change 'yesterday' within yourself, you will act differently today. For having killed once, you will not kill a second time (after the change), quite the opposite — you will save, and there will be no choice for you, you will not spare yourself.

So do not spare your own face, the one hidden inside, that people do not know. Look — there it is.

No dissimulation, everything is exposed—the right of the strong, the right to stand above all others, the right of the only one who knows what will make peoples' lives better, the right of the only possessor of the truth, cruel, cold, confident — the Face.

Like the guillotine, which also brilliantly fulfilled the purpose for which it was invented by nature and people. And not once did it ever occur to the guillotine that it was in the wrong. It was also simply carrying out its duty, while its blade was sharp, before the iron grew rusty, while there were guilty heads. It didn't matter — guilty of what against whom; and it didn't matter who controlled the guillotine — whether the first ones were replaced by the brothers of those the first ones were beheading yesterday.

Look, look at yourself — mind you don't confuse yourself with anyone else and don't forget how you have lived, and for what, even if you never had the right circumstances to show your full worth.

Never?

What about the Choice? And the thousands, who have been given Departure? And One Hundred and Five? But that was all the Official's doing, the time, the law, to which you, the Face-Maker, can merely submit. Lies! That time and that City depended precisely on you, and it depends on you who they will become tomorrow, and it even depends on you whether the person lying before you will feel pain — these were his thoughts, and his fingers were considerate and careful.

IX

Life seemed to have come to a standstill, time seemed to have stopped moving, like a cyclist who pedals for all he's worth until he's exhausted, only to find he's still surrounded by the same four walls and white ceiling — for beneath him there are only rollers, creating the illusion of a road. But then, why call it an illusion — the cyclist is actually moving and he is actually standing still, both of these are the truth; the heap of parings on the bottom of the basin kept on growing. It covered the bottom, and each face and each skin mingled with the skin of the ones removed earlier, and the faces remained only in the Face-Maker's memory, while his fingers kept on making the usual arched incision, raising the edge of the skin and removing the square, and then doing it all over again. The rollers span, the scalpel moved, the basin grew heavy, the days passed and time stopped. The person before him never moved, his eyes were open, and the Face-Maker always sensed when it was time for a break, although he could not understand how this happened. If it weren't for the eyes, the person lying before him might have been lifeless for all the Face-Maker could tell. But the eyes!

They showed the Face-Maker just how carefully he had done what he had done.

How scant and narrow his daily life had become — operation, break, rest, memories of the faces removed, blurred memories of pain and the sense of the Muse's presence. Sometimes it seemed to the Face-Maker that the operation would never be finished and he would never leave this place, this was simply the illusion of work, and in reality it was all just a cunningly arranged captivity. Although, why would that be? It would be so easy to deal with him in the simple, more customary manner — Departure, and then he wouldn't have to get so tired and suffer such agonizing torment and doubt. No, the Face-Maker told himself immediately, you are doing important work which only you are capable of doing — by virtue of right, experience and suffering — the creation of this new, hitherto unknown face, which he had never seen in any of the faces revealed to him. And when he finished the operation, let the rain carry on falling in the same old way, and let the City present its marble walls to his gaze in the same way it always had done — even so something would change deep inside it, because once they saw the new face created by the Face-Maker, women would become gentler, and men would become kinder, children would love those who loved them, because with this face it would be impossible to feel anything but love, and nobody would care any more what his number was and how his life would end. For life would be filled with kindness and trust. The daily round, yes. Monotonous labour, yes. But not in vain... for trust is everything that can make a man happy, it is when you can speak the truth, when you can say more than you do, and say what you intend to do.

His hands were growing heavier: how strange, the colder his heart was and the stricter his reason become, the greater the ease and the passion with which the Face-Maker worked. The more he wanted to work and the more happy he was in his work, the more heavily he breathed and the more effort each brush-stroke cost him, although perhaps he was wrong about that; there's always something happening to a man, everything in him keeps changing all the time, and every change makes it easier or harder to work.

It was not the first fright the Face-Maker had experienced, but it was a new fear. It was night, the patient was sleeping, with his head slumped to one side — smaller now, slimmer and almost in proportion with his body. The Face-Maker looked at him. An hour ago he had almost completely removed and reworked yet another face, but he had been thinking his own thoughts, scarcely paying any attention to what he was doing, and now as he looked up the light was dimmed and the sleeper's head was only half-illuminated. Suddenly darkness swam in front of the Face-Maker's eyes and he thought he was going insane — there in front of him was the face of the Image, the face that was the most important in the City at that very moment, the only face, the face that the Face-Maker himself bore. It couldn't be — that had been dozens of faces ago, and the ancient craftsmen had worked in a different manner. Different? Look at the stitches, look at the joinings, look at the tissue — it was all different! What about from this side? He turned up the light. No, from here the resemblance was not so strong. He turned it down again — the same effect. How could that be? Strangely enough, removing that face proved to be harder than anything else, because it was tailored in a fashion quite alien to him. After making a few of his customary incisions, the Face-Maker had to stop and start all over again. Yes it was put together quite differently. But this time too the work was quite perfect.

How good it was, even so, to work fenced off from the entire world by the massive marble walls, all alone with his patient, He-Who-Lay-Before-Him, relaxed, unspeaking and undemanding, and to think of what had been, and no matter how terrible what had been might be, it was only 'had been', and not to know what events were taking place in the City, to be free at least from whatever was happening.

X

Meanwhile, life in the City continues on course. Not the old course, when the City swung regularly and evenly around the 'Official-Great Face-Maker' axis, smoothly, on and on forever. Something out of the ordinary had fallen under the wheels this time — apparently it was no more than a few hundred heads and that speech from the Great One, but the wheel had risen up from the track where it was crushing them, and the axle had shifted out of true, cracking the bearing, and the wheel had begun to run crooked. They were still moving along, and still at the same speed, but the shaking was worse now, and it was transmitted to the people. There was nothing surprising in the fact that the wheels cracked heads open like nutshells — that was nothing special at all — but the Great One's words had not been crushed under the wheels, they had not been reduced to dust, but had simply popped out untouched, while the bearing had been cracked and the axle had been pushed out of alignment, and the wheel itself had started running lame and limping.

Yes, that was it — the word, having survived under the wheels, had created the possibility of independence from the wheels, and that meant the possibility of transgression of the law of the City — for the good, naturally, of every person who lived in it. And transgression of the law was understood by each one of them as the opportunity to win a new number or acquire a Name — no longer at some unknown point in time or by the end of your life, but tomorrow. However — and this was something every true City-dweller understood — this desire required a decent and respectable ideological formulation in order to make it acceptable to a citizen raised and educated to respect the law. And for this purpose the idea of the true face was absolutely ideal.

The city swelled up like dough made with yeast, like a river that has burst its banks in the spring-time, like an anthill teeming with fresh movement after the winter.

The citizens with names regarded the anthill with a curious glance from a squinting eye, and under this gaze the anthill was seen to separate into two uneven halves — the activists and the waiters. The waiters sympathized with the idea but their fervour was contained internally. Their external life was perfectly normal, and since all the rest was only internal, it was their personal business and had nothing to do with the life of the City — they were not the ones.

Remember the one who split female One Hundred and Five's breast in two with his scalpel — he turned out to be one of the waiters, believe it or not. Of course, the fact that he possessed such great internal reserves of nobility was no great comfort to female One Hundred and Five. And as for the activists...

Ideas are capable of producing children.

The activists came up with a neat trick. They disguised their work as love — meetings for this purpose were unofficially allowed in the City, without any restrictions. It was a splendid idea. Of course, some of the citizens turned out to be engaging in love under the guise of the idea, but the rest of them engaged in action under the guise of love. The Husband was quick to join the ranks of the former. How vast his opportunities had now become! He used to visit the houses where uncoupled women lived, but as I'm sure you'll agree, the best ones have always been taken for coupling, and who wants to keep using the things nobody else wants all the time?

Today the Husband had a good idea. He jerked open the door of his former apartment and the eyes of the new female One Hundred were there, looking at him. They watched him with enthusiasm over the shoulder of the new male One Hundred. The Husband recognized her immediately. He remembered her from back then, at the time of the Choice — sitting silently in the next row and staring fixedly at the Husband's face, even back then. Ah, how convenient this idea of the True Face was. The Husband opened his eyes wide and spoke the password. He didn't actually know the real password, but male One Hundred didn't know it either, he simply realized that he had to leave. Only female One Hundred knew that the password was something different — but why should she miss out on her chance?

Everything was arranged most conveniently. Male One Hundred went round to the neighbours without even putting on his cloak, apologizing nervously as he went. He respected those who had chosen to act — he was only one of the waiters — and he was even proud to think that his partner was about to participate in this dangerous undertaking of the bold. Unfortunately he was unlucky; at the neighbours' place there were half a dozen people already engaged in practicing the new idea, it was as dark as Sodom on the night before the end came, and the air was filled with the sound of sobbing and groaning. Male One Hundred realized that such intensive, demanding effort was only possible when people were working on a new idea, and that made him feel even greater respect for these people, so in order not to disturb them or be taken for a spy, he went out quietly, closing the door behind him. The most astonishing thing in all of this was that female Five could engage in this activity with male One Thousand Nine Hundred and Seventy-Seven, while male One Thousand Six Hundred and Sixty-Six could engage in it with females Forty-Seven or Seven, depending on the circumstances. That was another reason for male One Hundred to respect these people.

When male One Hundred went back to his own apartment, he did have just a momentary twinge of suspicion (like a fleeting glimpse of a bird's shadow through the window at night — perhaps it was real, perhaps you imagined it) when he saw his female One Hundred sitting on the Husband's knees, but they quickly explained to him that it was necessary for the conspiracy, since anybody at all might enter the apartment at any moment, and that would mean certain Departure. Male One Hundred admired them even more for this — her for her moral courage (he knew how his female One Hundred loved him), and the Husband for his strong body, which supported the body of his female One Hundred so easily. People like that won't let you down, thought male One Hundred, as he sat in the corridor for the three and a half hours which the courageous people he respected so very much spent in his home.

We must give the Husband his due, after this he began calling round regularly, and in time male One Hundred stopped getting in their way and sometimes, feeling like a terrible coward and yet at the same time respecting himself for joining in, he would even lend a hand, but without ever fully understanding the inner meaning of their mysterious activity.

The Wife arranged things for herself no worse. Now that she had masses of free time and a Husband who was always disappearing, she gave up the inconvenient effort of visiting the other houses nearby and began leaving her own door open, and anyone who found his way into her home always left feeling happy and tired. He might even forget all his exalted ideas for a little while, but he wouldn't forget to spread the word about the Wife, who was so generous and so indefatigable. The Wife could probably have satisfied the entire City, but the information was only passed on to close friends and through private channels, which restricted her practice to a certain extent. But then, there was still plenty of time ahead, and she could still hope eventually to receive the very last inhabitant of the City. This, by the way, was no purely private matter either, for the Wife undoubtedly exerted a certain influence on life in the City and the life of the new idea, which fluttered its wings anxiously at first, then began to mould and finally became quiescent, like a butterfly passed from hand to hand for everyone to look at — no matter how carefully it's handled, after six or seven hundred pairs of hands the wings have lost almost all their dust and therefore, all their attractiveness. As well as the ability to fly.

XI

After a while everything in the City settled down and even the crooked limping of the wheel began to seem natural. Those with names made the most of life and forgot the words spoken by the Great One. Except, of course, for the Husband — he remembered them alright, for his own convenience.

The secret and open participants in the movement for the True Face participated secretly and openly in this movement, moving always in time with the rhythm of the limping wheel.

The Official knew the secret and open participants in the movement to look at and from lists, or if he didn't, then his Commission did. From time to time the most active among them were condemned to Departure, and then the water in the canals ran more yellow than usual, and the City, limping along to the regular rhythm of that wheel, continued joyfully, secretly and openly on its course towards the new life, anticipating its own happiness in that new life, which was certainly no more than just, for each of them deserved happiness and had a right to it — such was the fundamental law of the City. The day and the hour of this encounter and its very possibility now depended entirely on the Face-Maker and his work, on his inspiration — but apart from the Official, the inhabitants of the City were quite unaware of that.

XII

The water turned yellow more and more often now, there were days when the yellow water flowed from morning till night, and even the rain, that constant, omnipotent force, could do no more than carry it away — it was beyond its power now to overwhelm the yellow colour and dilute it. The rain kept on pouring down, flowing together from all the streets and the squares in the City, until the water in the canals rose almost to the top of the walls, until it seemed one final effort would be enough to carry it over that granite threshold, and the yellow, glutinous flesh would go creeping through the streets, climbing up stairways and filling the houses, rising above the roof-tops until the entire City disappeared beneath an endlessly spreading, noisy yellow flood; but this had not happened as yet, and it merely seemed as though it might happen. The granite banks of the canals had risen noticeably higher and they were prepared to hold back the flood, but when the water reached the limits of the granite, the very top of those tall banks, it became clear that calm and unhurried work was no longer what was required. The Face-Maker was the first to discover this, together with the Muse.

The evening before she had laid on the floor after she came home from work and yelled that she was fed up with everything, she was fed up with the work, and the waiting, and all these Thirty-Sevens, Fifty-Threes, Sixty-Sixes, Eighties, Seventeens and the rest who opened her door almost every evening and pronounced the password which she now knew off by heart, after which, at first in a fury, and later with a smile, and then with total indifference, she threw out those idiots with the burning eyes and the sweaty hands accustomed to submissiveness that now reached out for her. Even her Name was no longer so all-powerful, and what was going on in the City, if even the Muse was so defenseless? Left on her own, the Muse trembled and shivered and curled herself up into a tight ball, feeling sorry for herself and almost forgetting about the Face-Maker — she was tormented by her own fear and impotence. And then, at the very moment when the Face-Maker, whose hand had been poised ready to work on the next square of skin, learned that his time was limited and the problem was not just to create something, no matter how long it might take, but to create something by tomorrow, the Muse became calm again.

She tidied up the house and washed herself, for the first time without that feeling of horror and revulsion for the water which had tormented her since that insane night when the Face-Maker had been led away at dawn. She stopped thinking only of herself, of how she was suffering, how she couldn't bear it, how she hated waiting, and she began simply waiting, without analyzing anything or feeling sorry for herself as she waited, calmly, with a clear mind, so that if it was necessary, she would be able at any minute to help the Face-Maker, if only by not tormenting him with her own suffering. When someone's dying more humanity is shown by a person who will give them a drink or an injection for the pain than by someone who screams and tears his hair out and beats his head against the wall, losing control in the face of his own suffering, forcing the dying person to think of compassion and to try not to torment the living with his pain.

The news that it had to be done by tomorrow had a sobering effect on the Face-Maker. He calmly lowered the scalpel in his hand to touch the skin.

The period of unhurried creative work was at an end, life had begun. Just a few more days of calm, painstaking work and there would be no one left to view the face which so far only his fingers and his memory and his imagination knew — the way a woman will pick out of a crowd the man who will be the father of her son, although she is still too shy to say hello to him, and will think that this is the man who will open her up and leave himself in a space deep inside her soul, so that her son will look at her with those same big eyes, so that his fingers will be strong and nimble like his father's. It's not the man she loves in the person she has met and recognized, it's her future, the continuation of her tribe, and even if it's impossible and even if she doesn't feel it or see it, this is a truth that exists without her having to know it. Just as He seeks for the mother of his tribe, recognizing her by the smell of her body, the colour of her hair and her light, hurried, staccato manner of speaking, which are like the pattern of fingerprints, never encountered twice. The Face-Maker had realized that he could no longer continue searching to find the one for whom he had come into the world. There was no time to wait, tomorrow was the last day, and if you want to continue the line of the tribe, better embrace the first one to come along, lying on the dirty, unplaned planks smelling of pine resin and turpentine somewhere at the back of the goods yard, behind the wall of a rotten, half-ruined shed, turning your face away from the old, stub-nosed, crumpled face, better give her your excess portion of life. Leave without looking back, because you won't do this, and there will be no continuation of your tribe, and your fingers will never grasp the scalpel and your eyes will never see your work, because there behind you the heavy goods train is already rumbling along the track, it has already picked up speed, and the brakes will make no difference, there's no siding to turn the train into, there is no force that can halt this juggernaut, and the driver, with hair as white as snow, can only watch as your stooped back approaches and feel sorry for you, as though his sympathy will help your head to part more easily from your body under the iron wheels and your bones will be reduced less painfully to the consistency of emptiness.

All the same, you've been lucky, Face-Maker — there in front of you lies the face your own hands are creating, your scalpel is sharp, your fingers are faithful and true, and the Muse shelters you with her love. Out there, where the walls of the houses await your return, the Muse is also waiting, no longer noticing all of the things that surround her, hardly even breathing, so that her breathing won't distract you from your work, and you can feel this waiting dissolved in yourself, you know that behind you, at home, everything is calm and safe, and the train approaching you from behind is not due for days yet, and the train approaching you from the front, which prevents you from hearing the other one, has never been a danger to you, because you're walking along the next track, and it will always approach and then go flying on past.

Thank you, Muse, for being so calm now and for serving me, even though you don't accept me, for being faithful in my work and in my bed. Thank you for suffering with my pain, the way the heart aches, when the eyes see peace and a garden clad in white, because hiding behind the trees there is a man with a knife and an axe and a trusty hand, waiting for his chance to raise his hand to your body, surely and soundlessly, the way the beloved Muse awaits the return of the Face-Maker. Thank you for shining with my light, the way the eyes of a man sinking into a swamp, wide with terror, are suddenly filled with the light of joy and safety, because there is firm ground under his feet and the swamp is shallow enough for him to stand in. Thank you for being kind with my kindness. What meaning have people's offences to you and each other when death's saw is sounding at the door, and if you put your foot over the threshold, your leg will be gone; if you bend down to the severed leg, your eye will be gone, if you lower your head in impotent humility, your life will be gone? What meaning have people's offences to you and others when they are not the ones whirling the metal disc, and the only path there is leads across that threshold?

XIII

Yes, everything changes quickly in a person. Only yesterday the Face-Maker had been glad that it had fallen to him to continue the line of his trade, to leave people a face which would reveal to them the secret of the miracle of love and tenderness for each other. Only yesterday he had been happy that he could work unhurriedly forever, reading, as he looked into the features of strange faces, the book left by humanity, a text which was visible only to him — the entire experience of all the City's masters, who had lived centuries before, was open to him.

And now, when there were only three or four days left to create a new face and be the first to see it, without having destroyed on the way a single feature of a single face, sensing with each movement the mastery of skill and of intention, he had to hurry. Lord, if he had known earlier that there was so little time, the Face-Maker would have ripped all of those masks from the face of Him-Who-Lay-Before-Him in two or three days, so that the patient would have writhed in agony, and then, in creating his face without having seen anything, without having learned anything, instead of love he would have put into it all his hatred for the one who had tested him and for the City, which is so dead in its eternal pursuit of ranking, in its desire to bypass, to overtake, to astonish, he would have put into it all the pain he had experienced, so that they would hate each other still more, so that, meeting once a year at the Choice, they would tear each other's faces, scratch each other's eyes out, break each other's arms and would be happy in this hatred — because this was what they had taught him each moment of each of his lives. But the Muse! The Face-Maker's thoughts come to a halt, they stop circling around, and they are no longer red, and no longer black, but purple, and yellow, and happy.

All the same he will have to remove several faces at once, and no one on earth will ever know what those faces were like. Let them be destroyed, the ones that were left, no one will ever know what they were like. But he will make his own face beautiful, the most beautiful in the world, because people must not hate each other, and their hatred must not swell up to become as immense as the air, so that a man cannot live anywhere without breathing it, because when that fire starts everything is destroyed and no rain is able to halt the flames, because hatred is stronger than rain.

While the thoughts were skidding and soaring in his head, changing his decision, changing despair into hope, then into fear, then again into hope, the Face-Maker's fingers saw only the small square on the surface of the skin, and this square was separated from the face, and there was nothing but a tiny yellow patch, which had to be exfoliated and preserved — let others do that some other time, it was easier to restore than to create. No one would do that except him.

XIV

The only way to resolve things was by work.

Like a gold-miner he began to rush over the skin, the eyelids, the lips, and there was no more time, or Muse, or concern about growing tired, or leaving anything till tomorrow, for there was no tomorrow. It was an only illusion that tomorrow was coming. When tomorrow arrives it becomes today, and there is no point in saving your energy, no point in sparing your hands, no point in sparing your soul — only once in a lifetime does the chance come to work as the Face-Maker worked.

The golden plough thrust its way into these furrows, these ruts, these depressions and uplands. An immense field lay before the Face-Maker, and it had to be ploughed and the sods broken, so that it would be transformed into green meadows and be yellow with wheat, and beautiful with the grains of bread which could feed people.

May the harvest come to your field, may the reapers come in time, may their work go well, and the sky — may the sky not send down hail and rain on your yellow field. Hear the ears of corn calling out like pregnant women, hear how their legs will be broken off beneath the blades of the machines and their bodies will be thrashed with flails, and there shall come to pass what must come to pass — the poor, ragged, hungry children, like the yellow leaves and the green leaves of the bog sedge, shall be given loaves of bread into their hands, into their transparent hands, and with their mouths watering, they shall sink their black, rotten teeth into the bread, and their faces shall light up, and their eyes shall grow more gentle and kind, and they shall stand up, and go forth into the field, and they shall meet the beasts, which shall go dripping blood on the ground, and shall not harm a single person. Knowing not what they do, the children of the bogs, having liberated people from fear and cruelty, shall go to drain the bogs and save everything that is left alive on the earth.

And this shall be because the golden plough creaks beneath the hands of the Face-Maker, and the black soil has already been turned over, and steam is already rising from the openings in the upturned blackness, which has never before seen the light of day, and moves like living earth. There is no City, there is no Him-Who-Lies-Before-Me — there is only craving, right and achievement. But then it is as though they have pumped out all the air, like before, and there is nothing left to breathe, and his lungs are stretched till they seem about to burst; but the Face-Maker knows what to do at such a moment, and his hands are raised upwards, and mercy is granted; it becomes easier to breathe, there is something to breathe now, and once again he can take up the handles of the plough, but he manages the earth clumsily, and it cries out in a voice of pain — or is it the rooks calling as they circle above the plough-field, their eyes fixed on the tumbled bosom of the earth, aiming their beaks at the chopped, bleeding worms turned up by the plough?

So that was why the face stirred under the scalpel, no muscles, no tissue — there are worms instead, the red worms have woven their bodies together and lifted up their tails or their heads, defending themselves and their families from the Face-Maker's knife. The worms share in immortality. For the faces have changed, wisdom has squinted through the eyes of cruelty, pain has emerged from tenderness, strength grinned in insanity — and only the worms have known the truth. They have borne it in their own bodies, and these bodies were constantly in motion, attempting to make themselves more comfortable in the close, stuffy darkness. And now here was a knife — was that any better than stifling in the darkness? Like snakes they raised their tails or their heads to meet the pain. They attempted to demonstrate their skill — one flat white body changed its form, and the Face-Maker recognized an expression of grief. Another one changed its pose, and another lowered its head, and the face was distorted in terror.

The Face-Maker swiftly tore his eyes away from this face, and immediately a short red worm hid itself among its fellows, and laughter curved the lips of Him-Who-Lay-Before-Him. And, setting aside the knife, with fingers that were blue, gentle, subtle, agile as musical sixteenths, the Face-Maker gathered these harmless, blind creatures from the bones, these creatures full of skill and slime, and dumped the mass of joy, pain and life into the bucket, then pulled off the last few who had grown into the bone and muscle. Why rely on worms, on their cramps and hunger, on their closeness and indifference? Let the soul weep — and the face, let it grow radiant, the face expresses the soul, even if the soul is a severe one — and the face is like it.

I don't need smooth-skinned intermediaries, I don't need intermediaries stuffed with my body that has been digested into shit. I want to smile and cry myself. I need a Muse, who sees me, and not them, pretending to be me. I need a City which will contain what is, not what pretends to be what is. I need a love which is as sincere and shameless and fearless as the love between bodies open to each other in trust.

Without looking at the red worms writhing and scrambling over each other, crushing the remnants of the husks of the faces, slithering down the smooth nickel-plated wall, yet clambering back up again, and devouring each other and the remnants of the material that they used to set in motion, the Face-Maker went on with his work.

He worked until the eyes opened beneath his hands, and they were like the eyes of those who had sent him on his way, who had no strength to crawl after him, whose bread he had eaten, leaving them to die of hunger; the eyes of those who had been kind to him while the woman died at the paw of the beast; his own eyes, which had remained hidden within him during the trial by fire on the square. These were eyes of forgiveness and hope, these were eyes of understanding and compassion — these were the eyes of the life which the Face-Maker was moulding with his own hands. These were the eyes of the Muse, without whom he was helpless and senseless.

Because if you live for no one, you are empty and your name is dust. Now the cheeks have already taken shape beneath the Face-Maker's fingers, like a field in which he has sown his own corn, and from which he has gathered his own harvest. And the nose, like a watchman, has taken up position above the field in order to preserve this harvest and protect the grain from the crows. And the lips have become ricks of corn, crimson from the setting sun and infused with the reaper's blood.

The Face-Maker stepped back, and looked at the person lying there, and he was blinded by the beauty and goodness of what he had created, and when his eyes had recovered and grown accustomed to the sight which had transformed them — the essence of Him-Who-Stands-Over-All was revealed to him.

And then the Face-Maker understood that he had only remade what was visible to the eye.

The master-craftsman of the flesh had not touched the soul.

The beautiful was external.

He-Who-Stands-Over-All is indifferent to how his face is seen and made by people, for his essence is devoid of flesh and eternally inaccessible either to skill or iron.

A reward?

Of course, the Face-Maker deserves one for his work.

It is not given to everyone to know the count of the days, especially as mercifully, as wisely and with such compassion as He-Who-Stands-Over-All had revealed this to the Face-Maker, whom he would never remember, and without whom he would in any case have brought about what could have happened even without Himself.

XV

The wide-flung doors of the House sucked in the people from the rain. As though a boa-constrictor had opened its jaws, elastic as a nylon stocking, and was gradually swallowing an entranced, defenseless, crawling animal which rustled its cloaks, smelling of the thunderstorm which had rumbled past above the City. At last its tail whisked in at the leaves of the door, and they all came together slowly and indifferently, probably initiating the process of digestion.

The chalice was full to the very brim with evil, and the Official's hand held it carefully. He had fulfilled his mission today as he had to and none of it any longer depended on him, it was time for him to take a break. Even the water in the canals was almost transparent today after the downpour. All that was left of the City, afraid of overflowing, was perched on the edges of its seats with all its eyes glued to the centre of the stage. It was empty. The image had disappeared, and in its place on the wall there was only a faint, dark square.

Its outline was only visible from the final rows, but from the first row, where the Official was sitting and from which he had viewed the hall when they were removing the image, the spot was invisible. The Official had smiled to himself at the time as he looked around. The Image had been stuck up there without being changed for so long, and when they took it down there wasn't a trace left. Stone doesn't change its colour.

But to those sitting high up, in the final rows, this visible square of emptiness was a sign of hope that today their destiny would change. Who knew who they might be when they left this hall? The front rows, who had seen so many changes in their time, had come to terms in advance with the pain of the usual corrections, and were expecting a spectacle, and laughing to themselves at the hopes of the rows at the back. But even they were gripped by anticipation, and in a few minutes, despite their self-assurance, indifference and readiness for the usual changes that changed nothing, without understanding what was happening to them, they became one with the entire hall, as though they were beginning to feel something that their brains could not understand — the way a dog howls on the eve of its master's death, although the master is still unaware of the expiry of his term. Faithful to the law of future causes, the flesh united the people. And the hall's immense heart began to beat regularly, only very slightly faster, as though it had been enlarged and strengthened so that without losing the general rhythm, each of them might look to the spot where He was to appear, the one whose existence the Great Face-Maker had surmised in opposing the Official. Seven days had passed, and that fable had turned the world upside down.

The Official held the chalice of the hall carefully in a steady hand. The hall's heavy heart contracted regularly, driving fear and hope, indifference and hope through the people's veins. Only the Official and the Muse had a life of their own. He winked at the Muse, who was sitting beside him. The Muse pressed her lips together in tense exhaustion — she alone was waiting for the Face-Maker, and not the person the rest of the hall was expecting.

The Official had promised her they would meet here. But she remembered very well the Official's phrase that he never spoke the truth, the phrase that meant he never had to justify anything he said or did. But strong as the Muse's hope to see the Face-Maker had been, in defiance of untruth, for an instant the hall tipped over in her eyes and then righted itself, and just a single drop — the Muse's teardrop — spilled over the edge when the Face-Maker sank into the chair beside her and took her hand with a palm still hot from work. There was no time to rejoice — the light on the stage was growing stronger, and in the hall it began to grow dim, as though it was being pumped from one vessel into another.

The quietness grew still quieter, and only a few hearts began to beat out of step, faster, and then the others caught up with them and joined the new rhythm, as though the train were gathering speed.

XVI

When the light in the hall was completely extinguished, and the shadow on the stone had quite vanished, the Face-Maker rose and pulled the Muse after him. She smiled in response in the darkness, as she had smiled when she waited for the Face-Maker, who was already close by, who was entirely with her an instant later — at this moment she was dying and being born to the light. The Face-Maker led her through the aisles to the exit.

The Muse's head was spinning, and she hardly knew what was happening or where she was, because she had waited for him too long. The people living in the darkness paid no attention to them, and just to be certain, they dug their fingers into the arms of the seats, so that they became part of the arms, in order not to lose their places just yet.

The Muse only recovered herself a little when the rain began to drum on her hood, when the Face-Maker's fingers, weaving their way round her back and under her arm, touched her through her cloak. And again the rain and everything around her disappeared.

There was no City, no pouring rain, no anticipation, no need to be back where they had just been.

She came to herself again for a brief moment when he lowered her shirt to the waist, and stroked her, and switched on the light, and leant over her. His chest touched her, and the Muse felt the great power of the moment, and she stretched out her arms and wound them around the Face-Maker's neck. She didn't understand at first when he removed her hands and placed them at her sides.

'Don't you love me any more?' asked the Muse, still not able to believe what had happened.

'I can't tell you anything, but you must believe that I'm doing what has to be done. I don't have much time,' said the Face-Maker, 'hardly any at all, but I'll try to do everything that I can.'

The Muse raised her eyes, and only now did she see that she was in the Face-Maker's laboratory, surrounded by white walls, lying on the operating table, that the Face-Maker was holding a scalpel, and the pain in the right corner of her mouth made her realize that the operation was already taking place. Just like that, without the face being prepared, without the skin being anaestheticized, on the living flesh. Why, the Muse wanted to ask, but she believed that if the Face-Maker was doing it, it was necessary. That meant it was important to them.

'Look at me,' said the Face-Maker, 'look at me, and it won't hurt so much.' And he pressed down still more heavily on her breasts, and she could feel his body and his pain, this Muse who knew him as no one else in the world knew him. The face of love and labour breathed above her, and it all became one — the love, the pain, the pressure of his body. It was no longer frightening to feel the skin being bent under her eyes, her lips growing heavier, her mouth filling with blood, the Face-Maker changing the cotton-wool in her mouth. The scalpel began cleaning the corners of her eye. She began to see the Face-Maker's real face, and it was different from what it had been yesterday. The taste of blood grows stronger and stronger, and the softness of the Face-Maker's body... But he works on, hurrying himself along and watching her face as it changes. Water and tears fall on to the Muse's exposed muscles.

'I'll get it done, I have to, even if it's not perfectly right, even if it's not absolutely accurate it will still be enough, and you'll wait for me.'

'I'll always wait for you, but why are you crying, and why are we here?'

'I'll tell you,' said the Face-Maker, 'I'll tell you, just let me get it done. Be patient and bear it.'

'Of course I will,' answered the Muse, 'that's not so difficult, I'll be patient.'

But it's not so easy to bear it. All the muscles of the face are exposed now and it's on fire, as though flames are creeping across the face and burning off everything that was on it, so that grass might grow here, so that flowers might grow here, so that this earth might give life to the Muse's new face, which is like her soul, like the face of Him-Who-Stands-Over-All. Ah, these flames, no body left, only pain. How long till the flowers? But now there is only fire, fire and smoke, and a smell of wool, and nothing to breathe, and nothing to live for, and nobody, no Face-Maker, no old face and no new one. Only endless kilometres of scorched steppe. And when will the first grass sprout again from the ashes, and when will the first flower bloom, and the first little green cricket sing its wise, clicking song?

The Face-Maker works on, and the tears fall on the steppe, and its hills lie beneath his chest, heaving slightly, ever more gently. It is so quiet that a bird flying by might startle you with its terrible noise.

Chapter Four

The New Face

I

It is so quiet that if it should get any quieter, the life will flow out of the hall, like water out of a chalice that has cracked in your hands or a mountain lake that empties through a cleft in its bottom — the way a train stops when it breathes out its last smoke, because the coal is all burned out, the wires have gone dead, the climb has defeated the wheels. But after lingering for a moment, the hall breathed out, and the pass was left behind. Like a canal filled by fresh water, the wires were newly charged with watts and volts, and the wheels began to breathe, and they picked up speed once again. There it is — movement, a tight feeling in their throats, hands gripping the arm-rests of the brass seats, heads thrust forward, eyes fixed on the spot where He-Who-Stands-Over-All is revealed to the hall. The first sight of the face, the glimpse that blinded everyone, astounding everyone sitting in the hall with its goodness, strength and mercy, is past now. Just as a person blinded by approaching headlights stops seeing anything round about him, but the flash of light remains fixed in his vision, although the car and its light are already far away. He can just see well enough to make out the road and turn off before he is hit by the next car, the one moving without lights. He would have turned off sooner, but for this light still in his eyes. Until they could grow used to it, each of them saw the face with his own imagination, with his own blindness. Yes, this was the face they had been waiting for.

But time passes, and the blindness from excessive light passes, a man's ear hears a word, and that helps him to see what the eye is unable to distinguish. The Official, who was keener-sighted and quicker-witted, was the first to see another new face — and fear crept into the Official's heart.

While the hall was jubilantly silent, a toad thrust its nose and eye into the Official's heart and blocked the valve through which the blood flowed to the Official's body, there was nothing left to breathe, and the Official gulped at the air, exactly like the Face-Maker stuck in the bell-glass from which the air had been evacuated. The Official ceased to breathe, but the Official gathered his strength: 'Now then, push, give it everything you've got' — and he squeezed this slimy green monster through the valve, which expanded into a mouth, and he began breathing calmly and evenly.

He-Who-Stands-Over-All had tricked him. The City would be saved; perhaps, there would still be life in it, and there would remain those whose faces, although not quite like the face of the Image, were nonetheless suitable for reworking. But the Official's face was too far beyond the bounds of this 'suitable'.

He felt cold and senseless inside, like a man who has been wandering in the desert for days upon days, knowing exactly where there is water. He has managed to crawl to the place, half-dead, and his hand is already stretched out to scoop up the water, to return to life and learn once again how to love, and how to fear the simple things (loss of power, abandonment by the one you have loved, or the realization that the work you've been doing all your life is confusion and absurdity), he has already pursed his lips, ready to moisten their dry, rough skin, cracked like the earth in a drought, but then before his very eyes, when he has crawled so far and lost everything on the way, abandoned everything on the long journey in order to get here, the water drains away, and nothing is left before him but a sink-hole in the sand, as dry and dead as a road built by man. The Official's lips turned down, as though a cane had been broken in the middle. The Face-Maker, the trials, thousands condemned to Departure with Departure executed so rapidly that the water in the canal became thick as oil, participation in acts of copulation under the guise of a member of the movement, all in the name of the City's good, each hour devoted to ensuring that the City lived as it had lived before the absurd quarrel with the Great One, whom he, the Official, would not now outlive by very long.

The Official rubbed his temples, closed his eyes and saw a thought. He needed the Face-Maker now. That was why he had taken the Muse out of the hall — in an hour the Muse would have a new face. That meant the Official had the same chance — while the hall was still listening to the words of Him-Who-Stands-Over-All.

The Official stood up, and in the darkness he walked slowly and quietly up the steps to the entrance: in his thought he had even seen precisely where to find the Face-Maker — in his laboratory. And no one paid any attention to the Official because down there on the stage was the light and down there the destiny of each one of them was setting out on a new journey along a new road. The Official pushed gently against the door — and the door was locked.

If anyone should know, then he should, that if the doors are closed, no one alive can shift them an inch. The Official became even calmer inside. He would stay here, in the final row, by the door, and when everything was over, he would slip out and find the Face-Maker. All was not yet lost — as long as his legs walked, his eyes saw, and there was air to breathe.

Like a cat ready to pounce, the Official sprawled in the seat right beside the door. The back rows were almost all empty. Too many had been given Departure in the last few days, there were not enough numbers left now to fill all the seats, for the procedure for registering as a number required an operation, and the rank-and-file face-makers simply could not work fast enough to replace the departed.

II

By this time the words of Him-Who-Stands-Over-All were filling up the space in the hall, the way water gushing into a newly excavated canal flows slowly at first, soaking into the earth, but then it picks up speed, and already the front rows are caught up in the flow of thought, they are beginning to feel dizzy with an excitement and strength which drowns out doubt and fear.

Desire, right, necessity, the inevitability of action, like seeds broadcast on rich soil, crack before their eyes to throw shoots high into the sky — the thought of Him-Who-Stands-Over-All flows on and the shoots grow higher in leaps and bounds.

Action — their bodies fill with strength like a rubber toy with air.

Each hears what he wants to hear. Each one with a Name understands the thought flooding his ears in his own way.

First row, seat six — he's even half-risen to his feet.

Damn it, a fight means something. Defending what you have is a sacred duty, victory is their form of life, everything remains just as it was. But now the stagnant blood, like a river at full-flood, will flow more merrily through his veins. And his hand feels along the arm-rest — this is the weapon with which he is destined to conquer.

First row, seat seven — the Chairman...

It's time to take the side of the back rows, the future belongs to them, to those he has not yet worked with, who, consequently, are still alive, and consequently, for them he is only the magnanimous, compassionate Chairman of the Commission — but he has a Name. He will renounce his Name, he is prepared to carry out his work namelessly, losing your name is easier than losing your life...

Third row, seat ten — the Husband...

He's only just achieved something beyond his wildest dreams and now he'll lose it. he'll beat them all on his own, the lot of them, fighting with teeth and nails and feet.

Seat eleven — the Wife...

Don't get involved, wait a while and see how things turn out — everyone needs a wife. She turned round, and the eyes of the hall looked past her, but there were so many eyes she knew well, they would defend her and keep her alive. Wait a while.

Seat thirteen...

That's fair. Yes, it's time to get started, everything from the beginning again. Better houses, better women, better... Of course justice is on the side of the back rows, and then there will be no shame inside, no fear or bondage in living by the law of the Name, without paying any attention your inner voice... of course, change sides right this moment, before they notice you.

Seat thirty-one...

For him the words of Him-Who-Stands-Over-All were a clear and palpable expression of the certainty of the victory for the names, in their status as chosen ones, in their professional ability, their right to stand over the City and command it — for what are these dull, ugly specimens, almost different faces, capable of by comparison with his face. This Other Image? That's what the face-makers are for, tomorrow they will all have that face, and tomorrow once again they will... better to lose your life than to lose your name. And he dug his fingers into the arm-rest of the seat, into the heavy green brass, a very axe of an arm-rest.

Seat thirty-three...

In the fervour and strength of their rectitude the front rows awaited the end of the speech.

III

Each one heard what he wanted to hear.

In the fervor and strength of their rectitude those sitting behind the front rows waited, motionless, for the words of Him-Who-Stands-Over-All. The wave of thought had already dashed against their ears, against their souls, it was already clear to each of them, even those who were in the back rows: so that was it, their neighbours and friends had not departed in vain, today the front rows would be taken over by them — in the name of their Departure, their homes, their gardens, their peace... They heard quite clearly that the old law was demolished. The new face was the measure of the new life.

All things are made new.

All places in the hall are free.

All they need to do to begin with is make the front rows knuckle under, to ring them dry with their hands, like drying a washed dog.

They can manage that, see how many of them there are, the whole hall row upon row, all who have never seen the Image so close up as the front rows, they fill the whole hall. Always they've had to fight in the darkness, breaking arms and heads, for what the front rows had without fighting: and even when, mutilated, battered, half-throttled, they nonetheless survived, they were still nothing and nobody for the names, and just like before the front rows didn't even see them and divided all the good things in the City between themselves. So that was it, the time of payment, here it was, the chance to obtain in a single minute — without work, without operations, that is, without pain, simply by making the effort — what belonged to them.

Glory to the Great Face-Maker for revealing to them Him-Who-Stands-Over-All. Their eyes sparkled merrily. The male One Hundred and Thirty-Two felt a paving-slab with his foot — it was loose, and he worked it to and fro. A good material, stone, not afraid of the rain, and for a fight you couldn't do better. The female One Hundred hid her hands on her breast, she had a lead charm, and her fingers quietly began to scrape through the linen thread on which the charm was hung. A charm is not the worst of weapons, if it's heavy.

The male One Hundred thought regretfully that he had not really taken part in the movement, except perhaps once, and that he would hardly get anything, but his partner, the female One Hundred... he stroked her elbow, which was just level with his lips — she was scraping through the linen thread. She just shifted her elbow slightly and the male One Hundred's lips split against his teeth, and the blood ran down his chin. 'Yes, yes, that's fair,' he thought, 'what she did, poor thing, and she loved me, and what could be worse than the pain of moral torment?' The blood was a salve to his conscience, it somehow expiated his passivity in the movement, and he kissed her elbow with his split lips. The female One Hundred didn't even wipe away the blood — she had no time.

Ah, how right he was, He-Who-Stands-Over-All.

Anything was allowed, if it was what you wanted.

Everyone had the right to be himself and occupy the position which he felt he was destined for. And nobody — each of them heard — knows better than yourself what you deserve.

Yes, the sweet music circulated in the human body with the blood, and if we were to lower into it a floating light which could be seen through the form of the body, then these are the words it would spell out in its motion: 'Behold, the truth'.

Each of them is right.

If he has the right.

Each has less than he deserves.

There it is, movement, and each of them is justified by results.

What was still new to them had already grown old. The old words were new in their essence — internally, in their meaning, not externally in their sound and their physical existence. And the hall accepted this in joyful excitement.

The time came when a new face was inevitable. And this face was recognized by the eye of the hall and avidly accepted by it — the way the dry earth accepted the rain.

After this the head of the hall thought lightly and fluently. The hall knew what to do, it was only waiting for the signal. It had all happened already, so far only within their bodies and their imaginations, but it had happened. Each of them had rehearsed his first movement, and each of them had chosen the seat which would be his.

Ah, what power that was — to allow a man to surmount with a wave of his hand the things that took everybody years, a lifetime, a generation. Ah, what power that was!

Like setting a wolf-hound on a wolf, its sets the province against the capital, drives the steppe into the mountains, pours the sea into the rivers, transforms the mountains into ditches, fills the graves with dirt, instantly circles the globe and returns unexpectedly from the other side, hangs itself, gobbles its own pups with horse-radish in oil, brings music into the world and leaves it attached to its umbilical cord, so that terror and pain should live on until both mother and child die, it changes gods the way junk-men change rags for money, chews broken glass with pleasure and a feeling of pride in its strong stomach, it deceives itself, then the second time around becomes the truth, the truth externally and its own opposite internally, and as a result as temporary as this power itself is.

Lord God, how much energy is wasted only in order to arrive back where everything started, and after such great losses!

This energy could turn so many wheels, move so many wings, bring so many children into the world, plant so many new forests, invent so many new words to replace the old ones that no longer mean anything, or new meanings which could be introduced into the old words like a bird into an abandoned house, and so many lives would not have disappeared without trace, like waves dissolved in the ocean... There could be so much extra warmth in every home in the world. Well then, pointsman, switch this energy to the main track, let it fly on without halting.

Go to the left and you'll lose your own self, go to the right and you'll kill a man. Go straight on and you'll end up back where you started. The wheels of the train spin, and there is no choice, you are moving onwards, the carriages fly along, and there's no way of telling the names from the numbers, just one hurtling mass that cannot be stopped or understood, but just let anyone try getting off and the speed will rip his head from his shoulders: 'No Exit' — the sign is lit up in the carriage, like the 'No Smoking' sign in the passenger cabin of a plane, where there's no need to write that there's 'no exit'.

And before everyone's eyes, which are turned back in on themselves, stands the new face, which has opened these eyes, which has taken on itself all their pains and sorrows, all their guilt.

This face!

How could the soul of the hall not believe in it, how could the ear of the hall not hear the new words, if people recognized themselves in the mirror? He-Who-Stands-Over-All was gone, and the words he spoke had vanished, hidden (the way the free bread-loaves disappear into bags in hungry years), but the hall was still sitting in silence and greedily absorbing the echo of what He-Who-Stands-Over-All had said, the way a beggar, having eaten his crust, gathers up the crumbs and greedily dispatches them into his mouth with his dirty, withered hands.

People were still seeing themselves in the beauty of the new face (a distorting mirror can make an ugly person beautiful), but the first grains had already split and the shoots had sprouted.

Female One Hundred, clutching the lead charm in her raised hand, crossed the border that no one could cross and brought down her leaden fist on the head of the Wife, yesterday this was her place in her imagination, and today by right, but the Husband did what anyone with a name had to do when a person with a number attacked — he caught female One Hundred's hand, when the fist grasping the charm was just about to touch the Wife's hair, and twisted the entire arm and the shoulder, so that blood spurted from the flesh, and the bone cracked, the axle snapped, and the first wheel span off into the hall. See it whirling faster and faster, off across the stones, along the edge of the precipice... The carriage keeled over, caught a sleeper, ripped it out of the ground, and tied the rails in a knot beneath itself, as though they weren't metal at all, but a thick brown thread that had been stretched under the wheels, and the carriage lay across the length of the train.

IV

The law was ended, and there remained only the truth that each one knew and which made him free. The seats began to creak, and those above came rushing downwards, while those below went rushing upwards, or first those below rushed upwards and then those above rushed downwards. Of course, there were some among them who would have liked to quit, who would have voluntarily surrendered what they possessed, who didn't give a damn for this illusion of a person's prospects — name and number. But... of what use to us is our wisdom when we are flying in a burning plane, or standing on the window-sill of the twentieth floor, which is blazing like an oil-tank, how wise can we be in the compartment of a train when the carriages are piling on top of each other? What good are our subterfuge, our cunning, our restraint, our diplomacy, our will, our foresight, our preparedness, our indifference.

Tell me, train, who set you sideways on the tracks? You've tied the cursed rails in a knot and tossed them off to the side. How precipitously it hurtled downwards, this iron monster stuffed with people, destinies, hopes, classes, numbers — carriage upon carriage, like a bull to a cow, like a dog to a bitch... The carriages landed on one another, and inside them arms were pulled off, and scratched-out eye-balls tumbled like spilled peas around the floor, tendons snapped with a noise like gunfire, heads burst under heaps of feet like balloons pricked by a pin. And the fists were working all the time.

The train hoots with its wheels up in the air, smoke pours out of the funnel. Tear it to sheds! There's a piston still flying through the air, still spinning from inertia, and all the glass! Crash it goes — into your eyes. Crack go the hands — breaking the skulls. What turmoil, God preserve us! Everyone has the same face, you can't tell whose is whose, everyone is beating everyone else, and no one knows who is who and who is on which side. If the Face-Maker could have seen this now, he'd have laid down on the floor like a dog between the chairs and howled at his stupidity. He put his life into this.

Into that?

Into THIS?

Run the film back a week, and he wouldn't have corrected the Husband's face, he'd have slit the Official's throat in a dark corner, he'd rather have been given Departure as long as it was for something worthwhile — but this hadn't happened then. If you can't create, then at least preserve. That's greater than creating, and more importantly, it does people more good. It may be more anonymous, but it does more good. A week's happiness for the Husband and the Wife was small reward for all this suffering. And the train would not have gone hurtling and twisting through the air and crushing those who were caught in its iron folds. And the flames, the flames! Did some fool couple a tank-car into the train for a joke?

The Husband's luck had soon deserted him, dropping him down just as it had raised him up — only lower than his life before the rise. Someone's feet trampled his head, someone's foot sank into his groin, and like a dog the Husband doubled over, and his life squelched out as his tongue came tumbling out of his mouth, and he could remember no one, the burning train turned upside-down in his eyes, and the lead charm tumbled on to the floor and rolled under the seat.

But life still goes on. Someone is storming the doors. They're swinging the Official against them like a log. The Official's head has long since been replaced by a spongy mass, but they keep pounding and pounding; others press around them and try to drag them away, but they keep on pounding like woodcutters, monotonously — like a pendulum, regularly — like a machine, fast — like breathing in and out, on and on inexorably... And look at the women, the women! Nails and teeth at work — and anything else they can think of — they've set the most zealous ones on fire. The flesh burns well, it runs around, it shrieks and burns, and still it keeps on fighting.

But nothing lasts forever.

V

It seems the carriages are all at the bottom of the slope now, the engine has burnt and smoked itself out and soot is all that's left. Everything seems to be dead, there's nothing but iron and silence. But even here life goes on. They begin crawling out of the iron junk-heap, some with a groan, some even calmly, some — you can't understand how they can possibly do it. It turned out not to matter in the fight, in that whirling tornado, who had a Name and who had a number, there are heaps of both lying there, tumbled together, uncounted, unsorted, between the chairs, in the aisles, on the stage. By the door a hillock has risen up, and is still stirring slightly as other people come scrambling back from non-existence.

The only thing is, however you may try to twist things, the numbers have more people killed, and more survivors too, and this fact, of course, has its own logic and its own justice. In the first place, even before the crash the names were merely an insignificant leaven among the masses, and everyone knows that nature respects proportion, and in the second place, after all, the majority smeared the minority across the walls and hacked them down with brass axes, and if it had turned out differently the scale would surely have been all wrong.

What had happened had happened, and now the survivors crawled out, stunned and listless, they crawled out, glanced around, gathered their wits, recovered slightly — crushed out of shape, twisted but still whole — and the veil of stupor fell from their eyes like the shell from the head of a chick newly emerged from the egg, and immediately the first to recover his wits (who appeared to be the most intact, even his shirt wasn't torn, which means he's an iron warrior, or perhaps, of course it was just luck, or — like the Wife — he simply sat it all out) barked out: 'Bind them in the name of the New Face'.

The numbers immediately understood who it was they had to bind, and they bound them. But what could you bind them with? They ripped the shirts off the dead women and men, they tore them up and bound the others, and if anyone half-resisted the numbers, still drunk on blood, struck him with a chair-leg or anything else they could lay their hands on, without bothering to think about it too much. And that was only right — what pity could there be when so many of their brothers lay all around the hall between the shattered rows of seats? True, there was still the question of who had put them there — but whose question was that? For the numbers it was clear —

the Names, of course, especially the ones who were still alive, these ones here. The iron man went up on the stage and asked his brother numbers to drag up the bound bodies. They dragged them up.

There weren't many with names left alive.

The Wife, of course, had not come to grief, come hell or high water, half-suffocated, she had sat it out under the chairs, covered in bruises but, like the iron man, almost unharmed — so there is a way out when the carriages are crashing on to one another?

No! But what about the Wife?

Coincidence — she wasn't the only one who tried to escape, to wriggle out of it, to sit it all out, there they are, still where they were under the seats, some had their heads kicked in, some had them smashed by axes. Pure coincidence, too, that the new female Joint Chairperson is alive, although, of course her profession is in some ways as much of a hell as the picture now resolving itself before her eyes, images draining away like rainwater into the earth after a downpour. Five living Names, less important ones, were all they collected. They included the Muse's Director, who had occupied an empty seat.

The numbers are at work, dragging whole seats — and what remains of what was sitting in them — closer to the stage, leveling them out, forming them back into rows, and almost without abuse, almost without quarreling, seating themselves in them — for what is there to quarrel about?

Here it is, success.

Nine Hundred and Thirty-Seven sits in the sixth seat of the first row as though he has been sitting there all his life. Sitting beside him is the former Three Hundred, and the others are not wasting any time either.

And there's our iron man, Nine Hundred and Ten, already settled into the Official's seat — not the old one, true, that was shattered or shredded — but a new one has been set in the same place. Not actually a new one, of course, there's the number Six Hundred and Sixty-Six still on the back of it, but the place is the Official's place, and that's what counts. He sat down as the iron man, but he rose as the Official.

And then it started.

'Well,' said the new Official. 'What shall we do with you? You have killed so many of our people.'

One of the bound prisoners snarled at him:

'You killed them yourself, nobody else did.'

The Official spread his arms sadly and shrugged his shoulders, people from the front row rose and went across to the slanderer. And with their bare hands, in the sight of all there present, as it says in the ancient chronicles, they strangled this louse, who had dared to contradict the Official (the depths these Names had sunk to, the old Official had been too soft on them) while he was speaking - for numbers love order too. They dragged the dead body aside. The Wife saw his tongue lolling out, and she shuddered, and he reminded her of her Husband in bed. Now the Wife realized why she had hated her Husband all her life — when he blew his fuse he was like a strangled corpse. She thought with relief that now she was free of her Husband, and she smiled.

'Are you smiling? Are you laughing at us?' The Official was absolutely furious. Like anyone who has only just seized power he was, of course, suffering from morbid mistrust in the sincerity of respect shown to his authority.

But the Wife just smiled even more broadly and said:

'I'm simply glad that a real man like you is in charge.'

She hadn't done the rounds of almost the entire male population of the City for nothing. What hadn't she learned in her varied life — getting round a man was child's play to her. She knew the higher diplomacy of relationships as well as a senior school-boy knew his multiplication tables — what to say and how at such a moment to the former Nine Hundred and Ten, for a position is all very well, but inside (with, of course, the additional experience of the crash) he was still as yet the former Nine Hundred and Ten, with his mind fixed on getting a number a bit higher (which he had), and a decent woman, from somewhere in the eight hundreds. As for the Wife — in this very hall just over a week ago he had sweated and snorted, and dug his fingers into the back of the seat in the course of the model lovemaking. Who could resist the charms of the Wife, whose body he, like everyone, knew like the back of his hand, and had carried for so many days in his heart? Reassured by her words, and encouraged by his desire, he said to the Wife:

'You have earned a pardon.'

And no one spoke a word from the hall, they respected order too. Only when she went over to him, sat beside him, put her hand on his shoulder, and he put his right arm around her and pressed her to him, several rows of the seats still standing squeaked, and no wonder — almost all of them were either broken or scarcely holding together.

The Wife thought how she had always lived with a sensation of loathing for her Husband and her life; and it was quite possible that the names were to blame for that, they had made her what she was. This thought reassured the Wife, and glancing around, and noting to herself the strong hand calmly lying on her shoulder, she thought that to be the Official's partner was success, and everything that had happened was for the best — she had been lucky. Glad at what had happened, she began to feel attracted to the man sitting beside her, and her hand grew hot, and her hips grew warm, and through the material the warmth touched the Official's legs, and he shuddered, and what he was doing at this minute was determined to a certain extent by this feeling of having a woman beside him.

VI

'Well now,' said the Official, 'we have before us the Joint Chairperson of our remarkable and excellent Commission. Whose brother or father or near number has not passed under this all-seeing eye? Look at this monster.' Everyone looked at this monster, and no one felt even the slightest stirring of doubt that he had to look, no one even felt the slightest stirring of regret that none of them felt the slightest stirring of doubt that they had to look. To listen to the other Official, the former one, would have been insulting to the spirit of the numbers who were left alive, but not listening to this one... Because he was them — and surely it's not insulting to listen to yourself? As for the habit and experience of obedience, they had plenty of that.

All of them, even those who had squeaked their rickety seats, looked at the Joint Chairperson. And the sight was worth looking at. The material at her breast and her waist and lower was tattered, exposing the beautiful pink young body, and only by the neck was there a bruise left by someone's misdirected blow with a chair-leg or some other sharp instrument, for instance a woman's nails.

'But we can't see what she's really like,' said the Official. He nudged the Wife in the side and she went over, and without untying the Joint Chairperson, she ripped the remnants of material from her body.

'Now you see.' The Wife raised her eyes to the seated company — there weren't many of them after all, and the eyes of many of them were familiar to her, but they were occupied with retribution and, of course, they could not allow themselves what they wanted and what the Wife knew all about.

'Now we see...'

The Wife was about to go back, but the Official stopped her:

'Wait, insofar as we represent our brothers who have here given up their lives'— he pointed into the hall — 'we must determine the degree of guilt of each of our enemies who is left alive.' The Official pointed first at the Museum Director — 'We'll start with him.' The prisoner twitched in his bonds.

'No, don't get up.'

There was no need to explain anything to the Wife, she had quickly mastered her new duties. At the words from the hall: 'He must hide nothing — away with their secrets!' the Wife tore the last few rags from the Director's body.

'Untie them,' ordered the Official, pointing to the Joint Chairperson and the Director.

The Wife untied them.

'Set them facing each other.'

The Wife turned the seats round and helped the Joint Chairperson and the Director to sit more comfortably. It was all done with sincere concern and kindness. 'After all, he's one of us,' the thought flashed through her head. 'I should do what I can.'

As she re-seated the Director, she even stroked him gently on the shoulder, but so inconspicuously that those sitting in the hall could not see it. Having carried out her duties, the Wife returned to her seat, and once again the Official put his arm round her and pressed her to him. He became tense and focused and leant forward.

'And now perform your duty,' said the Official to the Joint Chairperson, 'you're a professional, and if you do it well enough, perhaps...' he did not say perhaps what, but it was clear from his expression that Departure was one possibility, but clemency was not out of the question. The other prisoners had grown accustomed to their bonds and were still. It seemed now there might be a chance to serve the new Official. Lord, how far away was that peaceful time when they didn't need to make any choices, they could eat, sleep, go to work, and life was as clear as the name they had. No need to think about any new face. But then, He-Who-Stands-Over-All had been prophesied by one of their own, and their brains just couldn't make sense of that riddle. Yes, he was even more them than they were themselves, and there could be no two ways about it.

'Your Name?' asked the Joint Chairperson, who had also had an inkling of hope. She began to do her usual job, there was no more hall, no fight, no feeling that the Official was watching her and she had to make a special effort in performing her duties.

The accused had also conceived a hope: after all, it was quite clear that those sitting in the hall had been just as involved in the fight as he had, and he was no more guilty than they were. And then an interrogation in public is not the same thing as a *tête-à-tête* in the Joint Chairperson's office.

'Director!'

'For how long?'

'Two years now'.

'How many corrective operations did you have in order to receive this name?'

'Six.'

'Why was such great concern shown for you?'

The hall was indignant, not even in the most favourable of circumstances could any of them have counted on having two operations, one was the best they could expect.

'What was your initial likeness coefficient?'

'Minus twenty.'

The hall let out its breath. 'Monstrous!' They had been stuck in the middle numbers with a coefficient of minus ten.

The further conversation between the Director and the Joint Chairperson exposed such a large number of violations of the Law of Operations that in half an hour everything was quite clear. And despite all his attempts at subterfuge, the accused always came up against that single, central truth, one tenth part of which would have sufficed for Departure even in peaceful times — but today, in front of the numbers, after so many deaths... The Joint Chairperson, however, was merciless.

'Did you yourself believe in the justice of the Law of Operations?'

After he had replied no, but he had always honestly carried out his duties, and the entire City had been educated with the programs that he had produced, which had invariably reinforced the citizen's aversion for any other life, the Joint Chairperson asked a seemingly innocent question:

'And did it not seem to you that in reinforcing the aversion for any other way of life, you were developing an aversion for absolutely anything that was new?'

'Of course,' — the accused's response was immediate.

'And therefore,' the Joint Chairperson continued in a lazy, careless tone, she even smiled, 'for the new face too.'

'Therefore, for the new face, too.' The frightened accused breathed out the phrase, half-meaningless under the circumstances. His eyes were full of terror. Good God! he would never have thought of that, now he realized that he really did deserve Departure. And sentence was pronounced...

'Taking into account such and such counts of guilt,' said the Joint Chairperson, who had risen to her feet, but rather abruptly, so that the skin on her neck had tensed and pulled open her wound, and from beneath the crust of clotted blood there emerged a fresh, bright-red drop, which ran down across her breast, halted for a moment, crept across her belly, lower and lower, slid over her hip and finally spread out beside her right foot. A small puddle formed on the stage, but the Joint Chairperson was absorbed in her work and her triumph, and she did not notice it.

'Taking into account the understatement by the accused of the damage which he consistently inflicted upon the City over a period of many years, or to be more precise, which was inflicted upon the City under his direction,' pronounced the Joint Chairperson, as though reading from a sheet of paper in her hand, although in fact there was no sheet of paper, and she reformulated the text several times as she went through it, but in general she spoke smoothly and with genuine professionalism.

'Yes, that's real skill,' the Official took note, 'I should learn from that.' And he learned.

There followed another series of counts of guilt, to which the accused had not confessed, which had not been mentioned but which (and everyone understood this) ensued from the single confession of encouraging aversion for the new face.

As they carried out their new duties in the name of the new, in a manner not only quite irreprehensible, but demanding a heroic feat of service to a new idea, they were also thrown into a certain degree of confusion by the unexpectedly large number of counts of guilt which ensued from a single one, of which the accused had been unaware. Each of them began involuntarily to measure these counts of guilt against himself, and it turned out that to a certain extent they had all played the same role, although perhaps at a different level from the accused. The Official also began to ponder, but not along the same lines as the hall. As far as he was concerned now, there could be no question about those sitting in the hall... He'd have to think about that a bit later, he thought, and squeezed the Wife's shoulders still tighter.

'Enough,' said the Official, and everyone sighed in relief, because the Joint Chairperson might actually have begun to list the counts on which they too were guilty, and then... 'Since we are unable to administer Departure according to the rules... by the way, do you know how the rules define the method of Departure?'

In her agitation the Joint Chairperson shifted her feet and almost fell as she slipped on her own blood; it was a good thing that one of the accused held her up, she thanked him with a quick nod.

'No, that's not my area.'

'A pity,' said the Official, 'we'll have to improvise our own amateur methods. But you will also have to master a new profession. You are appointed Administrator of Departure.'

Approval lit up the faces of the hall. That's right, let them administer Departure to each other. After all, if they'd taught us about the new face in time, nothing bad might have happened in the hall today.

There was a pause, and then in the place of the severe, precise, harsh professional face concealed behind a mask of gentleness, they all saw a weak woman on the verge of howling out loud, that is, not actually howling, but the tears began to roll down her face. She didn't know — and this was the truth — how to administer even an improvised Departure. And not because she hadn't seen it done, but simply because she had devoted too much energy and too many years of her life to a different trade, a trade which was restricted to mere inquiry, accusation and examination.

Of course, the Official was not at a loss. He inquired of the accused whether the latter was able to administer the sentence of the court himself. The latter shook his head in a rather thoughtful manner, because he was sincerely tormented by his guilt and the sudden realization that the duties which he had punctiliously and religiously performed for so many years, had been so detrimental to the City.

'In that case, can you administer an improvised Departure to her?' the Official continued to demonstrate inexhaustible invention: he had accumulated so much energy during the years of hope with nothing to expend it on (you can't use up much of it editing broadcasts).

Yes, the Director is still the Director. Even if he is condemned to Departure and crushed by a sense of guilt. He was interested by the suggestion, and only one thought concerned him: 'What would he get for it?'

'A seat in the back rows of the hall,' the Official responded immediately.

'I can,' said the accused, without pausing for thought. And once again he saw before him not a woman with blood streaming down her body, but the stern Joint Chairperson.

'Then I also can,' said the Joint Chairperson, looking into the eyes of the accused, and then into the hall. Ah, how subtle and clever the new Official was.

'I think that the accused deserves to be punished twice: once for his guilt, and a second time for forgetting his guilt so quickly and accepting clemency which he does not deserve. But our court is both the most just of all that exist, and it is new. Since we have suggested it, first he will administer improvised Departure to her, and then we shall make our decision.'

The Director administered improvised Departure to the Joint Chairperson. He took this young and beautiful body by the legs, and he smashed the head of this young and lovely body against the floor of the stage.

'He administered it well,' said the Official, 'but we will reserve pronouncement of our final decision.' He squeezed the Wife's hip, turned to face the hall, and winked.

Having heard this, the Director picked up the Joint Chairperson, his right arm under her knees, his left behind her back, carried her to the heap of other bodies, and set her down carefully so that she could lie there comfortably, even adjusting the position of her head.

VII

'We appoint you in the interim to perform the duties of the Joint Chairperson.'

'The next accused!'

She was a young girl, only just past the threshold of maturity. The Wife recognized her, she was one of next year's candidates for the name of Wife, her future rival. The Official was suddenly extremely polite. He changed before their very eyes. A moment ago they had all seen a witty, somewhat over-familiar man full of energy, and now there appeared before the hall a man one might even call courteous, that is, if you couldn't see his hands — entirely unconnected with his kind, attentive face, or the clear expression of his eyes — as they fumbled with the thighs and the breasts of the Wife sitting with him. But what does that have to do with the matter he is dealing with? The girl was attractive. She was so attractive that the Wife did not carry out her new duties, for fear that the numbers' sensitive souls might be touched by pity — and the half-shredded material was left on the girl's thin body.

The Director, who has somehow managed to survive so far in this honest, new and just court, has already begun his interrogation, somewhat concerned that he will not be able to manage the investigation as professionally as his predecessor. But, whether because in the course of his own profession he had frequent occasion to investigate the guilt of his subordinates before handing them over to the Commission, or whether because of what he had just experienced (experience frequently makes us wiser and more sincere), or whether for certain other reasons, he demonstrated abilities as an investigator which had remained hidden until required at this moment. In their declining years many people begin to behave like youths, indulging themselves unnecessarily in love, or, in contrast, going into politics, and all entirely as a result of the fact that the unused experience they have accumulated longs to be exposed, to be demonstrated to others.

And so, after an interrogation of literally seven minutes, it became clear that there was in effect nothing to accuse her of — she hadn't worked anywhere, she wasn't involved in anything, she hadn't been a member of anything, she wasn't, in fact, guilty of anything. Of course, in the Official's place anyone else might have suspected the Director of tendentiousness and a desire to help his own kind, but the Official was sufficiently clever to guess that no matter how you tried it would be hard to get anything out of this frightened, fresh and lovely — at this point he glanced at the Wife — young girl. And she — the Wife — somehow seemed a little less attractive to him just at this moment... On the other hand, the Official was clever enough to understand that even if she was innocent, she belonged to the names, and therefore... After all, justice is supreme over all things, thought the Official, and the way a matter is begun will decide how it continues. And then, what's done here is one thing, but there's still tomorrow, and tomorrow we'll have to account for ourselves to the New Face.

We don't know what else the Official might have gone on to think about, involuntarily squeezing the Wife's hip tighter and tighter, until the effort of his thoughts was so great that the Wife could stand it no longer, but as an experienced and educated woman, of course, she didn't smack his face, she didn't insult him, she didn't protest, she didn't complain of his behaviour to those sitting around her (and their train of thoughts concerning the Official was about as long a train as the Official's concerning what he ought to do now). No. The Wife calmly stood up, went out into the centre of the stage, limping slightly (after all, there was nothing wrong with the Official's fingers), went across to the Director, took him by the nose — which, of course, made everyone in the hall laugh, she did it with such an air of caring sympathy — led the Director off to the side and sat facing the girl.

'Tell me,' said the Wife gently, 'next year you were to have been a candidate for the name of Wife.'

'Yes,' said the girl and hastily added that they had told her so and prepared her for it, but they had hardly made any corrections, just very minor ones, her face had a naturally high degree of likeness.

'That is, of course, to the old face,' specified the smiling Wife, polite as ever.

'But there was no other,' the girl answered guiltily, but sincerely, 'we simply didn't know any other.'

'Now, perhaps the last question I have for you. Next year, if you were selected as Wife, you would, of course, have faithfully endeavored to fulfill your duties?'

'Of course,' said the girl.

'And so have continued to serve what is now repulsive and unacceptable to us all?'

'That's right,' said the girl. 'Only I don't know how it would have been.'

'You would have served the propaganda of the old face,' saddened, the Wife spoke almost to herself, and she spread her arms wide and rose from her seat. And each within his own mind, the people sitting in the hall all rose from their seats and spread their arms in sympathy with her sadness.

The Director now performed the second part of his duties. Then he picked up the girl professionally — right arm under her knees, left arm behind her back, and carried her across to the same spot, to the same heap, and took just as much care putting down the body and adjusting the position of the head.

The Official was disappointed with the Director. The entire hall was disappointed with the Director in the role of investigator, very disappointed.

'Untie the three who are left,' the Official said to the Director.

The Director did it. The Wife at the same time sat back down, prepared to continue with duties so well begun.

'Are your hands numb?' asked the Official kindly. It was quite obvious that they were. 'Very well,' he said, 'our Director will now take you through a series of warm-up exercises. Please carry on,' he said to the Director. The latter dragged his weary body out to the centre of the stage, and it began.

'Hands up, and one, and two, and three... hands on your chest. Squat down, once more, straighten up, and one-two-three, and one-two-three, and one...'

No double the gymnastics would have gone on for longer, but the hall began to feel bored, and the Official cut short this magnanimous procedure with a gesture of his hand. It had clearly helped the accused, for their arms now seemed to obey them once again.

'And now,' said the Official, 'I think the time has come... How are your hands?' he asked the three accused.

'Fine,' a redheaded woman answered for all of them, making a few movements with her wrist, and smiling at the Official and the hall.

The Official continued with his speech, after smiling back at her:

'The time has come to keep the promise we made to punish the Director. In the first place — for his guilt, in the second place — for not punishing himself, and in the third place — for something which happened before your very eyes...' He appealed to the accused and the hall: 'He administered Departure to a woman who had refused to do so to him, that is, he showed no appreciation for her noble gesture, nor for our magnanimous decision to allow him the opportunity to demonstrate his moral capacities.'

The Official sensed that both the hall and the accused were on his side. There could be no misunderstanding here — each of them had felt a sense of disgust for the Director, and they had not the slightest doubt that in this situation they would have behaved in the same way as the poor woman who had refused to administer Departure.

Ah, what a difference support does make! The Official could now be humane and liberal. And he permitted the three accused — not ordered or insisted, but precisely permitted if, of course, they so wished — to administer the Director's Departure, which he had deserved merely for his behaviour during the last few hours of the hall's work.

VIII

The three accused, led by the redheaded woman, were not allowed enough time to finish administering Departure. The doors up above swung open, and a crowd burst into the hall. These were the people with different faces, ones who had neither names nor numbers. They lived on the very outskirts of the city, and only when the City gathered in the Hall of the House were they permitted to approach the square before the House, and standing under an awning erected for these rare and solemn occasions, to listen to the music wafting out to them from the walls of the House with a clumsy energy like a swan just before it alights on the water — but for them this was the great music of involvement in the main life of the City, the music of impossible hope and the music of non-existent prospects. Today, though, there had been no music, today He-Who-Stands-Over-All had transformed it into words and equal rights for them, the ones who had stood here on this square once a year century after century for the Choice of the Principal Couple, knowing only by hearsay what the proceedings were, not once setting foot inside the doors of the House and the houses in which the people with a name or a number lived — for them, who had no future, because the future was the same as the present. Today, He-Who-Stands-Over-All had transported them into that non-existent future. The town was given over to them, the people of the different faces and the different eyes, by Him-Who-Stands-Over-All. How could they not believe him, if while he spoke the very rain was stayed by his hand!

The service, the payment for this gift, was convenient, necessary and desired by Him — to exterminate everything living in the City which bore the old face, and it didn't matter that when He-Who-Stands-Over-All finished speaking the rain lashed down harder than it ever had in the City, as though the water which had not fallen during the temporary pause had merely been stored up and then poured down on to the earth. With their strength, with their pressure, with their right, with their bodies, the people had burst open the doors of the House and flooded in. Like a tank crushing a snail without even noticing it, like a landslide carrying away a slim sapling, like a plane smashing a bird to pieces — that was how the people still in the hall, and the accused, together with the Director and the Official disappeared beneath the torrent of arms, teeth and legs. In five minutes it was all over. All the people who had been in the hall had the old face, and the invaders knew just what they had to do — any old face of any degree of likeness had to be destroyed that day, like a captured bed-bug or a cockroach. And then the landslide, having swept through the hall, swept on out of the building, spread through the town, through the houses, through the laboratories, through the streets, thoroughly and deliberately destroying as it went everything that fell into its hands, the way a swarm of locusts devastates a field that happens to lie in its path.

IX

The Muse came to herself when the Face-Maker was pulling her shirt down on to her shoulders, he poured her a glass of ice-cold water which made her teeth ache, and having drunk it she wiped her lips, which were not hers — they had become softer and fuller. The Face-Maker showed her her face, and the Muse was astonished. It was a beautiful face. She moved her head, and her hair at the back seemed to be caught by a breeze, and it tumbled down the Muse's back.

'Is this me?' said the Muse. She saw her new, staring eyes, a long face, white and gentle, a thin, straight nose, and the face was severe and full of strength. Only it hurt. 'But why did you do it?' said the Muse. 'And why didn't we stay in the hall?'

But probably all people have their limits, even face-makers. Too much strength had been expended on Him-Who-Stands-Over-All and the Muse. The Face-Maker said nothing, and while he thought in silence, trying to answer for himself a question which only recently had been simple, and explain out loud to the Muse why he had done it, the doors opened and his surgery was flooded with the people who, after sweeping all before them in the Hall of the House, had spilled out on to the street and spread through the houses where those who had the old face had lived and worked. The flood halted only once — before the miracle — flowing backwards as though it had run into a wall. They had seen the new face — the face of Him-Who-Stands-Over-All, which was still alive in their memory — and after drawing back, they approached, carefully raised the Muse up on their outstretched arms, and slowly and solemnly bore her to the Hall of the House, in order to show her to everyone. They had become the Muse's slaves, but now she also belonged to them.

They did not look back as they left. What did they want with the man sitting in the corner with his hands resting on his knees, at such a solemn, holy moment they did not wish to soil the hands which bore the Muse, and the old face would not escape — those who were following would do their duty and swill the filth away.

The Face-Maker stood up, put on his cloak and followed them out almost indifferently, the way the dead give up their bodies to the worms, the way the dead give up their bodies to the fire and drift downwind as ash, feebly and slowly, like the burnt fragments of a letter from one who was beloved and now means nothing.

The Face-Maker lowered the hood over his face and slowly wandered down towards the houses, along the street which was deserted here, near his laboratory, but from down there, from down below, where the citizens' houses were, he could hear shouts and groans. The groans would break off and the shouts would explode into a merry rumbling of voices, then fall silent, and then again after a little while there was that almost subterranean rumbling — as though a volcano were churning its lava, as though the voices were playing a game of hunt-the-thimble, and when they were 'cold' it was quiet, and when they were 'hot' the volcano growled.

When the Face-Maker got down below the zone of the House he understood the principle that governed the alternation of silence and rumbling — the crowd rushed through the streets and some of its members ran in at the doors that stood open in every house in the City, while the crowd waited silently in the rain, and the rain lashed down on the threshold of the doors standing open, and flowed into the entrance-halls, and puddles stood in the entrance-halls, and then, splashing up the water of these puddles, the ones who had gone in dragged out the inhabitants of the houses who were still alive, and the crowd greeted their success with a roar, they all seized their victim, helpless in the face of their strength, and bore him off in their arms, up towards the House.

The Face-Maker halted beside the crowd without raising his hood from his face, melted into its ranks and began to wait with the rest of them by one of the entrance-ways, silently, as those around him waited silently for their prey. He saw them carry out of the entrance a person in tattered clothing, half-dead, with a face mutilated by blows. The crowd whooped in joy, they tore the last remnants of clothing from the man, the naked body was raised aloft on their outstretched hands, and like drumsticks the streaming rain beat on the man's body in a rhythm of triumph. The rain was joining in the festivities. In order to see this spectacle through to the end, the Face-Maker also put his fingers to the man's body and set off with the crowd up the hill towards the House. While the people were walking through the streets, no one took any notice of the Face-Maker. They were intoxicated with their mission, they, who only yesterday had not dared to take a single step on these stones, were today the authority, the inquiry, the court.

Perhaps the Face-Maker could have made the journey through the streets more than once, then sat it out somewhere, in order to see the Muse at least once more from a distance, and see the life of the new City with a new face, see the creation of his own hands. But it was his hands that gave him away — not the face, that was hidden under his hood. When the people went round the House and in through a side door into a hall which the Face-Maker, having lived a lifetime in the City, had never seen, and the light sprang up, striking the faces beneath the hoods and illuminating the hands, then at the condemned man's back, surrounded by the hairy, hooked, short, coarse fingers, the whiteness and slimness of the Great Face-Maker's fingers was suddenly highlighted, like a lily blossoming in a stinking bog in defiance of all common sense. A lily. They dumped the half-dead man on the floor and crowded round the Face-Maker, tore off his cloak and his clothes, and when they saw the old face, they began to shout in their astonishment at the shamelessness and lack of delicacy of their predecessors, and they were convinced yet again of the justice of their hunt. The very height of cynicism — to march in their ranks!

Raising the Face-Maker over their heads, they approached the Door of Departure, and lowered the Face-Maker down on to a narrow black landing, the upper step of a staircase leading downwards, and the Face-Maker met the eyes of the man lying on the floor, and smiled, and nodded, and then transferred his gaze to the people who were watching him from beneath their lowered hoods, so that it was hard to make out their faces. Maybe even some of them knew the Face-Maker — but then what did that matter? The man had fulfilled the purpose for which he was sent into the world. Departure is merely a question of time and technique, which are a matter of indifference to the person to whom it is administered. The people watched the Face-Maker and waited for his reaction — the ways in which they had seen their captives depart had been so very different, some had cried, some had fallen to their knees and kissed their executioner's feet, some had attempted to resist, and they had been forced to half-strangle those funny fellows to stop them making too much fuss before Departure. Once again the Face-Maker was astonished at himself: at this moment he felt neither fear, nor surprise, nothing at all apart from a dull curiosity, just as he hadn't had any fear when he led the Muse out of the hall, or on the streets of the city, or here now. Probably he had left his fear and love and desire in the face of Him-Who-Stands-Over-All, which shone so brightly for these people and was so omnipotent that in His name all was permitted, all was forgiven, all was justified. The staircase moved beneath the Face-Maker's feet, and began to slide downwards, the doors parted and closed behind him with a click — the way the mouth of a fish out of water closes in a silent convulsion.

While the doors were opening the Face-Maker laughed with his lifeless smile. The Muse was alive. It didn't matter that he wouldn't be there — the Muse was also the Face-Maker. These harsh, hooked fingers would love her, and she would teach them her tenderness, which she had discovered with the Face-Maker. The Face-Maker smiled again, perhaps at his own naivety, or perhaps at the truth which he saw, or wished to see in this way. The Face-Maker transferred his gaze from within himself outwards, and for the first time he saw the blue dome of the hall soaring upwards out of sight, and below and ahead of him a frozen motionless mirror of yellowish water, a mirror that was trembling slightly at the point where the staircase moving beneath the Face-Maker's feet disappeared under the water, and small circles ran out across the surface and disappeared again not far away — the water was heavy and sluggish, as though oil had been poured on to its surface.

Let the entire city and its new inhabitants in here throw them, shove them into the water, and there would not be a single splash, not a wave would heave up on this heavy surface, and such is human memory — it drowns without trace, it dissolves destinies, bodies and events, great face-makers and great ideas. The Face-Maker can depart calmly without knowing, and therefore without remembering, that the City has gone mad and time has fallen out of joint. The final Face-Maker will now move down towards that thick, green, heavy silence and oblivion, there will be no one to carve these faces into the standard features of beauty, nobility, severity, the new standard, for the secret of the craft and the art, together with the fingers, the slim, white fragile, sensitive fingers of the Face-Maker, and his intellect, equipped with the age-old ancestral ability to create a face, will melt away with this single, temporary, fleeting body which contained within itself the traditions of the clan. But the Muse, whom he had left to the people, she would grow old and eventually would depart as he had done, and if she should have children, they would not be like the Face-Maker's Muse, the man-made Muse, they would have their original faces, the ones that each inhabitant of this city had inside.

'The Muse's children will be like the people with no face,' was what the Face-Maker thought in his knowledge of the future. 'They will have their own faces,' was what He-Who-Stands-Over-All thought, who had known the future before it had even begun.

The City had gone mad, the City had been driven mad, and who can tell what awaits the person who has departed from repetition and example; in the entire history of the City, no one had ever returned to his primal state, but perhaps this is not a return to the primal state.

The staircase shuddered beneath the Face-Maker and stopped with only half a metre left to the water, and the Face-Maker swayed forward, but he held on, astonished that the movement had stopped. It was an illusion, the movement had simply become so slow that it was almost imperceptible. Now there were only centimetres left to the water, and it looked soft, and steam rose from it. The water was warmer than the air, its warmth drew him towards it.

The Face-Maker thought that now it was time to remember the Muse, and the City, and his work, which had brought him so much joy.

'Did it really bring me joy?' he asked himself.

'It did,' he immediately reassured the questioner.

'Are you afraid of what's happening now in the city? Or are you the cause of what's happening?'

'I'm afraid, but you know that you're not the only cause of what's happening,' he reassured the questioner.

'But if not for you — would it all have happened?'

'Perhaps not like this, perhaps it would have even been more terrible, and...'

The soles of the Face-Maker's feet touched the water, at first the warmth, and then the water. Yes, it was a familiar sensation, but there was no time left to remember what it was like, because his thoughts began to flow out through his legs into the water, and his legs themselves were becoming invisible beneath the transparent greenish water, they were melting, as sugar melts into boiling water, as a plane melts into the sky, as a snowflake melts into your hand, as the dawn melts into the morning. But there was no pain. The water was already working at his hips, his belly, his chest, but there was no pain, there were only weariness, peace and submission in place of a body, and his thoughts were becoming warm. Then the vault over his head began to glow red-hot, and this heat touched the Face-Maker's eyes and just as his body used to be covered with goose-pimples before it was warmed by the steam-bath, the Face-Maker's eyes froze, and the tears that had risen in them froze. Through the ice the Face-Maker attempted to see the vault and the water and what was still left of his body, but his vision began to be locked into this ice — the way a horse that has fallen through ice into the river may break the crust, but the sleigh still drags it down to the bottom — the way it is with a plane out of control — everyone is still alive, their hands still function skillfully and precisely, but the earth is rising up to meet it like a billiard ball — the way a dog trapped in the skin-merchant's cage struggles frantically in a futile attempt to break free. The oppressive heat finally overpowered the cold, extracted all the air, his throat swelled up and his cry emerged through his melting eyes, because his mouth was already in the water and was drifting downwards, drawn towards the exit by the current. His eyes cried up to the red vault, they turned red, they melted, and his pink eyes set, not as the sun sets in an eclipse, but as it goes down when it has served its entire term. The vault listened indifferently to this cry and gradually it grew calm and blue, as a house that has been burnt out will be grown over with grass and become transformed into a green wood, so that a century later no one can guess whether there was a powerful state here, or whether high towers stood here beneath the blue vault overhead, and down below the surface of the lake is frozen still without a single ripple.

There were only small circles now running out from the almost imperceptible movement of the staircase, while the eyes and thoughts of the Face-Maker went gurgling out through a narrow channel into the streets of the City and its eternal stone canals, and they were calm and serene, because ahead lay the long journey along the canal to the outskirts, beyond the limits of the City, into the waters of the river which received the canal, and then along the old channel to the ocean, which is eternal and constant, gazing up with its green eyes into the blue sky. But that would be later, for now he was surrounded by the usual houses, built of the stone which is not afraid of water.

The rain was falling as usual, and the Face-Maker thought that somewhere he could hear the Muse crying.

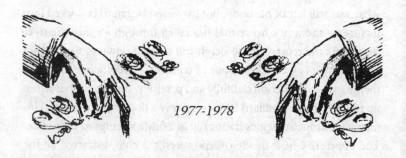

1977-1978